RE-FIGURING THEOLOGY

SUNY Series in Rhetoric and Theology
David Tracy and Stephen H. Webb, editors

RE-FIGURING THEOLOGY

THE RHETORIC OF KARL BARTH

STEPHEN H. WEBB

STATE UNIVERSITY OF NEW YORK PRESS

Published by
State University of New York Press, Albany

For information, address State University of New York Press,
State University Plaza, Albany, N.Y., 12246

Production by Marilyn P. Semerad
Marketing by Fran Keneston

Library of Congress Cataloging-in-Publication Data

Webb, Stephen H., 1961-
    Re-figuring theology : the rhetoric of Karl Barth / by Stephen H.
Webb.
        p.   cm. —(SUNY series in rhetoric and theology)
    Includes bibliographical references.
    ISBN 0-7914-0570-2. —ISBN 0-7914-0571-0 (pbk.)
    1. Barth, Karl, 1886-1968—Literary art. 2. German language–
–Rhetoric. I. Title. II. Title: Refiguring theology.
III. Series.
BX4827.B3W33 1991
230′.044′092—dc20   90-34275
                                                                CIP

10   9   8   7   6   5   4   3   2   1

CONTENTS

PREFACE

This is an exercise in theology and tropology — on the two assumptions that the *logos* of theology is in its deepest level 'word' in the fullest sense of that term: written, rhetorical, poetic; and that *how* you say what you say is to a great extent *what* you say. Thus, I have set out to display the figuration of the word of theology, and to achieve this I have chosen to focus on the words written by Karl Barth. John Updike first put me on the track of pursuing Barth's style. In his novel, *Roger's Version* (New York: Fawcett Crest, 1986), the main character, a divinity school professor, ruminates on two of the greatest theologians of this century. Paul Tillich, he decides, is tepid, uncertain, a lightweight in comparison to Karl Barth. What he likes about Barth, though, is not just his specific theological proposals but primarily his style: "the superb iron of Barth's paragraphs, his magnificent seamless integrity and energy in this realm of prose—the specifically Christian—usually conspicuous for intellectual limpness and dishonesty . . . it caresses and probes every crevice of the unknowable" (41–42). While I do not agree with many of Roger's theological judgments, I was prompted to consider his taste for rhetoric. Barth is more troubling, provocative and, in the end, exciting to read than any of his contemporaries — or, I am tempted to add, any of our own. Thus, I decided that Updike's insight was worth exploring in a systematic fashion.

The more I read Barth's early work, the more I realized that *only* a rhetorical approach could do justice to this theologian. Barth's early work is not about the Wholly Other God, dialectics, crisis, the failure of the church, the renewed importance of the Bible, the retrieval of the orthodox doctrines of sin and predestination, or the integration of socialist thought into theology. It is neither a return to the reformation nor an introduction to existentialism. All of these themes are present in Barth but they are subordinated to a dominant and disruptive style. His writing is such that he can never make a statement that is not qualified in some ironic way or contradicted with equal assurance, sometimes in the very same paragraph. If I have occasionally contradicted myself in attributing various positions to Barth, then I must say that it is only because I have tried to read Barth consistently. His early style subverts any attempt to label his thought or to place him in a school of theology; there is no Barthian "ism" that can be summarized in some propositional form. His attempts to make this clear in the several prefaces to *The Epistle to the Romans* should not be interpreted, therefore, as excessive modesty or the longing to "go it alone." Indeed, Barth could not found a school of theology because great style is, by definition, inimitable.

This style, especially, resists paraphrase or repetition. Barth was writing at a time when God was present only in an absent future, he thought, so he had to write against theology, against, in fact, himself, in order to make evident what was hidden. I trace this style through three moments which, although analyzed separately, overlap and interpenetrate each other. Barth's metaphors proliferate his sense of an eternally impending crisis, and yet that crisis is such that he can never fully comprehend it. Instead, he hyperbolically distances humanity from its perception of God and denounces all religious and cultural attempts to bridge the gap from here to there. This prophetic approach claims to know too much, however, and so it too is subject to the crisis. In the end, his own attempt to make sense of the crisis is rendered incoherent; ironically, he cannot mean what he has set out to say. Throughout each phase of this tropical journey, then, from metaphor through hyperbole to irony, Barth's work is nearly unreadable. Barth does not write about God but reenacts the religious situation by displaying a theology under an impossible pressure, a discourse deprived of its subject matter. There is, thus, an unavoidable connection between his style and the content of his theology; one cannot be understood without the other. This connection even continues into his later work, where his belief that God speaks first and the theologian must listen and obey is reflected in a realistic style in which the earlier twists and tensions of his rhetoric are straightened and relaxed. These, in any case, were the conclusions I reached after a careful reading of this great theological writer.

ACKNOWLEDGMENTS

Writing theology is such an intersubjective enterprise that only convention keeps this section — which is not a series of compliments but a witness to my many dependencies — from being incorporated into the main body of the text. This work began as a thesis at the University of Chicago Divinity School, and my dissertation committee was ideally suited to inspire and guide my explorations. I have benefited from Langdon Gilkey's lectures, writings, and conversations about the powerful effect of Karl Barth on his own career. Better than anybody I know, Gilkey communicates the passion of what has been called neoorthodox theology; yet, by not being limited to this theological position, he has shown me how to learn from it without repeating it. Gilkey's theological writing, by the way, is surely the best of his generation and gives me hope that style in theology is not a dead issue. Lynn Poland's knowledge of the field of religion and literature has been especially helpful. In particular, her book *Literary Criticism and Biblical Hermeneutics: A Critique of Formalist Approaches* (Chico, Calif.: Scholars Press, 1985) has been a model for my own work; her use of literary categories in studying theology has helped me to see how to examine Barth's theology for both its figuration and its realism. Finally, David Tracy has contributed to every stage of this project. In fact, I like to think of this work as an extension of his own: whereas he sees theology in essentially rhetorical terms, as an ongoing conversation, I have tried to offer a rhetorical analysis of one particular theologian, a theologian with whom he is often thought to be at odds.

Tracy's inspiration has been more than just pointing to a new direction in theology, which others can then develop. His reading of Barth as the principal representative of what he calls the trajectory of the route of proclamation, which is the preaching of the dual pronouncement of God's judgment and grace, as opposed to manifestation theology, which is sacramental in displaying the avenues of possible union with God, has shaped my own, more specifically rhetorical reading. (See *Analogical Imagination, Christian*

Theology and the Culture of Pluralism, New York: Crossroad, 1981, chapter 9.) Moreover, his analysis of pluralism in theology has informed my attempt, at the end of this book, to reread Barth's rhetoric in the light of the contemporary situation. Thus, I have tried to show that there are valuable rhetorical resources in Barth that can make contributions even to theologians working within the presuppositions which David Tracy so splendidly exemplifies. I should also note, in a personal aside, that his analogical and pluralistic imagination is as helpful in practice as it is in theory: he is always ready to make room for imaginations different from his own. Thus, at every stage of this project he has been a wonderful advisor and friend, full of encouragement and patience. Without both his work and his life this book would never have been launched, let alone completed.

Finally, I want to not pay but acknowledge some personal debts which I have incurred over the past several years. Dave Burgess, who teaches religious studies at Aberdeen University, Scotland, has been a constant source of wisdom and inspiration. Raymond Williams of Wabash College graciously came to my assistance at crucial junctures during my graduate studies. By inviting me to teach at Wabash, he gave me the best context in which I could begin and complete this project. Bill Placher, also of Wabash, has contributed many important suggestions and comments. His eye for detail is matched only by his insight into the larger movement of things. Although he basically agrees with my reading of Barth, he has drawn the opposite conclusion, believing that Barth's later realistic rhetoric rather than his early figures is more valuable for theology today. All three of these men, I should add, along with the late Eric Dean (who introduced me to Barth, not to any Barthianism), Hall Peebles, and David Greene (whose close reading improved this work immensely), have been my teachers, showing me that thinking, imagining, and being religious—as well as being good friends—are all of one fabric. Mary Gerhart, Hamilton Beck, and Ken Chase also offered valuable critical suggestions, and the following have been significant conversation partners: Andy Laue, Dan Clark, Clisson Rexford, Linda Margolis, Don Breen, and Victor Vogt. My parents, Carl and Helen Webb, have been more than generous with their support. Finally, Diane Timmerman helped me with the original German text of *The Epistle to the Romans,* although I alone take responsibility for my inability to improve upon the magnificent translation by Edwyn C. Hoskyns. Diane also is my best friend and loving wife, and to her this work — which she saw in its finished form long before I did—is gratefully dedicated.

READING KARL BARTH

RHETORIC AND THEOLOGY

Rhetoric, classically defined by Aristotle as "the faculty of observing in any given case the available means of persuasion,"[1] often has been set on the margin[2] of those discourses that fall short of (a perhaps unrealistic ideal of) the apodictic demonstrations of science. In this view rhetoric has been limited to the traditional dichotomies of means and ends (persuasion as opposed to demonstration) or form and substance (appearance as opposed to essence), functioning either to show what is already known or to convince when there is no known. Today, however, it can serve more theoretical than practical purposes by contributing diverse analyses to any field of inquiry: a theory of the many and mixed levels of argumentation employed in any pattern of persuasion; the location and reception of a text or event in particular situations with various audiences; an analysis of the relationship between discourse and forms of power in the formation of communities; and an examination of the employment of figures of speech and other literary and rhetorical categories.[3] In all of these cases, rhetoric, which now subsumes or at least cuts into such fields as philosophy of language, literary theory, linguistics, and aesthetics, facilitates inquiry into the ground and aim of communication; broadly construed, it is moving toward the center of the self-reflection of any discipline that becomes conscious of its own linguistic structure and communicative praxis.

Theology, in its attempts to make deep truths clear and to defend its own legitimacy, has always had a stake in rhetoric, and recently, following the lead of David Tracy, Sallie McFague, and others, theologians have begun the task of reflecting systematically on the many productive connections between these two fields. In *Plurality and Ambiguity,* for example, Tracy advocates an essentially rhetorical model for theology with his theory of conversation: because of the "dialogical reality of all human life," theology is, to a significant extent, constituted by its many dialogue partners and has no

single or simple structure or ground.[4] McFague also has done much to promote a rhetorical version of theology, arguing that religious reality can only
be imagined figuratively, not conceived abstractly: "The point is that difficult, strange, unfamiliar matters must be approached with the utmost cunning, imagination, and indirection in order for them to be seen at all."[5]
McFague suggests that it is not sufficient to acknowledge the poetic basis of
first-order religious language — scripture, hymns, confessions, prayers —
but that second-order theological reflection must also confront its rhetorical
construction.[6]

Yet many theologians, perhaps concerned over the charge of being
"merely rhetorical" and anxious over the precarious status of theology in
both the academic and wider publics, are hesitant to acknowledge the various claims of rhetoric.[7] Their concern is that rhetoric will detract from or
minimize the significance of specifically theological problems. This is the
case not only for theologians. As Michael Leff explains, "At base, academic
antipathy toward the study of rhetoric arises from the fear that, in pursuing
this subject, intellectuals might chart a course for their own destruction."[8]
When rhetoric is conceived as a tool of persuasion regardless of the content
of communication, many scholars are motivated to battle against it: rhetoric
is thought to be radically unsystematic and, therefore, threatening, reducing
all judgments to the question of immediate persuasive effect. Rhetoric is an
art, not a science, which manipulates words without showing any concern
for the objects with which words should correspond, thus implying an epis-
temologically disruptive separation of language and reality. At the root of
this view is a philosophical tendency to contrast rhetoric and reason; rhetoric can thus be opposed with the warning cry of relativism, which it is
thought to represent.

Even if rhetoric is treated in a positive manner, it is usually allowed to
function only if it is subordinated to the rules of reason. Questions of style,
some believe, should be contained by the canon of good taste and should
only serve to embellish the subject matter under discussion. Although this
view does not treat rhetoric as unsystematic and relativistic, it does manage
to demote rhetoric to a merely practical discipline, implying that it is void of
any philosophical significance of its own, not even as a representative of relativism. Rhetoric is thus good for certain problems of communication but
not worthwhile for the development and explication of theories. At best, this
position holds, rhetoric comes after the fact: that is, it helps to communicate
an already established theory or finding. This is evident in theology, where
any treatment of rhetoric is often relegated to the neglected field of practical
theology and the problem of preaching; note, for example, Schleiermacher's

influential *Brief Outline on the Study of Theology,* where the question of communication and style is raised only in the discussion of the structure of the church service.[9]

Some voices run counter to these generalizations. One recent model of the renewed use of rhetoric as a theoretical tool is Clifford Geertz, who fights against the usual prejudices in his attempt to offer a rhetorical reading of anthropologists in *Works and Lives, the Anthropologist as Author.*[10] Geertz argues that ethnographic texts are author-saturated (as opposed to author-evacuated texts, common in the natural sciences), and he tries to make this rhetorical basis of anthropology productive, not destructive. Those who criticize his approach, he argues, imply that, "Exposing how the thing is done is to suggest that, like the lady sawed in half, it isn't done at all."[11] To meet this objection, he tries to focus on the rhetoric peculiar to the anthropological texts he discusses, instead of importing rhetorical theories that might be foreign to his field's concerns. His goal is to show that anthropologists have particular styles that shape their observations, methods, and theories. Displaying this style does not detract from but instead adds to our knowledge of anthropology. This is a strategy I will follow, but, as chapter two will show, I will not forego theoretical reflection on rhetoric itself, something Geertz's book is lacking. Without such reflection it is too easy to view rhetoric as style separated from, even if important for, content.

One of the leading contemporary theoreticians of rhetoric has been Paul de Man. He argues that rhetoric has less to do with persausion than with an inherent capacity within language itself. He defines the rhetorical as any language that does not mean what it seems to say. In fact, he equates "the rhetorical, figural potentiality of language with literature itself."[12] Rhetoric is the flexibility that disrupts the one-to-one relationship between words and things. In order to defend this view de Man insists that rhetoric cannot be reduced to grammar; thus, the logic of language is never coincident with its structure. Indeed, language really does not have a logic: "Rhetoric radically suspends logic and opens up vertiginous possibilities of referential aberration."[13] Restricted to the realm of literature, this definition poses no problems; however, when rhetoric is connected to allegedly literal texts — a move which is part of de Man's project — rhetoric becomes a potentially explosive and controversial force. If the language of science and scholarship is less refentially stable that it appears, then the problem of interpretation can become nearly insurmountable. This is, in fact, de Man's position: rhetoric makes the otherwise seemingly simple process of reading problematic.[14] Indeed, to read a text rhetorically is to question the process of reading. Yet this kind of reading does not have to be narcissistic, con-

cerned only with its own inabilities; a recognition of the limits of interpretation and the ambiguities of language can lead to very sensitive, even precise textual analyses.

The question that remains is whether such a reading can be applied to
theological texts. Thus, before the interconnection of rhetoric and theology
can be cemented, the importance of rhetoric for theology *as theology* must
be demonstrated. To accomplish this, at least two issues need to be ad-
dressed: How is rhetoric crucial for theology? That is, in what ways is rhetoric pervasive throughout the entire theological spectrum? And what are the
benefits and limits of a rhetorical analysis of theology? In other words, how
can the analysis of rhetoric both deepen and challenge the self-understanding of theologians?

READINGS OF KARL BARTH

In order to initiate a response to these broad questions, I propose to
offer a figurative or tropical reading of Karl Barth as a test case of this inter-
disciplinary frontier. I want to show that rhetoric lies at the heart of theology
by giving a systematically rhetorical reading of Barth, which will reveal
Barth's theological depths. My decision to focus on figures does not exhaust
the resources and possibilities of a rhetorical reading of Barth. One could
also analyze the argumentative structures of Barth's thought; reconstruct
the history of the reception of his works; or relate his rhetoric to the social
and political powers of his time and to the present. However, I want to argue
that Barth's theology is especially suited for a figurative approach. In fact,
Maurice Wiles has suggested that Barth could be read best as a kind of theological poet.[15] I do not mean to imply that tropical readings of theologians
are best practiced on writers like Barth who wear their rhetoric on their
sleeves; on the contrary, as I hope to show in chapter two, every theologian
of any sophistication could be illuminated by a figurative reading. However,
Barth's case is particularly instructive because although he rarely discussed his own rhetoric, many have noted its power and, moreover, his theology did arise from a deliberate reflection on the problem of religious communication.

Barth spent about ten years as a pastor at Safenwil, a village in Aar-
gau, Switzerland, and much of his early work was a result of his many struggles over the question: How is preaching possible? T. F. Torrance has argued
that the problem of preaching is central to all of Barth's work: "His primary
concern then [in Safenwil] as now was the question as to what preaching
really is as a task with its own independent right and action."[16] Certainly this
problem is a key to the early Barth, and it gives his writing its characteristic

restless urgency. Barth wanted to preach the Word of God, but he was unsure of the ability of his own words to do it justice. In Barth's own formulation of this problem:

> Is one single word of mine perhaps *the* word I am searching for, a word which I out of my great urgency and hope would like to say? Can I speak in such a way that one word does not nullify another?[17]

Here, in an important passage, we can feel a significant tension in Barth's work: faced with the blank page of theology, he tries to erase his marks just as he is making them. Yet Barth could also make pronouncements on God with the most confident enthusiasm, portraying grace as a "shattering disturbance, an assault which brings everything into question."[18] In fact, when Barth speaks of God's grace as a lightning bolt, both illuminating and destroying human existence at the same time (*R,* 227), the reader today can only think of Barth's work itself, and the effect it had on the theology of its day. The contour of this anxious writing, as these examples make clear, wavers, I will argue, between bombastic exclamations and cunning retractions. The resulting mixture is often explosive, a style that has rarely been matched in modern theology.

This explosiveness is especially true of his early work, which has been called, and the image is both a compliment and a warning, a bomb thrown into the playground of the theologians.[19] The figure is appropriate because many of Barth's own metaphors and analogies from this period are military ones.[20] This helps to explain why Barth's early rhetoric was shocking, fascinating, intimidating, and even insulting to his generation. Recall, for example, his own ironic self-description from his early period as a wandering gypsy who, having only a few leaky kettles of his own, for compensation occasionally sets a house on fire (*RTM,* 79–80). The appeal of that inflammatory rhetoric, although not widespread, is still present today. Note John Updike's persistent obsession with Barth's work, an interest that is often expressed in writers' terms.[21] The question, then, naturally arises concerning Barth's writings: Why is he so troubling and seductive, even to those who vehemently disagree with him and wish to disregard him?

Langdon Gilkey perhaps best captures this reaction in a memorable reflection on his many careful readings of Barth:

> There is no arguing with this man *while* you are reading him — his thought has entirely too much dominating or overwhelming power. If you wish to dispute with him, close the book, lock it in a closet and move away — preferably quite out of the house. Then and only then can you succeed in constructing a critique.[22]

Even a theologian whose work has been a development of Barth's, Hans Frei, can write, "He was decisive, and could be frustratingly, even infuriatingly contrary and stubborn . . . Certainly Barth actually relished opposition even though he could drive opponents to distraction by his confidence that he was right."[23] Frei suggests that Barth often used irony to deflect and refract his more aggressive tendencies, an insight that I will try to develop in a systematic manner in chapter five.

Both of these theologians point to the fact that Barth's self-confidence, mixed with the clever candor of irony and the sometimes brutal exaggerations of polemics, leaves no room for an indifferent reaction. To say that Barth forces a decision on his own work from those willing to wade through the thick of it, however, is not to say, as many commentators have pointed out, that to follow Barth is an easy task. In fact, it is surely easier to disagree with him than to try to trace over the tortured logic and the fragmented prose of his early work or to step into the tightly structured and isolated world of his later thought. One reason for this difficulty is that Barth was a thinker of extremes, and as Hans Frei has pointed out, his various extremes could be mutually contradictory.[24] Especially in his early work he pushes theology to dialectial, paradoxical, and contradictory limits. Both prophetic and poetic, his work cannot be easily followed or simply paraphrased. How then can anyone begin to understand the cutting vigor and the broad but weighty expostulations of Barth's many theological travails?

This question can be restated simply: How can we best read Karl Barth? John Bowden is a good example of the way scholars note Barth's rhetorical power without reflecting on the implications of that observation. Bowden at first seems to understand that Barth's style is integral to his theological content, and he wrestles with an explanation of that style.

> Several analogies have been used to sum up Barth's style. He has been seen as an architect, building on mediaeval scale and with a mediaeval freedom that is not afraid of inconsistency. He has been seen as a poet or painter, setting down what has escaped less penetrating eyes. And probably most appropriately of all, he has been compared with the great musicians . . . 'Symphonic' is a good adjective for Barth.[25]

However, Bowden goes on to say that such attempts to understand Barth's style

> would be only to skate the surface. The long hours in the study were not spent polishing style . . . What he was like, how he put what he had to say, were immaterial in the face of the question whether what he saw was right, and whether he communicated his vision faithfully.[26]

Precisely at the moment of rhetorical insight, Bowden succumbs to the prejudice that rhetoric has nothing to do with reason and truth. Perhaps the problem here is that Bowden's stylistic analysis does not go deep enough; an analysis that could do justice to Barth's style might show that his style is more than just the immaterial surface of his theological constructions. In any case, Bowden is an example of the tendency of writers to praise Barth's style but also to draw back from the use of rhetoric as an explanatory tool in theology.

The most common answer to the problem of reading Barth has been to bypass the question of style altogether by extracting a theme from the Barthian corpus and demonstrating its significance and centrality.[27] Many such motifs have been put forward as candidates for the key to unlocking Barth's complexities. An abbreviated list of such attempts should include the Trinity, the Holy Spirit, the problem of Justification, the Word of God, the problem of the Other, political theology, grace, the church, and hermeneutics.[28] Most recently, George Hunsinger, wearied by the single-mindedness of this strategy, has argued that there is no single motif in Barth but instead there are five key themes.[29] While this work is surely an advance on previous scholarship, one is forced to wonder whether multiplying motifs is really the best way to resolve the problems inherent in the thematic approach. As Hunsinger himself has noted, the symphonic complexities and ceaseless self-questionings in Barth serve to resist the quest to reduce his work to one or even several different key themes. Barth himself requested that readers approach his book not with the intention of finding in it some school or theme (he was especially concerned that people would see him through the spectacles of Emil Brunner) but "to read it as though they knew nothing of those well-known glosses and catch-phrases" (*R*, vii). To disregard what has been made of *Romans* is not an easy task, but to pay attention to the specificities of the language of this book is surely a first step toward appreciating it "on its own merits" (*R*, vii).

When it comes to reading the early Barth, the problem of theme hunting is only exacerbated. Some of the defenders of the motifs catlogued above argue that these same themes pervade the early Barth as well. Berkouwer, for example, has argued that the triumph of grace was present in Barth from the very beginning. Others have found a greater divide between the early and late Barth, and they focus on themes distinctive to his early period, such as dialectics, the Wholly Other God, the idea of crisis, and the critique of religion. Many debates, therefore, have centered on the nature and development of this turn in Barth's thought. Hans Urs von Balthasar has claimed that a reconstructed principle of analogy and a Christological concentration separate the later from the earlier Barth,[30] and T. F. Torrance, turning Bonhoeffer's charge into a virtue, has argued that theological positivism and objectivism best characterize the later Barth, although he claims to find such methodological principles implicitly present even in the earlier Barth.[31] In chapter six I will put forward my own, rhetorical reading of the shift in Barth's thought in the 1920s. Even the early Barth, however, must now be divided into different periods, with Barth's earliest liberal writings giving way to the first and then the crucial second edition of *Romans*.[32]

I want to focus my own attempt to read Barth on this second edition of Barth's commentary on *The Epistle to the Romans,* published in 1922, which was one of the most significant, influential and extreme responses to the crisis situation of post-war Europe. By choosing this focus I cannot do justice to all of Barth's thought, especially his later work. Indeed, I want to take seriously the fact that he often dismissed the importance of *Romans,* as in the 1932 preface to the English edition: "When, however, I look back at the book, it seems to have been written by another man to meet a situation belonging to a past epoch." (*R,* vi) However, it is *Romans* that left the deepest and most disturbing impression on theology of all of Barth's works, and it is in *Romans* that the question of style in theology is most fervently raised. In fact, the style of *Romans* was provocative from the very beginning: one problem with the reception of the book was that nobody knew what genre it was—was it trying to be a scholarly commentary, an aid to preaching, speculative theology, practical edification, or some mixture of these? Indeed, some readers had difficulty in finding any coherency to the book at all, so that the translator for the English edition asked Barth to explain that it should not be treated as a collection of fragments (*R,* vii). These stylistic confusions continue to the present day, as I have tried to show. Commentators try to resist the essentially rhetorical configurations of this text by isolating and extracting themes. I want to suggest that such moves do not do justice to a real reading of *Romans;* as de Man has argued, to read a text rhetorically is to call into question the process of reading itself. Such a strategy will raise questions in the place of making generalizations. For this strategy, a theological rhetoric is required. My hope is that by learning how to read this work, its theological content will become more deeply understood.

BARTH AND EXPRESSIONISM

Fortunately, Hans Urs von Balthasar has put the answer to the problem of reading Barth on the right track by offering an aesthetic analogue to the *Romans* commentary. "In methodology," von Balthasar writes, "it is theological expressionism."[33] The lack of harmony in the work, the striking juxtaposition of images and ideas, the disturbing ambiguity and ceaseless striving after paradox, and the breaking of old forms combined with a hesitation to create new ones, all point to a revolutionary program that demands rhetorical as well as theological reflection. Expressionism thus serves as a stylistic or rhetorical precedent for *Romans,* which is markedly different from the usual attempts to find philosophical or theological precedents for the work—such as the search for Platonic idealism, Kierkegaardian or Hegelian dialectics, Overbeckian cynicism, Kantian dualism or religious socialism latent in Barth's thought, not to mention the influence of Luther, Calvin, Nietzsche, Dostoevsky, Feuerbach, Christoph Blumhardt, and Wilhelm Herrmann.

Other writers, including, for example, Wilhelm Pauck, have also made the expressionist analogy in describing *Romans,* so that it has now become commonplace in the secondary literature.[34] Yet none of these writers develop this observation with an analysis of Barth's style. In fact, von Balthasar at one point attributes Barth's style to his faithfulness to God: "He did not write well because he had a gift for style. He wrote well because he bore witness to a reality that epitomizes style, since it comes from the hand of God."[35] Both von Balthasar and Pauck use the expressionist analogy to label or place the power of Barth's rhetoric, but then they go on to examine isolated themes in *Romans* as if that rhetoric did not affect the substance of Barth's thought. I think this analogy is a helpful start for a rhetorical reading of Barth, but it is only that; it must be further developed in aesthetic and rhetorical categories if it is to prove to be more than just an incidental observation.[36]

One difficulty with the expressionist analogy is that it is a general movement that is exemplified in many different genres. Barth himself would not have found this analogy very helpful if painting were used as the representative of expressionism. Although his verbal imagination is indisputable, and his delight in Mozart is well known, his theological comments on the visual arts were "few and mainly negative in character."[37] I have found only one reference to artistic expressionism in his early work; he begrudgingly approves of it only because it is not art for art's sake.[38] He did make the acquaintance of two expressionist painters in 1921, but there is no evidence that he was especially interested in their work.[39] The painting he most often and almost solely commented on was Grünewald's *Crucifixion* from the *Isenheim Altarpiece,* which, interestingly enough, the expressionists considered to be one of their forerunners and Paul Tillich considered to be a great example of expressionism, but I will return to Tillich later.[40] It is interesting to note that what Barth always likes about Grünewald's *Crucifixion* painting is that John the Baptist's forefinger—exaggeratedly elongated—is pointing away from himself and imperatively toward Christ. In other words, Barth likes the painting because it does not draw attention to itself; he does not commend it for any of its intrinsic, or artistic features. If *Romans* truly is an expressionist work, then that is due not to any direct influence but rather to traits that both expressionism and Barth's theology hold in common.

What both do hold in common is their relationship to a culture in crisis. I will return to this theme when I examine Barth's use of the metaphor of crisis in chapter three. For now I merely want to note that Barth himself, in the several prefaces to *Romans,* is the best commentator on his uneasy relationship to World War I Germany and the later Weimar culture. He initially defended *Romans* as a reproduction of the biblical message, not a representation of German culture. In the preface to the first edition, published in 1918, Barth states that his purpose in writing the work is to demonstrate that the differences between biblical and modern times are "purely trivial" (*R,* 1). In the preface written in 1921 for the second edition, he reiterates this theme of a hermeneutics glued to the subject matter of the Bible alone. Barth wants to get to know the author of the epistle so well that "I allow him to speak in my name and am even able to speak in his name myself" (*R,* 8). This strategy of loyalty and obedience to the text has the goal of letting the text speak without translating it into concepts that might be foreign to its original intention.[41] It is an attempt to avoid the problems of rhetoric by reflecting a language already formed, and it is a move that Barth will more successfully accomplish in his later work.

Barth anticipates various objections to his method, including the criticism that he is a Biblicist, which he preempts with this bit of understatement: "When I am named 'Biblicist,' all that can rightly be proved against me is that I am prejudiced in supposing the Bible to be a good book, and that I hold it to be profitable for men to take its conceptions at least as seriously as they take their own" (*R,* 12). Yet, already in the preface to the second edition he expresses doubts about his hermeneutical program, realizing that an understanding of Paul "involves more than a mere repetition in Greek or in German of what Paul says: it involves the reconsideration of what is set out in the Epistle, until the actual meaning of it is disclosed" (*R,* 6–7). In the preface to the third edition, he begins to realize that his book was not written in the hermeneutical vacuum, which he had once supposed. He laments the irony of the modern situation that "a man says something, and then finding it echoed in the mouths of others, fears to say it again, lest its meaning be altogether lost in the noise of its echo" (*R,* 15). He is beginning to wonder if he said what the Bible said in his book or if he spoke to a more contemporary scene.

This concern is explicitly raised in the preface to the fifth edition, written in 1926, where Barth asks, "When I wrote the book, did I simply put into words what was everywhere fashionable — especially in Germany after the War?'' (*R*, 21). Barth's positive but uneasy answer to this question is given an ironic release:

> Every word I wrote against human — too human — vapourings, everything I wrote especially against religious vapourings, everything I said about the various causes and effects, seems now to be turned back against myself. I had set out to please none but the very few, to swim against the current, to beat upon doors which I thought were firmly bolted. Was I altogether deceived? Perhaps I was. For who is able to know even himself accurately, or to gauge his contemporaries? Who knows whether we are not being moved, just when we are moving others?... Am I after all one of those bad theologians who are no more than servants of public opinion? (*R*, 22).

Besides being a good example of Barth's taste for irony, this passage sets the pattern for his later criticisms of this early work. Barth came to feel slightly embarrassed by his first theological success and attributed it to youthful impropriety and a cultural moment now long past. This connection between the book and its cultural conditioning is finally admitted in bald terms in the preface to the sixth and last edition of the book in 1928: ''A great deal of the scaffolding of the book was due to my own particular situation at the time and also to the general situation. This would have to be pulled down [if I were to rewrite it today]'' (*R*, 25). Barth's original intention to create a hermeneutics of loyalty was reread, even in his own eyes, as a hermeneutics of assimilation, and he would have to begin his theology all over again to try to reach his goal.

These exaggerated self-criticisms of Barth should not be taken literally precisely because he was trying to distance himself from his early work in order to start anew. In fact, in chapter three, where I will discuss the metaphor of crisis, I will argue that Barth's notion of crisis is not identical to the pervasive sense of crisis that was present throughout German culture at that time. However, there are definite and obvious parallels between *Romans* and other currents in German culture, and the expressionist analogy serves to bring those shared traits into focus. Barth came to see not only that his theological style was, to a significant extent, a reflection of the style then dominant in the arts, but also that this style was on the way out, for as we will see in chapter six, as the arts turned to a new objectivity, so did Barth once again follow along.

The expressionist analogy, however, has never been closely analysed in its application to Barth, and I believe such an analysis quickly shows both its benefits and its limitations. The term is notoriously difficult to define and its range of application can be so broad as to force it to hold more meaning than is good for any such label.[42] It was first used in France in 1901, and it was applied to painting in Germany around 1911 and to literature around 1914. Eduard Munch and Van Gogh are usually considered its forerunners, and in Germany its most consistent representatives were the groups Die Brücke and Der blaue Reiter. Although most scholars claim that it is impossible to find a common denominator in all of its manifestations, nevertheless many definitions abound. A typical characterization focuses on its revolutionary aspects: "The expressionist practice springs from a violent anti-realism and is based on the refusal to imitate, repeat, reproduce that which already exists."[43] This rather negative definition paraphrases the polemical banner of the movement: *Die Welt ist da. Es wäre sinnlos, sie zu wiederholen.* (The world is there. It would make no sense to repeat it.)

Although expressionism was a repudiation of naturalism, especially in the form of impressionism, it was in no sense disconnected from reality. In most of its forms, in fact, it was an imitation of the human world, and only in its later phases did it become more abstract. Its mimetic practice, however, was not concerned with accuracy of representation. Instead, it wanted to distort, extend and even fragment and shatter the surface of reality in order to uncover something even more real hidden beneath the surface. Several scholars have pointed to exaggeration as one of its techniques.[44] Complacency could only be battled by exaggeration, and this gave the expressionists their prophetic edge. They were often caricatured as religious visionaries and ecstatic and eccentric irrationalists, yet they did not necessarily want to express their own, idiosyncratic emotions but the pathos obscured by the numbing normalities of quotidian existence. Some expressionists were, in fact, political as well as artistic revolutionaries, guided by dramatically utopian visions. After the Great War, however, their guiding visions became increasingly apocalyptic, obsessed with pain and suffering and the darker realities of life.

Ironically, the theologian who made the most of expressionism—using it as an apologetical tool, which was not prima facie inappropriate due to the religious and spiritual concerns of the movement—was Barth's theological nemesis, Paul Tillich. Although Tillich did not write in an expressionistic style, that art movement was formative for his theological development. He understood expressionism as a rejection of a portrayal of the world as natural, self-contained and finite "in favor of a view of the world in which depth and ultimacy were affirmed beneath the surface of reality as then perceived by society."[45] Tillich's use of the term is broad indeed; it denotes any painting or period that depicts the depths of existence. An expressionist work, he suggests, "does something with the surface of reality; it breaks it; it pierces into its ground; it reshapes it, reorders the elements in order more power-fully to express meaning. It exaggerates some elements over against others. It reduces the surface quality of natural reality to a minimum in order to bring out the depth meaning that it contains.''[46] It is not an art of despair, he contends, because of the courage that is needed to penetrate to such depths. However, in Tillich's interpretation expressionism does raise questions rather than offer answers, as in his favorite painting, Picasso's *Guernica,* in which, Tillich thought, the Protestant honesty concerning the fragmentation of meaning is most vividly presented.

Of course, expressionism was not limited to the visual arts; it also had a great influence on drama and literature, even though it is not a simple task to find the common ground that binds together expressionist literature. Some scholars have argued that the power of expressionist style in literature derives from a thwarted desire for a new reality.[47] The expressionists mix an aggressive defense of the highest ideals with self-contempt and a mistrust of the intellect. Such literature, which manifests a tendency to sermonize, makes its points by building menacing crescendos of exclamations and ques-tions. One scholar argues that the result is an "excessive use of figurative language, whereby the figures used were often bald and phantastic."[48] Expressionist writers use crass and shocking language, exaggerated and bombastic phrases. They do not care to set their observations in a detailed historical context, but rather want to stress the essential by any possible means. Some of their favorite techniques include the use of stammering, the overuse of exclamation points and dashes, experimentation with sentence structure, the reiteration of questions, the use of repetition, the expression of ideas antithetically, a tendency to play words against each other, and a ba-roque tendency to write in excess, that is, to say more than is needed to make a given point. One study has called this latter characteristic a "ten-dency to accumulation and enumeration."[49] Certainly many of these obser-vations could be directly applied to Barth's *Romans,* and this kind of analy-sis definitely informs my approach.

I should note that an analysis of Barth's expressionism is not only ab-sent from the theological literature, but it is missing from literary and aes-thetic criticism as well. In my survey of books on expressionism it is rare — even in books which focus on the religious aspects of expressionism — to find any mention of Barth.[50] Perhaps this is evidence that Frei's complaint is justified: "Had he not been a theologian, he would have been more widely recognized as one of the towering minds of the twentieth century."[51] And, I would want to add, as a great writer as well. Barth was not completely ne-glected on the latter point; he was given the Sigmund Freud Prize by the Academy for Poetry and Speech in 1968 for the quality of his academic prose. Yet the quality of that prose is explained only with such vague terms as volcanic, bombastic, explosive, overwhelming, and the like, hardly adequate explanatory analysis.

A CLOSER LOOK AT THE EXPRESSIONIST ANALOGY

Perhaps it would be helpful to play out the expressionism analogy by making it concrete with two examples. I want to explore the benefits and limits of this analogy by commenting on a painting and a film that are productively similar to Barth's *Romans*.[52] The painting is from Max Beckmann, a great expressionist, who wrote in the journal *Kunst und Kunstler* in 1914, "I want a style that, in contrast to the art of exterior decoration, will penetrate as deeply as possible into the fundamental nature, into the soul of things."[53] At first he was not as revolutionary as many of his contemporaries; he did not experiment with form or repudiate impressionism as much as some of the others in the movement. However, an early work, *Large Deathbed Scene* (1906), already shows his ability to evoke intense emotion by confronting tragic subject matter. After a nervous breakdown in 1915, his subject matter increasingly turned to suffering, despair, and death—to crisis. As one of his critics noted, "The war propelled the painter into reality."[54] As I will show in chapter three, this comment could have been made equally of Barth.

One of Beckmann's most powerful works is *The Night* (*Die Nacht*, 1918), painted the year Barth was finishing the first edition of *Romans*.[55] It is a horrifying scene of torture and murder. The picture is grotesque and joyless. Although the scene depicts the action of the murder of a family, the figures are stern and the arrangement is static, making the impression that the emotion in the work is carefully controlled. Beckmann is not expressing any sentimentality toward the victims; an open window above a sprawling woman mocks any hope for escape. The picture plane is filled with sharp, angular forms, thrown violently against each other. It is a cubistic arrangement: there is no order of linear or aerial perspective. Even the coloring is insensitively muted: cool greys and light blues, with touches of dull red and hints of a bland yellow and green. It is as if all the horrors of the war were squeezed into this one small room, and the faces of the two murderers that are most clearly visible show very limited reactions, one twisting an arm in gawking intrigue and hesitant disbelief, the other looking away out of a smug weariness, not willing to confront what he is holding in his very own hands, a struggling young girl. The male victim's silent scream (perhaps a quotation from Munch, to whom Beckmann felt close) is balanced by his outstretched arm and flattened hand, empty and beseeching. Finally, the room itself looks on the verge of collapse: slanted walls, a distorted window, a crashing ceiling, all claustrophobically encompassing a storm of brutality and agony. Beckmann's exaggerations are clear, even if they are disturbing. In his own words,

> There is nothing I hate so much as sentimentality. The stronger and more intense my wish to record the inexpressible things of life becomes, and the more heavily and deeply distress over our existence burns in me, the more tightly I close my mouth, the cooler my desire becomes to seize this frightful twitching monster of vitality and to cage it in glass-clear sharp lines and surfaces, to suppress it, to throttle it. I do not weep, I hate tears as a sign of slavery. I always concentrate on the essential thing.[56]

Matthias Eberle has written a study, *Max Beckmann, Die Nacht, Passion ohne Erlösung,* which argues that this painting is central to Beckmann's career. In interpreting the painting he draws several comparisons to Karl Barth.[57] His main point is that Beckmann's perspective of the world is similar to Barth's, but Beckmann does not allow for redemption, whereas Barth does. Eberle does not point out that Barth's first chapter of *Romans,* after an introduction, is entitled "The Night," and there his portrayal of humanity could be seen as a gloss on Beckmann's painting of the same name. At this early point in *Romans,* Barth is in no hurry to open the back door of human depravity to an easy exit of redemption. His driving rhetoric forces humanity into the very same room that Beckmann has painted. For Barth, the night is a time when we cannot see our way to God. "In this world men find themselves to be imprisoned" (*R,* 37). Life is a contradiction to which there is no solution. Even more importantly, our vision, like the numbed stares of the villains in Beckmann's painting, is too darkened for us even to begin to see our true situation. "Life moves on its course in its vast uncertainty and we move with it, even though we do not see the great question-mark that is set against us" (*R,* 43). The night is the time of God's wrath, and Barth portrays it with the same relentless courage combined with the same lack of sympathy that can be found in Beckmann. Both, in very controlled ways, are exaggerating and distorting the human situation in order to lay bare its very essence of pain, suffering, and ignorance, not willing to offer cheap answers as a way of avoiding and denying this fundamental reality, the never-ending blackness that is the night.

My second comparative example is one of the most celebrated artifacts of the Weimar Republic, *The Cabinet of Dr. Caligari (Das Cabinet des Dr. Caligari),* a film released in Berlin in February 1920, during the time that

Barth was rewriting *Romans*. The film's expressionistic sets (which look like the room in Beckmann's painting) and nightmarish plot make it an especially vivid representative of the crisis of post-war Germany. Peter Gay has described the original plot for the film, written by two pacifists horrified by the war.[58] It is a horror story with a revolutionary message, the story of the mad Dr. Caligari, who exhibits his somnambulist, Cesare, at fairs. Wherever Caligari goes, death follows. A student, Francis, wanting to solve this puzzle, creeps into Caligari's wagon and finds Cesare asleep. But while Francis is at the fairground, Cesare has kidnapped his friend, Jane. After a long pursuit, Cesare drops the girl and dies, and the police discover that what Francis had seen in the wagon was only a dummy. Now the plot begins to unravel: Cesare has been committing crimes at his master's bidding. Caligari eludes arrest by taking refuge in an insane asylum, where it is discovered that he is really the asylum's director. He has been experimenting with one of the patients of the asylum, Cesare, inducing him to murder. In the end, Caligari is restrained by a straightjacket. The message here is clear: authority has betrayed its trust and falls victim to its own machinations of power. Caligari represents the unlimited power of the German state, an authority that ruthlessly violates all human rights and values in its lust for dominion, while Cesare stands for the common person who, under pressure from the authorities, sleepwalks his way through murder and terror.

However, the director of the film, Robert Wiene, gave the original story a new frame, over the writers' vehement objections. The result was that the film now begins and ends in the insane asylum, and at the end it is clear that the student and his girlfriend are the real mad ones. Francis's belief that the director of the asylum, Dr. Caligari, induces Cesare, one of Francis's fellow patients, to murder is just one of his many delusions. Actually, the director is a compassionate man who announces that he will finally be able to cure Francis, now that he knows the nature of his psychosis. The original plot, therefore, has been turned into a chimera, an insane person's nightmare. Gay argues that the film was changed from a radical protest against authority to a rejection of rebellion itself and an acceptance of conformity, and because he interprets expressionism under the rubric, "the revolt of the son," he sees the final form of the film as confused and uncertain.[59] He misses, I think, the deeper message of the revision that brought the film so much critical acclaim and popular enthusiasm. The frame that Wiene constructed around the original plot puts an ironic qualification on all human perception and judgment. What seems so clear, especially in acute and serious situations, can really be so distorted. The film is not a conservative political statement but an indictment of the human predicament, an artistic portrayal of epistemological nihilism. Irony is its surest form: what is known is really not known, whom we distrust we should really trust — what we really need to do is distrust ourselves.

These examples illuminate the common cultural concerns and reactions of the period of *Romans,* concerns that Barth in his prefaces increasingly came to acknowledge as the basis of his book. In fact, the examples of Beckmann's exaggerations and Wiene's irony will set the pattern for my own rhetorical reading of Barth because of their use of precisely those two tropes: hyperbole and irony. Barth's work, I will argue, is a hyperbolic response to cultural crisis, and his vision of theology in this crisis is darkly ironic. Indeed, what one immediately observes from *Romans* is that this text is hardly a commentary in the traditional sense; it is not a comment on, or a development of, Paul's letter. In fact, it is a densely allusive book, which continually quotes from a number of different sources, so that the actual Pauline text often gets lost in the myriad of references. To the extent that it is "about" Romans, it is more like a rewriting of Paul than a commentary — a translation of Romans into a strange, new language, where everything becomes magnified, all the edges become sharper as in Beckmann's painting, and the images more intense. Barth forces Paul's letter to speak with his own voice, a voice so loud that the reader could not avoid hearing it.[60] This commentary is full of anguished cries and triumphant declarations; it is still resounding today, over and above the many theological criticisms that try to label and then dismiss it.

There is a panicked urgency in Barth's writing, not dissimilar to Francis's jumbled quest to find out the truth about Dr. Caligari. Barth's style is anxious; although the substance of his theology speaks of the impossibility of arguing one's way to God, his whole approach bespeaks a kind of rhetorical Pelagianism, which attempts to use that gap between God and humanity to convince humanity of the necessity for God. It is as if Barth thought that by piling up enough negative proclamations about God, some positive truth could finally be reached. However, negations can serve as only shaky foundations at best, and this is the source of much of the anxiety and panic the reader is forced to feel in the text. Can Barth's Sherman-like march through the battlefields of a defeated liberal theology leave anything but destruction in its wake? It is as if Barth identifies with the Francis of the film and knows that all of his quests for knowledge, even in negative form, will be futile in the end, will, in fact, show that he was deluded from the very beginning. He confronts this problem in the preface to the fifth edition, where he suggests that *Romans* should have been a failure, should have shown that theology cannot really be, but instead it "has gained the applause by which it is condemned" (*R,* 22). Too many people read it as the first, original plot of Dr. Caligari rather than the second, ironic version. Ironically enough, Barth's irony failed, and his vision of the failure of our knowledge of God was turned into still one more positive theological program.

These points will have to be further developed in the course of this work. What von Balthasar and the expressionists have taught me, however, is the crucial lesson that in *Romans* there is sytle and not method, but that observation can only be the beginning of a rhetorical examination of Barth; indeed, it is the task of rhetoric to expose the method in the style of a writer. The expressionist analogy can set up signposts for such an analysis; it can point in the right direction, but it cannot do much more than that. For one reason, the term itself is so vague that it is hard to define, a problem I pointed out with regard to Tillich's use of it. For another reason, style itself is an individual phenomenon. Paul Ricoeur has argued that style is uncovered if one sees a work as the resolution of a specific problem. ''The singularity of the solution, replying to the singularity of the problem, can take on a proper name, that of the author.''[61] Expressionism can illuminate the fact that the problem Barth is responding to is the perception of a crisis. Crisis is his ruling metaphor, and his particular solution to this problem involves the tropes of hyperbole and irony, nicely developed by Beckmann and Wiene.

Already, though, these remarks are leading further away from expressionism and deeper into a rhetorical analysis of Barth's text itself. Barth knew that he shared a style with expressionism, but he also knew that he did not share a common subject matter with that movement. He came to think that his subject matter, the Word of God, needed a style all to itself alone. Precisely what Tillich liked in expressionism — its relationship to a philosophical anthropology, which could be exploited by Christian apologetics — forced Barth to push expressionism further and further away. Yet Barth's subject matter, even in his expressionist period, gave his style a particularity and individuality that warrants attention and analysis as a rhetorical triumph of its own. To accomplish that analysis, I will need to develop a rhetorical method — a theory of tropes — to which I will turn in the next chapter.

CHAPTER 2

TOWARD A TROPOLOGY

THREE THEORIES OF TROPES

Rhetoric has always been concerned with figures of speech, those perceptible forms of language that are to ordinary discourse what features or traits — the figure of a person's face — are to the body. Tzvetan Todorov, who suggests that "the day is coming when rhetoric will be no more than an enumeration of figures," laments a rhetoric infatuated with figures alone, arguing that it is not only indistinguishable from literary theory, but it also abdicates the question of truth and the search for ideas.[1] However, many language theorists today do not defend the distinction between form and content on which Todorov's criticisms rest. These scholars contend that an analysis of form is itself a substantial activity; figurative language, in other words, has cognitive import. Moreover, as Paul de Man argued in chapter one, figures are the essence of language, allowing words and sentences to have a multiplicity of meanings and uses. To understand what a given discourse means, then, its figural potency cannot be ignored. In this chapter I will try to explore this position in order to develop a foundation for a figurative or tropical reading of Karl Barth.

Of course, a rhetoric of tropes is not the only strategy that rhetoric has to offer other disciplines. In a programmatic essay, John Nelson has described seven such strategies, of which a tropics of inquiry is only one possibility. On his rhetorical map, tropes are important but not central to rhetorical practice and theory. "Tropics of inquiry," he states, "consider investigators' descriptions, explanations, and theories as sets of tropes. As figures of language, these tools and products of inquiry evoke the directions, conditions, aporias, and repressions that structure inquiry."[2] Nelson's concern is that tropes should accomplish, not replace, argumentation, and that tropes should not become detours by deflecting arguments into irrelevancies; correspondingly, the analysis of tropes should not detract from the primary concern of rhetoric, which is argumentation and communication. Underlying Nelson's position is the fear that tropes can become traps, for both the writer and the inquirer; to get around this trap, the main road of argumentation must be closely followed.

Nelson expresses a concern over the role of tropes in discourse and analysis that has a long and varied history. He thinks that tropes are important as long as they are kept in their place — that is, as long as they do not interfere with rational argumentation and analysis. This tradition, to which Nelson does not actually belong although he comes close to being an at-large member, is often called the substitution theory of figures.[3] In its simplest form it holds that figures are decorative and expendable parts of language, which can be replaced by equivalent and literal statements when maximum clarity is being sought, as is often the case in history and philosophy, not to mention the natural sciences. This tendency to regard rhetoric as a dispensable and ostentatious flourish, which serious discourse can do without, is commonly traced back — along with many other modern philosophical entanglements — to Descartes (1596 – 1650), although its roots go deeper, of course, into the very beginning of philosophy. Socrates, himself a master of rhetoric, did not think well of those like the Sophists who argued with (allegedly) less noble purposes, and Plato's treatment of the poets in his ideal republic has been much debated and denounced. Yet Descartes provides one of the major points of origin for the modern period, and so his approach to language and reason is close enough to our own to make it seem especially important to analyze and amend.

With Descartes, epistemology became the centerpiece of philosophy; he was writing during a time when scepticism was accepted as a real problem, the logic of probability had not yet been developed to mediate between the two categories of demonstration and authority, and authority itself was increasingly questioned as a source of knowledge.[4] Descartes set out to make knowledge secure; having formed his ideals of knowledge by reflecting on arithmetic and geometry, he tried to discover the essentially simple, and therefore utterly clear and distinct, ideas upon which all knowledge must rest. To do this he developed a method of universal doubt; by clearing away all derivative and inconsequential beliefs, he thought he could uncover the innate and intuitive truths, which would commend themselves directly and immediately to the natural light of reason. From these truths, then, a system of propositions could be deduced. Although the nature of Descartes' program has been variously interpreted, Richard Bernstein argues that his influence, what he calls "Cartesian Anxiety," is clear: the thinking person should not rely on opinion, prejudice, tradition, or external authority but on the authority of reason alone.[5] The implications for language are enormous: language is a tool, which should aim at accuracy of representation, clarity, transparency and concision. Descartes offers language a great either-or: either language aids the search for the foundation for reason, or it abets the anxiety of a self-destructive relativism.

Two thinkers who make explicit the debilitating effects of this anxiety are the British empiricist, John Locke (1632 – 1704) and the French champion of the Enlightenment, Voltaire (1694 – 1778); they are worth quoting to give a taste of their polemics against figures. Voltaire actually holds a version of the substitution theory often called the emotive theory, because he argues that figures appeal to the emotions, and thus are untrustworthy. (Underlying this theory of figures, of course, is a theory of the emotions that is at least equally questionable.) Although he often speaks of figures in terms of metaphor, he really criticizes figures for being exaggerations, or hyperboles:

> Ardent imagination, passion, desire — frequently deceived — produce the figurative style. We do not admit it into history, for too many metaphors are hurtful, not only to perspicuity, but also to truth, by saying more or less than the thing itself.[6]

Locke's pursuit of clear reason leads him to similar conclusions concerning the need to see through language to "the thing itself." In a notorious passage in *Essay Concerning Human Understanding,* Locke denounces rhetoric with a passionate eloquence that has been seldom matched in these disputes. In fact, his own exaggerated rhetoric leads him to identify figurative speech with "the fair sex":

> But yet if we would speak of things as they are, we must allow that all the art of rhetoric, besides order and clearness; all the artificial and figurative application of words eloquence hath invented, are for nothing else but to insinuate wrong ideas, move the passions, and thereby mislead the judgment; and so indeed are perfect cheats; and therefore, however laudable or allowable oratory may render them in harangues and popular addresses, they are certainly, in all discourses that pretend to inform or instruct, wholly to be avoided; and where truth and knowledge are concerned, cannot but be thought a great fault, either of the language or person that makes use of them . . . It is evident how much men love to deceive and be deceived, since rhetoric, that powerful instrument of error and deceit, has its established professors, is publicly taught, and has always been had in great reputation: and I doubt not but it will be thought great boldness, if not brutality, in me to have said thus much against it. Eloquence, like the fair sex, has too prevailing beauties in it to suffer itself ever to be spoken against. And it is in vain to find fault with those arts of deceiving, wherein men find pleasure to be deceived.[7]

Locke's brutality — born out of a jealousy over the charms of a force that cannot be captured and a suspicion and resentment against pleasures that seem too strong — pivots in his own words on the ability of a discourse to "*pretend* to inform and instruct" without also offering pleasure and calling attention to itself. It is too easy to debunk these critiques of vanity and opacity in language by pointing to their own rhetorical configurations; the more important response is to defend a theory of tropes that does justice to both their aesthetic and cognitive dimensions. In other words, the choices that these writers offer us, their own private dualities, between pleasure and knowledge, language and truth, emotion and reason, are false and forced alternatives that must be overcome if the truth of tropes is to be fully understood.

An opposite discourse on tropes exists, less ancient but presently more respectable, one that accepts the dichotomies of the substitution theory but inverts their orders. Instead of reason and truth having the upper hand, language and the pleasure of figures are placed on top of the hierarchies. This tradition could be called the displacement theory, because it argues that tropes continually usurp the attempt of literal language to take their place. Vico, for example, in his rejection of the quest for Cartesian certitude in *The New Science* (first edition, 1725), argued that the true (*verum*) is actually the made (*factum*); what we can know for certain is only that which we ourselves have made.[8] This premise led Vico to place a new priority on history and language, both much neglected by Descartes. In fact, figures play a significant role in Vico's thought. In his historical investigations he surmised that metaphor is chronologically prior to and only gradually replaced by what is called literal description. Primitive people took their metaphors quite literally: metaphors structured their worlds and organized their thinking. Vico's larger claim is that the structure of language is the key to understanding past cultures. Implicit in this position is that minds are formed by language, not language by minds.

It is a short step from this kind of thinking to an even more radical inversion of the traditional roles of reason and language. If metaphors are chronologically prior to rational discourse, then could they also be ontologically prior? That is, could reason itself be in debt—and unable to pay off its debt—to figurative language? This is the position that Nietzsche takes when he argues that dead metaphors — metaphors that have been accepted into language and thus treated as literal — are really not so dead after all. For Nietzsche, dead metaphors are the very source of thought, and if you resuscitate such metaphors, you will certainly upset the slumber of thought. Nietzsche states this in a striking way:

What is truth? a mobile army of metaphors, metonyms, anthropo-
morphisms, in short, a sum of human relations which were poetically
and rhetorically heightened, transferred, and adorned, and after long
use seem solid, canonical, and binding to a nation. Truths are illusions
about which it has been forgotten that they *are* illusions, worn-out metaphors without sensory impact, coins which have lost their image and
now can be used only as metal, and no longer as coins.[9]

More recently Derrida has carried this insight to extreme and playful ends.
In "White Mythology: Metaphor in the Text of Philosophy," he argues that
philosophy intentionally erases the origin of metaphors in order to use them
for "spiritual," rather than "sensual" purposes.[10] Thus ancient fables are
replaced with vague, modern concepts, which not only are anemic (as are
white men?) but also attempt to dominate and control language (as white
men in fact have done, thus the phrase, white metaphor). In Derrida's view,
metaphors cannot be dominated by philosophy. As he puts it, philosophy
cannot make a profit from an investment in metaphors because philosophy
cannot free itself from metaphors in order to arrive at some stable certainty
that is independent of figuration. Philosophy is written, and thus it, too, is
subject to all the vagaries of rhetoric.

A third approach exists that takes a middle path between these two extremes of substitution and displacement. This approach tries to do justice to
the cognitive importance of figures, portraying them as unique avenues to
insights that are not reducible to emotional impact or prosaic paraphrase.
Yet it also defends philosophy's ability to analyse and illuminate figurative
discourse. In other words, figures and concepts are not involved in a struggle from which only one can survive. This approach is best represented by
the famous article that helped to initiate it, "Metaphor," by Max Black, first
published in 1954. In that essay Black develops what he calls an "interaction" theory of metaphor, and Janet Soskice has noted the success of his
view, suggesting that it "has met with considerable general acceptance, and
'Metaphor' has indeed come to be regarded as a seminal article."[11]

MAX BLACK ON METAPHOR

Black begins his article by recognizing the prejudices with which he is
working. "To draw attention to a philosopher's metaphors is to belittle him
—like praising a logician for his beautiful handwriting."[12] He even jests that
philosophers live by the commandment, "Thou shalt not commit metaphor." (These criticisms are a bit dated; today, thanks in part to Black him-

self, philosophers *must* write about metaphor, even if they are excused from writing metaphorically.) Black traces these biases to three defective theories about this figure of speech. The first theory I have already mentioned, the substitution view. "Until recently," Black argues, "one or another form of a substitution view has been accepted by most writers (usually literary critics or writers of books on rhetoric) who have had anything to say about metaphor" (*M*, 31). The second theory he criticizes is the comparison view. Here metaphor is considered to be a condensed or elliptical simile; it serves to present an underlying simile or analogy in a decorative or compact fashion. The third view is, to return to Voltaire, the emotive explanation. This approach is quickly dismissed by Black: "The principle behind these 'explanations' seems to be: When in doubt about some peculiarity of language, attribute its existence to the pleasure it gives a reader. A principle that has the merit of working well in default of any evidence" (*M*, 34).

Actually, all three views make the same mistake and thus are variations on a single theme: they all assume that metaphors say something that can just as well be said—or even better said—in a literal or paraphrase form. Black makes this clear when he argues that the comparison view is really a special case of the substitution view.[13] One could also say that the comparison view is the justification for the other two views. The reason why a metaphor can be substituted by another expression, and the reason why metaphors appeal to the emotions and not to the mind, is that a metaphor makes a comparison in an implicit way. Similes and analogies make clear that at which the metaphor only hints. The metaphor, then, is only a diversion— perhaps due to its ability to entice the emotions—and if clarity, or truth, is sought, one must turn to more explicit forms of speech.

These views fail, according to Black, because they do not recognize the fact that metaphors often create the similarity or resemblance they imply; metaphors do not necessarily formulate a similarity that is antecedently existing. Moreover, metaphors often say something that cannot be said in any other way. Good metaphors are precise in what they say; we mean exactly the metaphor, and we would not be satisfied with any other expression. To do justice to the metaphor, then, Black develops what he calls an interaction theory. At this point he acknowledges his debt to I. A. Richards, who wrote in *The Philosophy of Rhetoric,* "When we use a metaphor we have two thoughts of different things active together and supported by a single word or phrase, whose meaning is a resultant of their interaction."[14] Black voices some differences with the particulars of Richards's formulation but agrees with its basic outline: in a metaphor, the old or literal meaning of the words and the new or figurative meaning are held together in a dynamic or tensive form.

Just how this occurs is difficult to say, and Black has to struggle to make his meaning clear. His theory rests on the assumption that in a metaphor some words are used metaphorically while the rest are used nonmetaphorically. A metaphor results when two sets of words are brought together to make one new meaning, which actually changes or can change the meaning of both word sets. The word or words used metaphorically Black calls the "focus," which in turn is set in a literal "frame" provided by the rest of the sentence. The problem is to explain the change of meaning that is brought about by the interaction of the focus and the frame. To do that Black becomes more suggestive than precise. He argues that in the interaction of a metaphor, both the focus and the frame entail systems of associated commonplaces that are mixed together in a new way. More precisely, when you use a word metaphorically, you evoke the system of commonplaces associated with that word, but you suppress some of those commonplaces and emphasize others. Take, for example, the simple metaphor, "Man is a wolf." Here wolf is being used metaphorically, so that only those characteristics of a wolf that could be applied to human beings are relevant to the expression. Black refers to this as a filtering process. A metaphor filters together the two word sets to make a new expression. Black also uses other metaphors to clarify this process. For example, the metaphor is a screen that allows us to see a subject in a new light.

Whatever the merits of these metaphors of metaphors — filters, screens, focuses — Black's intention is clear enough. A metaphor does something that is unique and important. As Black says about the wolf metaphor, it "organizes our view of man" (M, 41). It brings together two sets or systems of meaning in such a way that a new truth is gained. Black goes further to argue that literal paraphrases of nontrivial metaphors result in cognitive losses. "The relevant weakness of the literal paraphrase is not that it may be tiresomely prolix or boringly explicit (or deficient in qualities of style); it fails to be a translation because it fails to give the insight that the metaphor did" (M, 46). Black goes on to argue that the importance of metaphors does not mean the end of analysis and reason. "But 'explication' or elaboration of the metaphor's grounds, if not regarded as an adequate cognitive substitute for the original, may be extremely valuable. A powerful metaphor will no more be harmed by such probing than a musical masterpiece by analysis of its harmonic and melodic structure" (M, 46). In fact, Black's own article is an example of the need for and illumination of rational analysis of metaphor — even if such analysis is limited, especially in its use of yet more metaphor. To say that metaphor begets metaphor is not to say that all language is metaphorical; Black's talk of filters, screens, and frames are second-order metaphors, which serve to clarify the figurative process as a whole, and thus offer the hope for some conceptual understanding of, but not domination or replacement of, language in its most poetic form.

Even though, as Soskice has pointed out, Black's article has created a new consensus in figurative theory, it has also provoked many critical discussions of his terminology as well as the basic premises of his argument. I will return, at the beginning of chapter three, to a further consideration of metaphor when I look at Barth metaphorically. Here it is sufficient to note that Black's work urges us to understand metaphors as, in their own way, cognitive devices. To make an extrapolation, tropes are powerful ways of organizing our knowledge about the world. Yet this generalization is so far unwarranted. Black's article only dealt with metaphor; it did not offer a general theory of tropes. Moreover, it leaves us with several unanswered questions. Just how important are the use of tropes? Black seems to think that figures are very important, and yet he never shows us how and why philosophers and poets alike should be interested in them or dependent on them. Are tropes something that can be used if the need arises, or are they more basic than that? Are tropes so fundamental that they shape and inform all of language, above and beyond their actual use in a specific speech situation? Furthermore, how can one reject the substitution theory and thus affirm the uniqueness of metaphors without falling into the displacement theory and thus denying the power of reason? To answer these questions I need to turn to more general and basic reflections on the use of tropes, and I will begin with Paul Ricoeur.

PAUL RICOEUR AND LANGUAGE

Black's treatment of metaphor was one step in a direction toward which many philosophers have been heading; this direction has been called the "linguistic turn" in philosophy.[15] In fact, the general claim could be made that there has been growing consensus in the fields of philosophy of language, linguistics, and literary theory that language is not only or perhaps not at all reflective of reality but instead constitutes what it sets out to purportedly describe and imitate. That is, language is not the servant of an already existing "something out there" but rather mediates, shapes and even creates what loosely can be called knowledge: our intuitions, perceptions and conceptions of what really is. For example, Richard Rorty, working in the American pragmatic tradition, argues that philosophy has been captured by visual and in particular mirroring metaphors that mislead it to seek a stable and certain—the term he uses is Cartesian—foundation for all of knowledge.[16] Against this view, Rorty, like Vico before him, argues that the mind is not a mirror of nature that needs to be continuously polished and repaired by philosophy. Truth is not an increasingly accurate representation of reality (a matter of "seeing") but an endless conversation (a matter of "doing") that seeks to edify and enhance our lives rather than to control and explain nature. Rorty's concern is that we understand our language because language is how we understand ourselves: language is not a mere dressing or cover that can be stripped away to show the naked essence of reality.

As Heidegger would have it, language is, and in its being is all that is; we dwell in the house of being, but that house is constructed from language.[17] Moreover, as Heidegger tried in his later work to show over and over again, the ground floor of that house, and thus the foundation for all of our knowing and doing, is the most primordial level of language: poetry. This is one step that Rorty's pragmatic antifoundationalism cannot take: Heidegger argues that precisely in poetic language we find the mysteries of being in the most direct way, without losing sight of being in the abstract and ultimately defeating detours of conceptualization and explanation. Poetry speaks, and all other language merely mumbles. The problem with Heidegger's position is that poetry is never satisfactorily defined. What I want to argue in this chapter is that the creativity of language need not imply either Rorty's relativism or Heidegger's poeticism. Instead, the creativity of language can be understood according to the well-known features of the various tropes, which are, after all, the very forms of poetry.

If there is a consensus on the importance of language in philosophy today, then surely Paul Ricoeur has been one of its primary architects. His own work follows Heidegger in focusing on the role of poetic language in thinking and acting. However, Ricoeur can also agree with Rorty that Heidegger's project exhibits a nostalgia for being and a desire to begin philosophy all over again that is provocative but unrealistic to most philosophers today.[18] Yet Ricoeur also wants to go beyond Rorty's flirtations with relativism by arguing that in poetic language as well as in conceptual discourse truth is really at stake. Ricoeur thus follows the basic outline of Black's article on metaphor: figures are unique and important, but conceptual clarification can be productive as it arises from but does not need to replace figurative discourse.

These brief comments on Ricoeur — situating him with reference to Heidegger and Rorty — cannot, of course, even scratch the surface of his many complex writings. In fact, his work on figures is itself only a small part of his overall philosophical project. He began his career firmly entrenched in the phenomenological tradition of Husserl. His concern, however, was not to further the researches into a phenomenology of perception but to expand phenomenology to uncover the dynamics of volition. *Freedom and Nature* was an attempt to write a phenomenology of the will without abandoning the method of describing the essential structures of consciousness.[19] What Ricoeur discovered in *Fallible Man,* however, was a gap between the structures of the will—project, motive, character, the unconscious—and the historical or empirical conditions of the will as it is subject to the passions and prone to evil.[20] As he states, "The servile condition of the evil will seemed to elude an essential analysis of phenomena."[21] Ricoeur found that human fallibility can only be spoken of in symbolic or indirect language, and he was thus led to develop a philosophical hermeneutics, which would explore language and not consciousness. Don Ihde has argued that even after this hermeneutical turn Ricoeur's project was still phenomenological: the goal of philosophy is still reflective self-understanding.[22] The difference is that now Ricoeur argues that self-knowledge can only be achieved indirectly, not as the result of introspection. To paraphrase the closing comment of a book by Ricoeur on hermeneutics, it is indirect — figurative, rhetorical — language, due to its power to disclose and create our world, which gives a self to the ego.[23]

     This project of a philosophical hermeneutics was launched in *The Symbolism of Evil,* where Ricoeur sought to explore the most primordial and spontaneous expressions of evil in those cultures that most influence Western history.[24] Here Ricoeur is basically following Heidegger's intuition that poetic language best expresses the truth of the human situation. In fact, Ricoeur often writes in very Heideggerian terms:

> My deepest conviction is that poetic language alone restores to us that participation-in or belonging-to an order of things which precedes our capacity to oppose ourselves to things taken as objects opposed to a subject.[25]

Yet Ricoeur is not content merely to let symbols speak again to deafened modern ears, and here he breaks with Heidegger's persistent attempt to return to the origins of thought at the expense of conceptual clarification and explanation. Ricoeur's intention is to promote symbols to the rank of existential concepts by means of a dialectic of explanation and understanding. Philosophy, he argues, must follow the road of reflection to the very end; yet it cannot give an exhaustive interpretation of symbolic language because such language precedes thought and is itself the basis for further reflection. The symbol is the origin of thought and "beyond the desert of criticism we wish to be called [by the symbol] again."[26] But how can thought return to the richness of the symbol when thought itself tends to dissolve and reduce symbols in reflective explanation?

Ricoeur's wager at the end of *The Symbolism of Evil* is characteristic of his approach to hermeneutics in general. His solution to this problem is encapsulated in the now famous maxim: the symbol gives rise to thought (*le symbole donne à penser*). Hermeneutics is caught in a circle: "Hermeneutics proceeds from a prior understanding of the very thing that it tries to understand by interpreting it."[27] Influenced by Gadamer's rahabilitation of the notion of prejudice and his idea of effective historical-consciousness,[28] Ricoeur argues that interpretation is always situated in language and history before it can attempt to free itself from its presuppositions in order to accomplish the critical act. But Ricoeur does not follow Gadamer in separating truth from method or in opposing understanding and explanation.[29] Interpretation for Ricoeur begins with a naiveté before it turns critical, but it cannot remain naive just as it can never completely turn away from its own historicity and linguisticality. The goal of interpretation is to return to itself in a second naiveté, to understand its own beginnings after an explanatory or critical interlude. Understanding must give way to explanation, but the goal of explanation should always be further and richer understanding, what Ricoeur often calls appropriation. Later, I will show that this same dynamic, which makes the hermeneutical circle productive and not vicious, governs Ricoeur's theory of the imagination and thus his philosophy of the tropes.

This process of interpretation can be seen clearly in Ricoeur's work on the problem of evil, where he carefully excavates the ruins of discourse about evil to discover some ancient truths, which we no longer know. Ricoeur begins with myths, which, even though they are broken by historical consciousness, are closer to us than symbols, and thus are easier to understand. Ricoeur defines myths as symbols that have been developed and placed in a narrative form. Myth, then, is already an attempt to explain and articulate the symbol: myth is a step from symbol toward philosophical thought. Symbols, on the other hand, are immediate and spontaneous in a way that is lacking in myths: the experience that leads to the story of the myth can be found in its purest form in the symbol. Ricoeur demonstrates this hypothesis with an analysis of the symbols of stain, dread, and terror as precursors to the mythical elaborations of sin and guilt. Thus, Ricoeur shows in a very concrete way that poetic or symbolic language is the origin of thought at least in this instance, and that thought cannot grasp evil without continually returning to the symbols that best display the problem of evil and make thought about evil a possibility in the first place.

How does a symbol work? How does it allow for mythical development and philosophical elaboration? This is the area of Ricoeur's thought that is most relevant for my purposes because it constitutes his first sustained attempt to defend a theory of indirect or poetic language, and his answer in this case influences the later development of his theory of tropes. According to Ricoeur, the symbol is a sign that intends something, but it is unique in that it is a sign that conceals a double intention. The basic level of the symbol's intentionality is derived from ordinary experience: it is the conventional nature of the symbol, what it means on a literal level. Upon this intentionality is built a second level of intentionality, which "points to a certain situation of man in the sacred."[30] For example, the simple sign of a stain can function as a symbol of humanity's guilty relationship to God. As Ricoeur explains, "The first, literal, patent meaning analogically intends *a second meaning which is not given otherwise than in the first*. This opaqueness is the symbol's very profundity, an inexhaustible depth."[31] In later language Ricoeur will call this the surplus of meaning inherent in all figurative discourse. Double intentionality, then, is the source of the symbol's complexity and power.

Ricoeur's hermeneutics continued for a time to focus on the symbol. In *Freud and Philosophy* he defines the symbolic function as "to mean something other than what is said."[32] Hence the symbol is any species of language that has a double or multiple meaning. This means for Ricoeur that "the problem of symbolism has turned out to be coextensive with the problem of language itself."[33] Hermeneutics thus becomes the central task of a philosophy of language because the symbol by its very nature raises the problem of interpretation. Symbols are overdetermined; they allow for interpretive strategies that are both suspicious and generous, seeking to reduce or to retrieve the symbol. Yet Ricoeur became dissatisfied with this approach because the symbol is a broad category that can be understood in many different ways. He began to refine his theory by focusing on more specific literary and rhetorical categories. If language is the key to self-understanding, and if poetic language lies at the origin of thought, then, Ricoeur decided, poetry itself should be investigated. Ricoeur often approvingly quotes Monroe Beardsley's claim that metaphor "is a poem in miniature."[34] Thus Ricoeur can turn from symbols, without leaving behind any of the conclusions he has already established, to the more specific problem of metaphor.

RICOEUR AND METAPHOR

In following Ricoeur to the problem of metaphor, I do not want to repeat any of the claims I have made in relation to Black's famous article. However, as the discussion above serves to demonstrate, Ricoeur's analysis of metaphor is situated in a philosophy of language that allows it to answer some of the questions with which I left Black behind. For Ricoeur, metaphor is not something incidental to a philosophy of language, no matter how im-

portant. Instead, his discussion of metaphor is consistent with his hermeneutical project as a whole. With metaphor he both tests his claims concerning the power and primacy of poetic language and shows in concrete terms
the relationship between the poetic and the conceptual. His wager is that by
uncovering the mechanism of the metaphor something significant can be
said about interpretation and language themselves.

In *Interpretation Theory* Ricoeur summarizes his postion on metaphor
in terms that expand upon Black's article in detail and in historical sophistication but do not contradict its main points. He argues that the ancient tradition of rhetoric dealt with metaphor by taking the word as its unit of study.
Metaphor was classified as a single-word figure, concerned with the problem
of denomination. It belongs, then, to the language game that governs naming. Ricoeur claims that this approach to metaphor was first developed by
Aristotle, with later contributions from Cicero and Quintilian. It presupposes that words can be understood in isolation from each other, each word
with its own signification. In figurative language there occurs a deviation
from the ordinary or lexical meaning of the word. The purpose of this deviation, according to ancient rhetoricians, was the need to fill lexical gaps in
language or to ornament language. In some cases, as Ricoeur explains, "Because we have more ideas than we have words to express them, we have to
stretch the significations of those we do have beyond their ordinary use"
(*IT,* 48). In other cases, if a suitable word is available, a figurative word
might be chosen in order to please or persuade an audience. This reflects Aristotle's definition of rhetoric, which began chapter one. Finally, Ricoeur argues that at the heart of this rhetorical tradition is the idea that metaphor
works by resemblance: one word is substituted for another word on the basis of some similarity or likeness they share.

Ricoeur argues that writers like I. A. Richards, Black, Monroe
Beardsley, Philip Wheelwright, and Colin Turbayne have shifted this perspective on metaphor in several crucial ways.[35] First, "metaphor has to do
with the semantics of the sentence before it concerns the semantics of the
word" (*IT,* 49). More precisely, it is a phenomenon of predication, not denomination. This change in defining the metaphor is important for the points
that follow. Second, metaphor operates by inducing or playing on a tension
between two different interpretations of the metaphorical utterance. "In
this regard, we can even say, in a general fashion, that the strategy of discourse by means of which the metaphorical utterance obtains its result is
absurdity" (*IT,* 50). The absurdity is revealed through trying to interpret the
metaphor literally. "Thus, a metaphor does not exist in itself, but in and
through an interpretation. The metaphorical interpretation presupposes a
literal interpretation which self-destructs in a significant contradiction" (*IT,*

50). In this tensive process — when the literal becomes figurative — there is imposed on the words a twist of meaning.[36] Third, the result is not achieved through resemblance, as in the classical account, but a calculated error, or what Gilbert Ryle called a category mistake.[37] The metaphor "brings together things that do not go together and by means of this apparent misunderstanding it causes a new, hitherto unnoticed relation of meaning to spring up between the terms that previous systems of classification had ignored or not allowed" (*IT,* 50). Fourth, the achievement of the metaphor is the creation of new meaning, not the substitution of one word for another. Ricoeur argues that this cannot be seen in dead metaphors (like "the foot of a chair"); it must be seen in live metaphors (like Shakespeare calling time a beggar). True, live metaphors are sometimes adopted into our lexicon and become part of the dictionary meaning of words, but real metaphors are not translatable, not found in the dictionary. "A metaphor, in short, tells us something new about reality" (*IT,* 53).

At this point in his researches, Ricoeur has substantiated Black's claims that metaphors are unique and yet their structure can be explained. The main thrust of Ricoeur's definition, in fact, is essentially the same as his understanding of symbol: there is a double intentionality in the metaphor, a tension between the ordinary or lexical use of words and their figurative use, which is the result of a configuration not accounted for by ordinary word associations. Soskice labels this the dual sense or dual truth theory, and Ricoeur himself, in later work, calls this the split reference of the metaphor, its ability to refer to a new meaning through the destruction of its literal reference.[38] Soskice is unhappy with this position, arguing that the literal meaning of the metaphor is never assumed by any interpreter; the metaphor has only one, figurative meaning, and to read it in any other way is not to find its basic, literal meaning but to read nonsense. She suggests that Ricoeur's theory comes dangerously close to the comparison view by claiming that metaphors redescribe reality rather than create something new. Her criticisms, then, force the issue of the relationship between figurative and conceptual discourse, a relationship for which I originally turned to Ricoeur but have not as yet discussed. In fact, in *Interpretation Theory* the metaphor is still seen only in terms of the symbol; "metaphors are just the linguistic surface of symbols," he writes (*IT,* 69). Ricoeur has still not delivered on his promise to relate metaphor to his overall philosophy of language and interpretation.

He does this in the encyclopedic *The Rule of Metaphor.*[39] Here he not only develops his earlier argument on metaphor in detailed form, but in section eight he answers the question: Is there a philosophy implied in this analysis of metaphor? Has this rather technical discussion been ruled by some philosophical presuppositions — prejudices, in Gadamer's terms — which now need to be disclosed? In this section we find the real reasons for Ricoeur's double intentionality theory, which Soskice criticizes, and we also find Ricoeur's own clearest statement of the relationships among poetics, philosophy, and hermeneutics. Ricoeur's basic position is simple: "I should like to plead for a relative pluralism of forms and levels of discourse" (*RM*, 257–8). He does not want to go so far as Wittgenstein to argue for a radical heterogeneity of language games, but "it is important to recognize in principle the discontinuity that assures the autonomy of speculative discourse" (*RM*, 258).

To establish the autonomy of speculation, he must first do battle with Derrida, and in fact he argues against the article, "White Mythology," which I briefly discussed earlier. Metaphor, for Derrida, functions, in Ricoeur's words, "behind our backs" (*RM*, 284). Metaphor disrupts and displaces metaphysical discourse because it can never be captured by conceptual language. Derrida makes this point in his essay by reading an eloquent section of Hegel's *Aesthetics*. Hegel argued that philosophical concepts are initially sensible meanings transposed to the spiritual order. Hegel adds that the establishment of properly abstract meaning necessitates the effacement of what is metaphorical in the initial meaning. "Where Hegel saw the innovation of meaning, Derrida sees only the wearing away of meaning and a drift towards the idealization resulting from the dissimulation of this metaphorical origin" (*RM*, 286). Derrida thus enters "the domain of metaphor not by way of its birth but, if we may say so, by way of its death" (*RM*, 285). In fact, truth is, for both Derrida and Nietzsche, a worn-out or dead metaphor. Ricoeur points out that this concept of wearing away (*usure*) is itself metaphorical: it connotes the wearing down of the features of a medal or a coin. The importance of the wearing away is that it marks the "ascending movement that constitutes the formation of the concept" (*RM*, 285). There is then an incompatibility between live metaphor and concept. "Henceforth, to revive metaphor is to unmask the concept" (*RM*, 286).

The fading of the metaphor marks the production of the concept, which, in turn, must erase the trace of metaphoricity if it is to pretend to achieve philosophical universality. Metaphors strive toward conceptuality, which can be attained only by self-sacrifice. The problem is that philosophy has begun a transformative process, which it can never completely understand. Ricoeur accurately states this apparent paradox: "There is no discourse on metaphor that is not stated within a metaphorically engendered conceptual network. There is no nonmetaphorical standpoint from which to perceive the order and the demarcation of the metaphorical field. Metaphor is metaphorically stated" (*RM*, 287). The theory of metaphor is caught in a vicious circle of metaphoricity: in the end, metaphor cannot decipher itself. If one were successfully to establish order in the field of figures, still one metaphor would escape the order: the metaphor of metaphor. So the field of figures can never be closed.

Ricoeur deals with this complicated argument in several ways. Most directly, he argues that the phenomenon of dead metaphors is really "less interesting than it seems at first" (*RM,* 290). Dead metaphors are not metaphors at all but instead are associated with literal meaning. Derrida has thus inflated the significance of dead metaphors, which merely contribute to our ordinary use of words. In fact, reanimating dead metaphors does not display the origin of concepts but amounts to a new production of meaning. Thus, the two operations of the wearing away of the sensible meaning of a metaphorical utterance and the production of a concept are distinct. Ricoeur makes this point in his strongest argument by inquiring into the conditions of Derrida's own theory: the assumptions that make Derrida's discourse possible defeat his own conclusions. "If these two operations were not distinct we could not even speak of the concept of wearing away, nor of the concept of metaphor; in truth, there could be no philosophical terms" (*RM,* 293). Philosophy, thus, cannot doubt its own existence because such doubt presupposes a conceptual apparatus, which itself affirms the efficacy of conceptuality.

Ricoeur's deeper argument, though, is to suggest that the alignment of metaphor and conceptuality occurs at the level of live and not dead metaphor. Metaphor, by nature of what it is, opens up the space for philosophy. This is a suggestive and at times obscure argument; Ricoeur does not want to claim that the semantics of the metaphor contains a ready-made and immediate ontology, which philosophy only needs to articulate, although he does say, suggestively, that the seeing-as which is characteristic of metaphor is correlative to an ontological being-as. Instead, "It can be shown that, on the one hand, speculative discourse has its condition of *possibility* in the semantic dynamism of metaphorical utterance, and that, on the other hand, speculative discourse has its *necessity* in itself, in putting the resources of conceptual articulation to work" (*RM,* 296). Speculative discourse is possible because it "possesses the reflective capacity to place itself at a distance and to consider itself, as such and in its entirety, as related to the totality of what is" (*RM,* 304). The work of metaphor allows conceptuality to seize its own task, which, in the end, must remain independent of figuration.

Conceptuality must be kept distinct from figuration because thought is, according to Ricoeur, the capacity of language to remain free from itself.[40] But thought is still embedded in language, and so the question arises: where does language gain this capacity for critical distance from itself? The secret to that question is found in the explanation of the metaphor, which is consistently approached by Ricoeur, as I have tried to show, in terms of a double intentionality that was originally attributed to the symbol. Ricoeur concludes his book on metaphor by suggesting that poetry, "in itself and by itself, sketches a 'tensional' conception of truth for thought" (*RM*, 313). Unfortunately, this claim is only sketched by Ricoeur, but the explication of his meaning can be found in his idea that the metaphor says both 'is' and 'is not.' The metaphor, by saying something new through the innovative arrangement of what is already known, "prefigures the distanciation that speculative thought carries to its highest point of reflection" (*RM*, 313). Philosophy does not arise out of dead metaphor but is inspired by the capacity of live metaphor to see what is not through what is, and thus understand what is in a totally new way. Concepts imitate the capacity of metaphor to create meaning by new constellations of groups of words; but what metaphors do spontaneously, concepts accomplish consciously, using the metaphorical genius for synthesis to reach new understandings of the structures of reality.

The faculty for this capacity of metaphor—and the final link, for my purposes, between Ricoeur's theory of metaphor and his general philosophy of language and hermeneutics—is the imagination. Ricoeur wants to reject any understanding of the imagination as completely passive. The imagination makes the metaphor possible because it enables the construction of a resemblance out of seemingly dissimilar elements. "To see the like is to see the same in spite of, and through, the different."[41] Thus, Ricoeur can say about the *Rule of Metaphor* that "it was my purpose to demonstrate that there is not just an epistemological and political imagination, but also, and perhaps more fundamentally, a linguistic imagination which generates and regenerates meaning through the living power of metaphoricity."[42] The inventiveness of human language is due to the power of the imagination to synthesize, or more exactly, to initiate a shift of distance in logical space. This is, Ricoeur argues, what Kant called the productive imagination—the capacity to schematize a synthetic operation.

The full scope and operation of the productive imagination is seen most clearly in the three-volume work, *Time and Narrative*, which Ricoeur suggests forms a pair with his work on metaphor: they were conceived together, even though one is an investigation in genre and the other a research in tropes.[43] In both narrative and metaphor the same sematic innovation is involved: whereas metaphor is the result of an impertinent yet synthetic attribution, plot is a temporal unity, which is synthesized from the resources of language about goals, causes, and chance. The plot grasps together and integrates into one whole scattered and multiple events, just as the metaphor fuses together words not ordinarily associated with each other in order to create new meaning. The plot thus works according to the same logic of double intentionality that we saw with metaphor: it takes the ordinary and makes it extraordinary. Here Ricoeur develops the action of the plot, and by implication the figure of the metaphor, in more detail, according to the model of hermeneutics which I discussed previously.

In fact, the plot is involved in the same three moments of preunderstanding, explanation, and appropriation that determine the character of hermeneutics. Ricoeur calls this the threefold mimesis of plot. The first level of mimesis is the ordinary world from which the composition of the plot must draw its resources. Here time is structured by discourse about agency and causation, but time is not yet understood in any coherent way. Time is, as with Augustine, distended and enigmatic — confused, unformed, and even mute. The second level of mimesis brings coherence to language about time by grasping together its chaotic elements into one synthetic whole, the plot. This is the act of configuration, and here Ricoeur plays off Aristotle against Augustine. Aristotle's notion of plot is a resolution of Augustine's reflections on the aporias of time: the story is followable, that is, the reader can move forward through the plot to make the connections that guide the story to its fulfillment or conclusion. Time is thus, in a way, explained by emplotment, or perhaps better put, what was once understood in an implicit way is made explicit. The third level of mimesis completes the full circle of Ricoeur's analysis: the configuration of the plot only has its full meaning when it refers back to the ordinary world of thinking and acting. Thus, the prefigured world is refigured by the configuration of the plot; the result is that through the imaginative detour of the plot we have a deeper understanding of our world, seeing it as though for the first time. Or as Ricoeur is fond of saying, the language of narration makes time human.

Ricoeur's detour through poetics — symbol, metaphor and plot — can be seen, then, as really a detour: the main point is to get back to a phenomenological analysis of existence. This detour is, it should be noted, not just very important but essential to philosophy: "Conceptualization cannot reach meaning directly or create meaning out of itself *ex nihilo;* it cannot dispense with the detour of mediation through figurative structures. This detour is intrinsic to the very working of concepts."[44] But the detour remains an excursion that has only one direction. Whereas figures can be conceptualized, the creativity of concepts is that they are inspired by figures (the conclusion to *The Rule of Metaphor*); they must follow the configuration of genres and figures before they begin the work of refiguring the world (the conclusion of *Time and Narrative*), but they are not themselves subject to figuration. This whole problem is raised from the start by the title of Ricoeur's book on metaphor: Who does rule figurative discourse? One commentator, Dominick LaCapra, has been prompted to comment that, "Ricoeur's central thesis might be summarized by saying that metaphor is all right in its place, but it must be kept securely in its place."[45] He goes on to suggest that this work is "one of the strongest reaffirmations of a basically traditional understanding of philosophy, literature and interpretation in the face of what would seem to be its most disorienting and uncanny challenge."[46] Ricoeur thus limits his tensive account of metaphor to the level of metaphor itself; that is, there is little tension between levels of discourse, as each keeps to its own autonomous sphere. Philosophy seems to imitate the tension of the metaphor, but it is not actually generated by metaphors. In fact, Ricoeur says that philosophy creates itself, inspired by the good example of metaphor but basically speaking a language completely different from figuration. Philosophy's birth is prefigured by metaphor, but the work of philosophy is independent of the work of figuration; in fact, it could be said that for Ricoeur figuration serves as a dispensable metaphor for the work of conceptualization. Concepts imitate figures, but they do their work in a completely different medium — a thought freed from language.

Yet surely LaCapra's criticisms, which come from the standpoint of deconstructionism, are one-sided: as Ricoeur has argued, how does deconstructionism do what it does if philosophy does not have a voice of its own? Of course, the debate about deconstructionism — Derrida's attempt to unmask the figuration of philosophical texts without committing himself to a constructive philosophical position, which itself would be subject to further deconstruction — cannot be pursued here. LaCapra's point, though, is well taken. My own complaint with Ricoeur is that he appears to see only a one-way relationship between figurative and conceptual discourse. He argues quite well that a conceptual analysis of figurative language can enhance such language without being subject to further figuration. Concepts can illuminate but need not, indeed should not, replace figuration. However, on the other side of the street, he is not willing to allow for a figurative reading of conceptual language. The relationship between figures and concepts in Ricoeur's thought is completely asymmetrical. If concepts can illuminate figures, then why cannot figures illuminate conceptual language — without in turn reducing such language to the figure's own ground? Backed into a corner by the deconstructionists, Ricoeur seems to think that once figures are given priority over concepts, then the autonomy of speculation is doomed and all thought will run out of control into the worst kinds of relativistic dead ends. However, the deconstructivist reading of conceptual discourse is not the only possibility here. In fact, my entire thesis is based on the possibility that a tropical reading of conceptual discourse can profitably illuminate that discourse without replacing it with or reducing it to an unstable collection of figures. In fact, figures and concepts are not involved in a competition from which only one set can emerge as victorious: my wager here is that both can illuminate each other, without confusion or reduction. To make this claim I will have to turn to Hayden White, who also nicely serves to expand this discussion from an unhealthy obsession with metaphor to a more encompassing view of the tropes.

THE TROPICS OF HAYDEN WHITE

Hayden White, like Paul Ricoeur, comes to his conclusions about tropes through a detour: his final destination is the understanding of the deep structures of the historical imagination. He complains that although history is often considered to be part science and part art, it is usually treated more as a science, and its artistic component is left unanalyzed. White wants to redress this imbalance by arguing that historical works are more like literature than science.

> In my view, history as a discipline is in bad shape today because it has lost sight of its origins in the literary imagination. In the interest of appearing scientific and objective, it has repressed and denied to itself its own greatest source of strength and renewal.[47]

In fact, he argues that it was no accident that the great philosophers of history were also philosophers of language. "That is why they were able to grasp, more or less self-consciously, the poetic, or at least linguistic, grounds on which the putatively 'scientific' theories of nineteenth-century historiography had their origins."[48] In his major work *Metahistory* and the essays collected in *Tropics of Discourse,* White sets out his argument that history is essentially a literary enterprise by treating the historical work "as what it most manifestly is—that is, a verbal structure in the form of a narrative prose discourse that purports to be a model, or icon, of past structures and processes in the interest of explaining what they were by representing them" (*MH,* 2).

The problem is that most scholars treat history as realistic discourse —that is, as objective and transparent prose, which describes a preexisting reality. In fact, history is often set against the mythical "as if the former were genuinely empirical and the latter were nothing but conceptual" (*MH,* 3), and then the realm of fiction is located somewhere between these two poles. Literature is realistic according to the extent to which it imitates history and avoids myth. As I will point out later, this could serve as a fair description of Ricoeur's position, which attempts to keep history and fiction in separate compartments, much as he tried to separate poetics and philosophy in his treatment of metaphor. According to White, however, historiography is not necessarily a final standard for the measurement of realism, and so the distinction between history and literature is blurred at best. History is creative in the sense that it too creates; it does not merely represent its data but actually contributes to the shaping of its field of inquiry and creates a final order by what can only be called a fictive act.

White does admit that history, unlike literature, is made up of events that exist outside of the consciousness of the writer. However, historians do not find the stories they relate ready-made. Instead, the historian must exercise the art of emplotment—a process of exclusion, stress, and subordination—in order to make sense of the data. The historian's analysis must be followable, and this narrative element is not incidental to historiography but is one aspect of its explanatory power. Following the work of Northrop Frye, White argues that there are four basic plot forms that historical writing follows: romance, tragedy, comedy and satire. Emplotment, however, is only one of three strategies of explanation that shape a historical text. Historians also explain by formal argument, which also divides into four categories: formist, organicist, mechanistic and contextualist, and by ideological implication: anarchism, conservativism, radicalism and liberalism. Much of White's work is focused on discussing historians in terms of the combinations of these three strategies of explanation. In fact, he defines historical style as a particular combination of modes of emplotment, argumentation, and ideology; there are affinities among the various modes, but the creative tensions in many historical works result from the effort to wed modes that are inconsonant with each other.

The next step of White's argument is most important for my purposes: a theory of tropes is developed to explain these different explanatory combinations as elements in a single tradition of historical writing. With this theory White thinks he has penetrated to the depths of the historical imagination. Before historians can bring to bear upon the data of the historical field the conceptual apparatus they will use to explain it, they must first prefigure that field. At its most basic level, then, the historical operation is poetic: the historian "*pre*figures the historical field and constitutes it as a domain upon which to bring to bear the specific theories he will use to explain 'what was *really* happening'" (*MH,* x). What White means by prefiguration is something very different from Ricoeur's use of that same term, and I will return to that difference later. For White, prefiguration is the act that constitutes a field as an object of mental perception and conceptualization, and this act is a tropical gesture. ''That is to say, before a domain can be interpreted, it must first be construed as a ground inhabited by discernible figures'' (*MH*, 30).

White calls this process of prefiguration encoding or the construction of a linguistic protocol to prepare the field for subsequent analysis, emplotment and explanation. This act is precritical and precognitive; it is foundational in the sense that it both creates the object of analysis and predetermines the modalities of the explanatory strategies that the historian will use. The result is that White is able to classify and explain various historiographies — and indeed the development of history itself, from the eighteenth century to the present — according to a tropological pattern.

> I contend that the recognized masters of nineteenth-century historical thinking can be understood, and that their relations to one another as participants in a common tradition of inquiry can be established, by the explication of the different tropological modes which underlie and inform their work (*MH*, xi).

Tropes are sanctions or funds for historical explanations, or said in a different way, history consists of formalizations of poetic insights. White generalizes his position to cover not only history: ''In any field of study not yet reduced (or elevated) to the status of a genuine science, thought remains the captive of the linguistic mode in which it seeks to grasp the outline of objects inhabiting its field of perception'' (*MH*, xi).

There are four basic types of prefiguration, which White has labeled, following Kenneth Burke, the four mastertropes: metaphor, metonymy, synecdoche, and irony. White notes that the use of tropes to explain various phenomena is nothing new; for precedents of his own work he refers to Roman Jakobson's use of the metaphor-metonymy dyad for a linguistic theory of poetics, Claude Levi-Strauss's use of the same dyad for his analysis of the naming systems of primitive cultures, and Jacques Lacan's use of figures for analyzing the linguistic structure of dreams. White, however, likes the more traditional fourfold pattern rather than the more limited use of metaphor and metonymy. He realizes that some rhetoricians have viewed synecdoche as a kind of metaphorical usage and irony as a kind of metonymy, while others have argued that both metonymy and synecdoche are really variations of metaphor. He prefers, though, to draw his inspiration from Vico, who utilized the fourfold distinction of tropes to differentiate the stages of the development of consciousness from primitive to civilized cultures. By keeping to the fourfold pattern, White is able to construct an impressive overview of historical writing: the four tropes serve as organizational and presuppositional models for the four modes in each of the three strategies of explanation, thus preserving the symmetry in White's complex scheme. Style is thus explained by reference to the ruling or governing trope of the historian's work.

The importance of White's work, then, is to show that although the description of a trope might arise from an examination of its use in an individual utterance, the trope's activity is not limited to this range but can provide a model for how a larger discourse functions to create new meaning. Each figure represents a strategy, which can be used in one utterance or by an entire discourse. More specifically, each of the four mastertropes signifies a particular way of organizing the historical field. The metaphor is essentially representational, bringing together materials on the basis of presumed similarities. "My love, a rose," for example, literally asserts an identification, but figuratively love is represented as a rose. Metonymy is the substitution of the name of a part of a thing for the name of the whole of the thing. For example, "fifty sails" can be used for the expression "fifty ships." Metonymy is, White argues, an essentially reductive trope: the whole is reduced to one of its parts. Substitution is also at work in synecdoche, but here a term is used to designate a whole which represents some organic quality of the whole, as in "he is all heart." This trope is integrative. These three tropes are "paradigms, provided by language itself, of the operations by which consciousness can prefigure areas of experience" (*MH*, 36), and White expends much effort showing the various connections among these tropes and the possible modes of the three strategies of explanation.

These three tropes, however, are naive. Each assumes that it has correctly ordered reality, while White argues that 'facts' are capable of engendering an indefinite number of explanations and representations. In fact, "there is no such thing as a *single* correct view of any object under study [but] there are *many* correct views, each requiring its own style of representation" (*MH*, 47). This situation is recognized and reproduced in the fourth trope, irony. Irony is the self-conscious counterpart to the three other tropes; by it authors signal a real or feigned doubt or disbelief in the truth of their own statements. "The aim of the ironic statement is to affirm tacitly the negative of what is on the literal level affirmed positively, or the reverse" (*MH*, 37). Thus, the statement "he is all heart" could be ironic depending on the tone of its utterance or the context—if the person referred to is known not to possess the quality of compassion, for example. In this sense irony is metatropological; its prefigurative operation is radically self-critical. Its fictional form is satire, and it can easily lead to relativism and skepticism. On the positive side, White suggests that it "prepares consciousness for its repudiation of all sophisticated conceptualizations of the world and antici-

pates a return to a mythic apprehension of the world and its processes''
(*MH*, 10). I will keep this in mind when I turn to Barth, because his own
tropological development ends in irony, and he found it necessary to pass
through this trope to a more objective view of theological reality.

White's development of this fourfold pattern of tropes makes irony
seem to be its inevitable outcome. In fact, he admits that his own study is
ironic. His method is formalistic in that it views histories not in terms of the
events they try to explain but as texts that need to be properly read apart
from their referential contexts. The figurative root of this formalism is irony;
there is a self-conscious recognition that any history always could have been
written in a different way, and so the authentic historian must exhibit doubt
and self-criticism as a warning against any pretension to absolute truth.
However, White is not happy with this prospect; he maintains that the recognition of irony as one tropical mode among other possibilities—''each of
which has its own good reasons for existence on a poetic and moral level of
awareness'' (*MH*, 434)—shows that irony itself is not necessary. Each of
the tropical modes must be judged according to the consistency, coherence,
and illuminative power they afford a historical analysis. The decision to
choose one mode over another is ultimately aesthetic and ethical. Thus
irony is not privileged over the other tropes because there are not reasons
generated by the historical field that force a choice for any trope over
another.

Yet everything about White's theory seems to drive him toward acknowledging the triumph of irony in the historical imagination. Not only
does he fail to give any practical advice about how irony can be transcended,
but his very description of irony as only one among several tropical strategies is, ironically, a situation that irony itself is both capable of and committed to recognizing. In other words, the fact that the ironic consciousness can
see other tropical possibilities is no ground for suggesting that irony is therefore overcome; it is inherent in the dynamic of irony to see ever-new possibilities. What irony cannot do is accept any one possibility as a certainty; in
this way, irony is not so much the counterpart to the other three tropes as
their parasite, always capable of turning against them in a skeptical attack,
but also willing to postpone any announcement of victory for itself. The
problem is that once White has unanchored history from its explanatory
field, irony does seem a necessary navigation for a discipline with no clear
constraints and only unpredictable direction.

My guess is that White refuses to give irony its due for the same reasons that Ricoeur defends the autonomy of speculation: both are worried
about the troubling implications of Derrida and his deconstructionist co-
horts. In an essay included in *Tropics of Discourse*, ''The Absurdist Moment

in Contemporary Literary Theory," White makes this worry explicit. He distinguishes between what he calls normal criticism, which believes that literature not only has sense but makes sense of experience, and absurdist criticism, which reduces literature to "a final paroxysm of frustration, to chatter about silence" (*TD*, 262). Among the absurdists White includes Foucault and Barthes as well as Derrida; their literary criticism, according to White, is not really criticism at all, but an attempt to mystify the text. They conceive criticism as blind or, at best, as a carnival, which exists for its own sake. White argues that Derrida's own favorite trope is "catachresis, the ironic trope *par excellence*" (*TD*, 281). From the viewpoint of irony, Derrida can claim that "there is only figuration, hence no privileged position within language by which language can be called into question" (*TD*, 281). I should note that many of these criticisms are hardly fair to Derrida,[49] and I do not summarize them to illuminate Derrida but rather to explain White himself. White has privileged the trope of irony, yet he must ultimately reject it, fearful that it will undermine his own project of describing the foundations of history.

Why does White's work end in this apparent paradox? The problem here is twofold. First, it is not clear why there needs to be a fourfold tropological pattern, a kind of tropography of the imagination. By writing about tropes in terms of a developmental or cyclical pattern, with irony as the last stop on the tropical route, White invites the criticism that he is leading not only his own work but also the historical imagination in general into the dead end of irony. White never really justifies his fourfold pattern, claiming only that it is traditional, that Vico used it to great effect, and that it fits well with his various tables of explanation. But he himself has admitted that, "The literature on tropes is as great as, if not greater than, that on the theory of the sign — and growing daily at a frantic pace, without as yet, however, giving any sign of a general consensus as to their classification" (*TD*, 23).

This situation is exacerbated by the second problem, which is the lack of clarity over the ontological status of the four tropes. In the introductory essay to *Tropics of Discourse*, White suggests that this tropical pattern is embedded in consciousness itself, and he even interprets Piaget as providing evidence for his position. At other times he argues that the tropes are the work of language. Dominick LaCapra interprets White as ultimately more interested in consciousness than language. "Language and discourse," he writes, "are seen predominantly as instruments or expressions of consciousness."[50] Consciousness for White is constructive rather than mimetic, and the tropes serve as constitutive categories that focus the projective consciousness. The point of this rather Kantian philosophical position is, similar to Ricoeur's, to keep the tropes in line. Consciousness, not language, is in control, yet irony, as White well knows, threatens to suspend that control. LaCapra suspects that White, in the end, is closer to Derrida than he would like to admit, which would explain why he reacts so strongly against him: "For the things Derrida discusses *are* inside White."[51]

Ricoeur would actually agree with LaCapra's criticisms of White. He congratulates White for being one of the first to show how history exploits the resources of narrative in explaining past events. However, he argues that, "A gap remains between narrative explanation and historical explanation, a gap that is inquiry as such. This gap prevents us from taking history . . . as a species of the genus 'story.' "[52] Ricoeur clarifies this gap by suggesting that historians, unlike novelists, are "subject to what once was. They owe a debt to the past, a debt of recognition to the dead, that makes them insolvent debtors."[53] The historian must render the past its due. It is at this point that Ricoeur criticizes White. Ricoeur argues that history is not a constructive but a *re*constructive activity: it is constrained by the reality of past events. White, by claiming that poetics creates the field which history explains, not only "runs the risk of wiping out the boundary between fiction and history"[54] but also covers up the intentionality of historical discourse which is directed toward past events. Here Ricoeur is being consistent with his analysis of metaphor. The tropes of history do not create reality but *re*describe the past. This referential emphasis on tropology is made possible by Ricoeur's own use of White's key term: prefiguration is comprised of the ordinary language about sociality and temporality, which both fiction and history, in their different ways, must reconstruct. Prefiguration for Ricoeur is not a poetic act of consciousness but instead entails the basic structures and languages of existence to which poetry just as much as history must respond. I cannot follow Ricoeur further in his attempt to show how history and fiction are distinct but interwoven in their configurative acts; actually, by showing the autonomy of inquiry from figuration in his work on metaphor, Ricoeur has already made his argument about the separation of historiography and poetics. My point here is only that Ricoeur echoes LaCapra's conclusion that White is closer to the absurdist critics than he thinks by, in Ricoeur's words, rejecting history's debt to the past.

However, both Ricoeur and White agree that tropes are something more than occasional flourishes of language, content to please or persuade but hardly meant for more serious purposes. At the end of the section on Ricoeur, I argued that he stops short of allowing for a figurative analysis of conceptual discourse. This deficiency is generously compensated for by White, but the case can be made that White, in turn, goes too far. His refusal to pay history's debt to the past comes about because his approach, in the final analysis, is not formal. Instead of developing a tropology as a guide to a formalistic reading of historical texts, he aspires both to ground this tropology in an ontology of consciousness and to suggest that its fourfold pattern is a necessary sequence of development. Because the tropes are really masks for the developing operations of consciousness, irony is indeed privileged over the other tropes. Because irony is the last trope, the killer-trope, White is forced to argue that the tropes do not respond to the historical field but create it and, finally, the tropes must turn their backs to history altogether.

I have no interest in writing a tropology of the theological consciousness. What I want to use from both Ricoeur and White is the idea that tropes are not incidental to language but are the basic forms of language from which inquiry must make its start. Tropes, then, can be understood as models of discourse. To the extent that language is referentially flexible, capable of carrying an excess of meaning, then language is at its base figurative. Even conceptual language, therefore, should be susceptible to tropical modeling. With this claim I basically agree with White over Ricoeur: tropes are the basic forms of discourse as a whole and are not limited, as in Ricoeur, to the level of the individual utterance. However, this claim does not jeopardize the autonomy and integrity of conceptual discourse, especially if I do not decide to follow White's ontological speculations. Tropes, as Ricoeur has shown, can also be modeled by concepts. The fact that the two can illuminate each other does not mean that one must come out on top. That is my pesonal wager, and I am willing to subject my claim to a quite pragmatic test in my reading of Karl Barth.[55] In this work, then, I will examine the relationship between figures and concepts in theology: I will try to uncover the tropes that shape Barth's discourse in order to show how the figurative process is essential to his theological reflection. Moreover, because I am free of White's commitment to a fourfold pattern of tropes, I am able to read Barth according to his own particular tropical development, one which I have understood as a trajectory from metaphor through hyperbole to irony.

METAPHOR OF CRISIS/CRISIS OF METAPHOR

METAPHORS AND MODELS

In closing chapter two, I suggested that figures of speech could serve as models for discourse as a whole. Now I want to argue that one of Barth's metaphors, the metaphor of crisis, which he shares with expressionism, so serves to structure and organize *Romans* that it must be considered one of that text's principal models. In other words, Barth does not only use the metaphor of crisis, but his entire text is constructed according to the specific features of this metaphor.

At this point two questions could be raised. It could be objected that Barth understood culture under the literal, not metaphorical, description of crisis. After all, the devastation of the Great War was very real, not merely figurative. Nonetheless, when Barth speaks of crisis he is not talking about the social dislocation that took place after the war. Instead, he is talking about a spiritual shift, which can be pictured as a kind of collapse, like the collapse of a building. The term crisis, therefore, synthesizes a variety of observations and serves to focus the urgency of the situation. That it is metaphorical is obvious from the way that Barth realizes that many people will not notice it; the collapse of a building, on the other hand, can hardly be ignored by those who are in it. All of this will have to be demonstrated later in this chapter.

The second question concerns the relationship between metaphor and model. More exactly, what kind of model can a metaphor be? The literature on metaphors and models is vast. Most discussions not only connect metaphor closely to models, but they also imply that metaphors function as quite simple and direct models, making sense of a given field of experience. Thus, a metaphor is a compact model, which can be explicated — or unpacked — by prose discourse; the prose explains, or fills in the space opened up by the metaphor, but it is not itself shaped by the metaphor. In contrast to this view, I will argue that Barth's metaphorical model is operative throughout all of his discourse. What is important is not that he writes about crisis but that his writing follows the contours of this crisis. Moreover, I will argue that Barth's distinctive use of this metaphorical model cuts across the usual discussion; the metaphor of crisis does not make sense of a chaotic background but rather calls into question the very field it purportedly sets out to explain.

Max Black, whose article on metaphor I examined in chapter two, has also made a seminal contribution to this discussion, which is a good place to start. Black's work can be found in "Models and Archetypes," where he begins his argument by distinguishing between literal and metaphorical models.[1] Literal models are constructed to be identical to their original objects except that they are different in scale. For example, a model of the Queen Mary will look like that famous ship, differing from it by being proportionally reduced in size. Black calls these examples scale models; they function to represent an object by stressing some properties or features especially relevant or essential to the original. This kind of a model is, in Peirce's language, an icon, literally embodying the features for which it stands.[2] The scale model serves a fairly specific purpose: it is a means to an end, showing in a simple or direct form what might be difficult or inconvenient to imagine or understand.

In contrast to the scale model, Black uses the term analogue model to refer to models involving a change of medium. While scale models are mimetic, relying upon a relationship of identity to represent their objects, analogue models are guided by the more abstract aim of reproducing the structure or web of relationships of the original. "The analogue model shares with its original not a set of features or an identical proportionality of magnitudes but, more abstractly, the same structure or pattern of relationships" (*MA*, 223). What makes this kind of model remarkable is that the same pattern of relationships can be embodied in a great variety of media. This is the level, Black suggests, at which most scientific models operate. Here Black introduces his previous discussion of metaphor in order to uncover the operation of such complex models. Scientific models say that certain phenomena can be looked at in certain ways, but they actually go further than that. To claim that 'x' can be considered *as if* it were 'y' is to make a comparison or draw an analogy, and Black has already persuasively argued that metaphors are not comparisons or analogies. What Black wants to say is that most scientific theories take the form of 'x' *is* 'y' (like light waves and time warps, for example), and *that,* of course, is the form of the metaphor.

The risk with such metaphorical identifications, Black realizes, is that the model might be taken literally, thus deterring further investigation and research. Or, conversely, the model might be considered only as visual aid, a picture soon to be replaced by mathematical definition, and thus the richness of the model would be overlooked. Black wants to argue that the scientific model should best be treated as a good metaphor: it is both irreplaceable—for the time being—and also informative. "A promising model is one with implications rich enough to suggest novel hypotheses and speculations in the primary field of investigations" (*MA*, 233). The model, in fact, arises from the very same conditions that encourage the use of metaphor: when ordinary language breaks down and a new way of understanding a phenomenon is needed. A model, just like a metaphor, achieves insight in a unique manner, by bringing together two disparate fields and showing a relationship between them that was as yet hidden and unknown. Models do not describe an already known situation; they create a new field of knowledge, which can then be further questioned and explored. Such exploration might lead to the demand for new models, but it cannot replace or exhaust the old model completely because good models like good metaphors serve to point in a direction and not to establish a proposition, allowing for much interpretation but never any conclusive paraphrase or summation.

However, just as there were questions about Black's earlier article, there are some problems here. Black is unclear, in the end, about the relationship between models and metaphors. Are models actually metaphors, or are they just similar to each other? How do actual metaphors contribute to models? Moreover, he comes close to describing models as more like analogies than metaphors. For instance, he writes, "The term 'metaphor' is best restricted to relatively brief statements, and if we wished to draw upon the traditional terms of rhetoric we might better compare the use of models with allegory or fable" (*MA*, 238). Perhaps the problem is that the complexity of most scientific models makes the comparison between models and metaphors strained at best. Black does go further than Hayden White by arguing that science too relies on figuration. "For science, like the humanities, like literature, is an affair of the imagination" (*MA*, 243). However, by trying to load metaphors with some of the analytical and explanatory tasks of science, Black raises more questions than he answers.

Janet Martin Soskice, whom I also discussed in chapter two, tries to answer some of these questions. She criticizes Black for conflating the categories of metaphor and model, a mistake also made, she argues, by Ian G. Barbour, who discusses models as "systematically developed metaphors,"[3] and Frederick Ferre, who treats the difference between the two as largely a matter of degree and not kind.[4] Barbour and Ferre think that metaphors propose analogies, Soskice argues, and this constitutes a lapse into the comparison theory of metaphor, which Soskice wants to avoid. To counter this tendency, Soskice suggests that often metaphors arise on the basis of models; for example, if we think of the brain on the model of the computer, then we can speak of the brain in the metaphorical terms of input, feedback, and programming. But from where does the model itself come? Here Soskice argues that the model does not act as a metaphor, so that there need be no confusion between the two. The real connection between them is that the model is often proposed by a metaphor. In other words, the model can be — but does not have to be — presented in the form of a metaphor. In the example just cited, the metaphor would be: "The brain is a computer." Soskice calls these statements theory-constitutive metaphors.[5] She thinks this avoids several confusions: some metaphors can propose models (which in turn generate more metaphors), but metaphors do not themselves function like models, and models do not necessarily take the form of metaphors.

The implications of these kinds of discussions for theology are enormous. Ian Ramsey, for example, has done the most to popularize the idea that religious language is rich in models and that this fact constitutes the most significant similarity between theology and the sciences.[6] Ramsey's intention is basically apologetical; he wants to show that science can pose no ultimate threat to religion because both modes of knowledge operate on a common ground. Soskice's purpose in clarifying the relationship between metaphor and model is also theological. She argues that most discussions about this subject imply that scientific models are explanatory and dispensable, whereas religious models are affective and necessary. Her response is to argue that the reference of religious models is every bit as objective as scientific models, and she defends a kind of theological realism to make this point. Theory-constitutive metaphors in religion refer to and explain the divine just as their counterparts in science depict and explain the natural world. At this juncture in her work, though, she runs the same risk as Black; by trying to connect religious and scientific metaphors and models, she faces the danger of confusing these two categories by making metaphor do the work of model.[7]

This same problem infects the project of Sallie McFague, who begins her work in the book already quoted in chapter one, *Speaking in Parables,* by arguing that religious language is inherently poetic or, more specifically, metaphoric. She relies on current scholarship to argue that Jesus' parables, for example, are extended metaphors, that is, brief stories that have the same impact as a metaphor, showing the strange or the uncanny through a tensive account of the ordinary. She develops her argument by claiming that metaphor is at the heart of all religious language, and religious belief is only possible by the appropriation of metaphor through the mediation of narrative. Narrative, in the forms of confession, testimony, and autobiography, allows a person to express the truth of a metaphor in the context of an entire way of life. This mediation is necessary because, "One does not move easily from poetic forms to discursive discourse, for metaphor is not finally translatable or paraphrasable."[8]

Metaphorical Theology continues this line of thought, but with this book the focus on models begins to replace the concern with metaphor, a trend that reaches a culmination in McFague's most recent work, *Models of God*.[9] In *Metaphorical Theology* she connects metaphor to model. "The simplest way to define a model is as a dominant metaphor, a metaphor with staying power."[10] She then moves to connect religious models with scientific models. The net effect of this argument is that the use of metaphors-as-models in religion is subject to the same revisions and modifications as scientific models. Thus, in *Models of God* she can argue that the metaphors of God as mother, lover, and friend are better than the metaphors of God as father, lord, and king, because the latter are paternalistic, hierarchic, and triumphalistic, while the former better serve an ecological worldview, which should imagine the world as God's body and not the world as external to and ruled by God's fatherly power and strength. One can agree with McFague's critique of traditional theological language — and accept her alternatives — without assenting to her treatment of such language as models that can be easily modified rather than metaphors that need more careful attention and transformation.

McFague and Soskice both serve as examples of how quickly a discussion of metaphor can become an analysis of models. In fact, in all of the works so far discussed in this chapter, metaphors are understood to function as or like models, thus being subject to a variety of criticisms and revisions on the basis of how well they explain and illuminate human experience (in the case of religious metaphors) or the facts of nature (in the case of scientific metaphors). This position is perhaps best developed and defended by George Lakoff and Mark Johnson in their *Metaphors We Live By,* where the authors argue that metaphors are pervasive in all aspects of human thought, governing everyday conceptual systems as well as the theories of religion and science.[11] Unfortunately, these positions end up devaluing what has been called the "ontological flash"[12] of insight that is given by a good metaphor: that is, the metaphor's capacity not to fund a conceptual delineation but rather to alter a perspective, distort a previously known, radicalize an orientation, or even provoke a conversion. This is precisely how I will approach Barth's metaphor of crisis. If this is Barth's model for understanding God and doing theology, then it is a strange model indeed because it does not illuminate or explain a field of experience but rather calls all such explanation into question. In fact, the metaphor of crisis is actually a crisis for metaphor because it means that the theological field cannot be simply modeled or prefigured but must be further re-figured by other tropes.

Moreover, when I speak of Barth's metaphor of crisis as a model of *Romans,* I do not want to imply that it is a model he consciously used and manipulated, in the way that a scientist, say, would use a model—although he was not unaware of its central importance to his thought. Instead, what I want to understand by using tropes as models for discourse is something different from the dominant discussion on this matter, which I have tried to summarize above. Tropes model discourse in the way in which Hayden White tried to show: they serve as the general forms of the basic moves of a given investigation of a particular field. Tropes are, then, similar to what Gadamer calls presuppositions: they govern an interpretation, and are themselves only discovered by further interpretation. This view of tropes, which is not necessarily in contradiction with the more dominant discussion but could be seen as a compliment to it, sees tropes as more fundamental than their operation as directly visible models subject to revision and modification would suggest. In my view, tropes are the sometimes hidden, sometimes evident forms of the dynamic of a given discourse. This is, as I understand it, what is meant by discussions about "root" metaphors. Stephen C. Pepper was the first, as far as I know, to use this term. In an attempt to classify the various metaphysical systems of Western philosophy, he developed a theory of their foundation and origin:

> The method in principle seems to be this: A man desiring to understand the world looks about for a clue to its comprehension. He pitches upon some area of common sense fact and tries if he cannot understand other areas in terms of this one. The original area becomes then his basic analogy or root metaphor.[13]

Such root metaphors are developed in a set of categories; the metaphors do not explain anything—the categories do that. Root metaphors are judged according to the explanatory power of the categories they beget. David Tracy has adopted this theory in a theological position, which argues that the root metaphor of Christianity is "God is love."[14] Root metaphors are not models in any obvious sense; they serve to structure a discourse from beneath, so to speak, monitoring the moves that a discourse makes while only occasionally making their presence directly known. However, both Tracy and Pepper imply that only metaphors can serve this purpose, while I will argue that any trope can function in this way, focusing on three such tropes in Barth.

I want to claim, then, that the metaphor of crisis is the root metaphor of Barth's *Romans*. Barth saw literally all of reality under the sign of crisis. What initiated this perspective, I will argue, was a reversal in his confidence in history. History was no longer seen as carrying culture on an upward journey of ever-increasing accomplishments. Instead, when Barth saw through this illusion of history — the unwarranted idea of inevitable progress — he was forced to view reality — epistemological, political, cultural, and religious — as in a state of crisis. I should note that Barth was not alone in this move. In an essay entitled, "The Burden of History," Hayden White has argued that the twentieth century is marked by an insistent desire to escape from history:

> In the decade before the First World War this hostility towards the historical consciousness and the historian gained wide currency among intellectuals in every country of Western Europe. Everywhere there was a growing suspicion that Europe's feverish rummaging among the ruins of its past expressed less a sense of firm control over the present than an unconscious fear of a future too horrible to contemplate.[15]

And Allan Megill has written a book, *Prophets of Extremity,* in which he argues that the major thinkers of our time, Nietzsche, Heidegger, Foucault, and Derrida, were all writing in response to a perceived crisis of culture, and shared similar antihistorical and hyperbolically critical perspectives.[16]

Karl Barth, I want to argue, also belongs in this group: his perception of crisis is thorough and comprehensive, and his response is also ruthlessly hyperbolic. His solution to the crisis of his time is to intensify it, and his voice is surely prophetic and extreme. As Langdon Gilkey has written, "Barth's view of history is the modern historical consciousness radically 'secularized,' i.e., stripped of every one of its elements of progressive meaning, and thus for him utterly separated from the redemptive activity of God."[17] History is completely deprived of any immanent principle of redemption. This is not a view which Barth took lightly, nor did he come upon it easily. It broke forth from his writings like a flood, but it is possible to trace the beginnings of the build-up, which was to wipe away an entire period of theology. It is also necessary to show how this presuppositional metaphor demanded further figurative elaboration in hyperbole and irony.

THE ORIGIN OF CRISIS

Many commentators, aided by Barth himself, trace the origin of Barth's preoccupation with crisis to the outbreak of World War I.[18] On August 1, 1914, the day the war began, 93 German intellectuals issued a manifesto identifying themselves with the Kaiser's war policy, and the document was published in *Die christliche Welt,* a leading journal of theological liberalism for which Barth had served as an editorial assistant in 1908 and 1909. Many of the signers of this manifesto were theologians, and Barth — who had long admired these men—was clearly shaken by their capitulation to the war ideology:

> The unconditioned truths of the gospel are simply suspended for the time being and in the meantime a German war-theology is put to work, its Christian trimming consisting of a lot of talk about sacrifices and the like . . . It is truly sad. Marburg and German civilization have lost something in my eyes by this breakdown, and indeed forever . . . (*RTM*, 26).

> Disillusioned by their conduct, I perceived that I should not be able any longer to accept their ethics and dogmatics, their biblical exegesis, their interpretation of history, that at least for me the theology of the nineteenth century had no future.[19]

The war served as a shocking catalyst to Barth's reappraisal of the liberal theological situation. It was a formative experience: no longer should theology trust in any alliances with the political or philosophical powers of its day. No longer should theology take God for granted as an adjunct to human affairs. In fact, Barth was to decide that theology itself was part of the problem; the crisis of the war merely unmasked a deeper rift at the heart of theology itself.[20]

   As much as the war makes for a dramatic starting point for any account of Barth's early theology, it is misleading to begin only there. Whereas it is true that Barth's earliest theological work was conducted in the liberal paradigm then dominant, even at an early stage he showed signs of tension with and dissent from liberalism. Indeed, his break from liberalism was made possible by an inside acquaintance with the strengths and weaknesses of this position; he was, then, a product of the world he would later discredit. For example, in 1906 he studied in Berlin under Adolf Harnack, and at that time he discovered Schleiermacher: "I was inclined to believe him blindly all along the line" (*B*, 40). It was also in Berlin where Barth first read Wilhelm Herrmann, who "was *the* theological teacher of my student years."[21] In 1908, after spending time in Berne and Tübingen, he fulfilled a longstanding dream to study with Herrmann at Marburg. Although Barth chose not to continue his theological researches in the academy, opting instead to become a pastor (and he served in Geneva for two years, 1909–1911, before he went to Safenwil), the result of his studies was a thorough indoctrination into theological liberalism: "At the end of my student days I was second to none among my contemporaries in credulous approval of the 'modern' theology of the time" (*B*, 51). Yet even then there was a presentiment of the need for change: Barth speaks about his pre-war attachment to liberalism as a "passable conviction," which held because "for the time being I did not see a better way before me."[22]

The better way—the advent of crisis—might have come as a sudden flash of metaphorical insight sparked by the war, but it was also made possible by a gradual dissatisfaction with theological modernism. Barth wrote several early articles elaborating these difficulties, and three of them fall into a natural group, which I want to examine, looking for clues to the origin of the crisis. The first is "Modern Theology and Work for the Kingdom of God," published in 1909 at the end of Barth's Marburg studies and before his Genevan ministry.[23] Here Barth states the position of liberal theology in his own terms by asking why modern theology makes the practical work of ministry so difficult to face. He defines modern theology as the demand for intellectual integrity—which means the exposure of religion to the historical sciences—and religion is defined in individual and inward terms. These two tenets of modern theology are borrowed by Barth from Herrmann and mutually implicate each other: the historical sciences disallow the acceptance of events, persons, or creeds as absolutes, identified with God's revelation; therefore, religion must be a personal, private matter. Because religion cannot be based on history, it must be grounded in the individual Christian consciousness. Barth thus sees himself in basic agreement with Schleiermacher: the task of theology is to explicate the structures of religious experience. This means that the superiority of the Christian norm can only be confessed, not demonstrated, but that is quite acceptable to Barth: "Religion is for us experience in an intensely individual form."[24] The religious individual should not be concerned with proving such an inner act of faith. Yet a question still remains at the end of this essay: how is the act of faith to be harmonized with a skeptical and relativistic—an ultimately corrosive—historical science?

A second important article, "Christian Faith and History,"[25] written in 1910 but not published until 1912, reiterates the problem of inner faith and outer reality as the main dilemma of theology. How does the theologian relate the present experience of God—the inner life of the Christian—to the whole history of Christianity? "How can a historically represented *then* be normative for an immediately experienced *now*?"[26] Barth defines faith as a direct consciousness of an absolutely transcendent power. In faith the individual is lifted out of time and history, but faith is also a social fact: the individual exists only in time and history. The dilemma is that the Enlightenment dissolved all external supports for faith and forced people to seek authority in their own consciousness; yet the Christ that is known from within is also the Christ of history. Barth concludes this article without relieving any of the tension: the content of faith is found in Christ, but that content only takes life in the individual's consciousness.

This dilemma is not resolved but only intensified in a third article, "Faith in the Personal God,"[27] presented as a lecture in 1913 and published in 1914. Here Barth agrees with Schleiermacher that religious experience is the source of all theological statements but disagrees with his antipathy toward the idea of personality in God. Barth thinks that religious experience demands a God as an active subject. Such a God, though, is not like us. God does not change — yet God is both eternal and active. Barth realizes this is conceptually messy: God is both transcendent and personal. The problem is a genuine one: the demands of experience impose a constraint on conceptual discourse. As one commentator puts it, "an irreconcilable contradiction exists between the finitude necessarily ingredient in the concept of personality (as a thinking, willing, becoming 'I') and the infinitude required by the concept of the Absolute."[28] The result is that even at this early stage Barth's theology is anxious and restless: "The incomparability of Christian experience makes it resistant to the very theological expression it demands."[29] Theology is ironically limited by the very experience that gives it birth. Already, then, Barth is developing a theology that cannot — say, as in Harnack's concept of theology as a science — speak easily or simply of its own object. Here we have the first glimpse that theology — and behind it religion in general — is incapable of achieving the goals it sets for itself; we have the first hint that theology not only fails to explicate religious experience, but it also fails to understand God.

These dissatisfactions, however, are still enumerated only within the liberal paradigm; they do not threaten to break from that model of theology. Nevertheless, such difficulties prepared Barth to be open to the possibility of doing theology in a completely different way. This paradigm shift in Barth's thought is not easy to map; many factors contributed to it. There are signs of change not only in his academic publications and lectures, but also in his sermons and in his politics. First, take Barth's politics. Socialism was both a spur and an outlet for his increasingly radical theology. When he came to Safenwil in 1911, it was a small agricultural village, but it was becoming increasingly industrial. This raised the problem of the trade union movement. When he was not writing his weekly sermon, Barth began studying factory legislation, union affairs, and economics. He began to give lectures at the Workers' Association. True socialism, he came to believe, was the true Christianity for our time; true socialism, however, was not what the socialists were doing but what Jesus taught and practiced.[30] Yet Barth accepted the main tenet of socialism, the class struggle — he could see it in his own village — and he also believed that Jesus was on the side of the workers, even if they did not go to church regularly or count themselves as Christians.

Influenced by prominent religious socialist figures like Hermann Kut-
ter and Leonhard Ragaz, Barth began to attend conferences on this topic—
where many of his earliest and most important lectures were given—and in
January 1915, he joined the Social Democratic Party. For a while Barth was
very enthusiastic about socialism: it "was the movement that was to us the
most impressive parable, if not the substance, of the Kingdom of God,
which we preached on Sundays."[31] Socialism did what Barth wanted from
the Kingdom of God: it broke the bonds of bourgeois complacency and demanded a new social order. However, when the socialists, like the liberal
theologians, became nationalists in support of the war, Barth also became
disillusioned with them. His commitment to socialism as a political movement decreased—as we will see, it, too, had to stand under the sign of crisis
—even though he continued to be influenced by its critique of the status quo
and by its specific political measures.

Barth did not spend all of his time criticizing Safenwil industrialists; in
fact, most of his effort was spent on the Sunday sermon. I have already noted
in chapter one that his theology grew out of a struggle to preach. At Safenwil, Barth was a difficult preacher, and he would later often think back to his
congregation with sympathy for what they had to put up with. Many Sundays attendance was very low, and Barth felt like a failure. Yet he insisted on
making his sermons demanding and honest: "My calling is to speak and to
speak clearly . . . If I wanted to be liked, I would keep quiet" (B, 63).[32] Barth
was struggling to let God speak without speaking for or about God. He
wanted to put into human words the devastating consequences of divine activity, while at the same time he did not want to trust too much in his own
very human formulations. "Through Jesus all standards are turned upside
down," he preached one Sunday, and another time: "There is only one kind
of work for the Kingdom of God, the work that God does himself" (B, 63).

This combination of hyperbolically announcing the judgment of God
and ironically qualifying every statement about God can be seen clearly in a
sermon given in 1916. Here Barth argues that the church is a place of great
disturbance, not refuge. The church is not one house among many. "You
cannot go in and come out peacefully."[33] What makes the church dangerous
is the Bible: Barth compares it to a river, which has burst its banks, spread-
ing destruction and yet also fertility everywhere. The message of the Bible
is too great to be stated in anything but exaggerated form. Barth also turns
this same destructive power against himself, claiming that the preacher is
not exempt from the power of the proclamation: "Everything in my position
and words that you now think is directed against you was really directed
against me and my own life long before."[34] In the pulpit, then, Barth could
both rave about and recoil from the Christian message. Yet for all the pronouncements he could exclaim and all the hesitations he could demure in the

pulpit, Barth was perplexed by theological reflections in his study. "Why, I had to ask myself, did those question marks and the exclamation marks, which are the very existence of the pastor, play really no role at all in the theology I knew?" (*B*, 90) Barth sought some way to transfer the excitement and anxiety—the peculiar combination of being allowed to make hyperbolic pronouncements while feeling ironically unable and disqualified to say anything at all—of the Sunday pulpit to the academic text.

As this last comment suggests, Sunday sermons and forays into socialism were not enough. Barth needed, above all, a new theological beginning. He was becoming more critical of the present state of the church and theology, but he was not sure what he himself wanted to say. One pastor's meeting, he wrote, filled "me with the greatest unrest and anguish . . . When I want to shout out in the room, I have neither the voice nor the words, and I hang there wriggling like a roofer on his rope" (*B*, 87). The pressure building inside of him had to burst; however, what was needed was not just another human option or theory but a way to let God overcome everything human: "Above all, it will be a matter of our recognizing God once more as God . . . This is a task alongside which all cultural, social and patriotic duties are child's play" (*B*, 89). Barth needed to focus his thought on one thing worth saying well. He wanted to speak about God, but to do that in a direct or straightforward fashion would only instigate yet another theological school or program. The metaphor of crisis, as the organizing principle of *Romans*, would allow Barth to talk about God in a completely new and disturbing way—by speaking through the collapse of all attempts to do just that, to talk about God.

Barth reaches the full implications of his understanding of crisis in several lectures and publications prior to the second edition of *Romans*. One of the first indications of his coming theological shift was an address given in 1916, "The Strange New World Within the Bible."[35] Here Barth not only announces his intention to return to the Bible for theological sustenance, but he also reveals what he finds in that return: in the Bible, he suggests, we are aware of the tremors of an earthquake or the thundering of ocean waves. Barth admits that the Bible gives to people what they are seeking: you get what you are looking for. Yet there is something else, something "other" in the Bible that transcends everything we project onto it. This excess is what Barth calls "a strange, new world: the world of God" (*WG*, 33). The Bible, then, does not give us any answers to our questions but rather questions our questioning by posing the question of God. Barth does not think, for example, that the Bible is very helpful as a book about morality. It often glorifies war, and it is not very specific about business, marriage, government, and so on. "It offers us not at all what we first seek in it" (*WG*, 39). Instead, it is an "other," which stands against us and questions the answers we bring to it. In the end the Bible speaks only the tautology that Barth will continually repeat throughout this period: the Bible says, "God is God" (*WG*, 48).

Another 1916 lecture, "The Righteousness of God," continues this discussion by focusing not on the Bible but on God. Here Barth suggests that God is the deepest and most certain fact of our existence, a fact that is attested to by our own conscience. "We must let conscience speak, for it tells of the righteousness of God in such a way that that righteousness becomes a certainty" (*WG*, 10). As this remark shows, Barth is still caught in the web of liberal theology in an attempt to ground religion in subjectivity. He is also hopeful about the possibilities that religion—once revealed—will transform the world. Barth speaks of another life that, once this life is uprooted, must grow in its place. He speaks of a new world, which must emerge once this world is eclipsed. Barth later rejected such optimistic language about the evolutionary coming of the Kingdom of God. In fact, even in this article Barth warns against any attempt to make the new world our own. The new that is to come must come from God alone. Barth can even initiate, here, a criticism of religion, which he will later expand: "We should above all be honest and ask ourselves far more frankly what we really gain from religion" (*WG*, 20). Indeed, the whole point of the article is to stake out a disjunction between the righteousness of God and the righteousness of humanity. The God based on the righteousness of humanity is an idol; God's righteousness can only silence the uproar of religion and culture. This God, God considered as God, is Wholly Other (*WG*, 24). This article, then, notwithstanding its attempt to place theology in a reflection on subjectivity, contains many of the elements Barth will later bring together in *Romans*. It is a testing of some very disturbed waters: "It remains to be seen whether the quaking of the tower of Babel which we are now experiencing will be violent enough to bring us somewhat nearer to the way of faith" (*WG*, 27).

Barth's own first major attempt to quake the tower of liberal certainties and presumptions was the first edition of his Romans commentary, which was written between 1916 and 1918 and published in 1919.[36] Barth decided that he needed to return in a systematic fashion to the Bible for his theological resources, and so he began a private study of Romans for himself and his friends. The result was both exciting and disturbing: "During the work it was often as though I caught a breath from afar, from Asia Minor or Corinth, something primaeval, from the ancient east, indefinably sunny, wild, original, that somehow is hidden behind these sentences" (*B*, 98). Rebelling against the practice of trimming Paul to fit the contemporary situation, Barth wanted to let Paul speak in all of his strangeness.

What makes Paul so striking to Barth is his witness to the coming

Kingdom of God. In this edition Barth writes with a passionate enthusiasm about the new age, which began with the incarnation and is now ready to break into the world as a mighty power. Jesus is the hinge of history that opens the door to the new period, which transcends this world and yet is more real than this world. The reality of God is the true history, which accompanies and overturns earthly history. Von Balthasar calls this theme dynamic eschatology, a movement from a doomed temporal order to a new living order ruled by God. He has argued that this position is couched in Platonic terms: an idea exists, is broken, but is restored. For Barth, history was now moving toward the original unity with God, which humanity had broken. At its base, then, this position advocates a relationship of identity between the world and the divine. Humanity needs to recall this original unity in order to begin an irreversible process of restoration.[37]

The movement of restoration follows the course of God's own activity from Adam to Christ. David Paul Henry has noted that Barth often draws the distinction between this side *(dieseitig)* and the other side *(jenseitig),* two aspects of reality that correspond with each other in this process.[38] Victory is assured because it is accomplished on the other side; on this side, a gradual, organic process is increasing evidence of that which has already happened. Restoration is a kind of second creation which, through the second Adam, reverses the flow of the stream of history. This side is always a distorted, nonchronological reflection of the decisive *jenseitig* events; nevertheless, possibilities of unity with God, once initiated, become concrete actualities as the dissolution of this world is replaced by the world to come.

James Smart has suggested that a translation of this first edition of *Romans* would have made more friends for Barth in the English-speaking world than the second edition.[39] Here Barth's language is optimistic about the possibilities for social progress and spiritual growth. It is almost as if he has transferred the old liberal belief in the progress of earthly history to hope in the growing work of divine activity. True, many of the elements of the later edition are present in muted forms. For example, Barth is serverely critical of the church. However, he is not indiscriminate in this criticism, being quick to point out that there is both a true and a false church. Barth is also ambivalent about religious subjectivity in this book. The seed of divinity has been planted in humanity, but because of the power of sin people cannot simply try to remember the divine. When that attempt is made, idolatry and self-deification are likely to result. What is needed, then, is not Platonic recollection but an acknowledgement of the unique work of Jesus Christ in manifesting the new age. Clearly, Barth is trying to announce a new theological attitude toward the church, subjectivity and God, but the framework within which he is working does not give him much room to maneuver. Thus, when the publisher wanted a second edition, he decided that he had to start all over, so that he could claim about the revision that "no stone remains in its old place" (*R*, 2).

Before he began his revisions, however, he gave a lecture in 1919 at a conference on religious socialism in Tambach that made his name known throughout Germany. Barth called "The Christian's Place in Society," a "rather complicated kind of machine that runs backwards and forwards and shoots in all directions with no lack of both visible and hidden joints" (*RTM*, 47). Busch has argued that this lecture marks Barth's farewell to religious socialism (*B*, 111). Barth takes as his theme the point that the Christian in society is not the Christian, but Christ, that within us which is not ourself. This paradox must be stated in order to counter the tendency—present in, among other movements, religious socialism—to reduce God to an aspect of the temporal order. God, Barth argues, is not a part of this world; God is not the guarantor of any human movement. In fact, "Society is now really ruled by its own logos; say rather by a whole pantheon of its own hypostases and powers" (*WG*, 279–80). Secularity is accepted as the very condition of modernity.

Here Barth begins to break with the first *Romans* by stripping away from history any possibilities for redemption and renewal. History is utterly secular, so that even religious socialism cannot contribute to its redemption. Barth also confronts the one crucial problem of this move: If there is nothing in this world that can be the basis for our talk about God, how then can we dare that talk? If the Christian does not have a place in this world, then how can the Christian speak of the other or divine world, which is no place at all? Barth answers these questions with his first hints of a truly ironic vision of theology, a point I will have to elaborate in chapter five. Barth must admit that he can really say nothing at all about God, and he uses the analogy of trying to draw a bird in flight. "For our position is really an instant in a movement, and any view of it is comparable to the momentary view of a bird in flight" (*WG*, 282). It is ridiculous to try to draw the bird flying, Barth suggests. "Almost unavoidably it ends in making the movement a theme in itself, a fact in itself, entirely apart from the motion" (*WG*, 283). Somehow, Barth must learn to speak without letting his words mean what they seem to say.

In another transitional article, "Biblical Questions, Insights and Vistas," an address delivered in April 1920, Barth sets out to make two points, which are central to his new project. First, he wants to argue that the Bible is a theological document, which confronts us with the most profound questions. Barth admits that the Bible is a human document, too—that is, it is subject to historical and psychological researches. However, "This judgment, being announced by every tongue and believed in every territory, we may take for granted today. We need not continue trying to break through an open door" (*WG*, 60). Historical criticism, Barth is saying, has already triumphed; it does not need any more help or support. What is needed is a theological retrieval, which will examine the special content of the Bible. That special content is Barth's second point. "Biblical piety is not really pious; one must rather characterize it as well-considered and definite refusal to regard anything as sacred" (*WG*, 66). Biblical piety, then, is in opposition to ordinary church piety. The problem with religion is that it forgets that it has a right to exist only when it considers itself as a dispensable manifestation of God's grace. Religion should not try to be a competitive power over against other such powers. At best religion is a means and not an end in itself. Moreover, biblical piety is not even concerned with religious experience. "In biblical experience nothing is less important than experience as such" (*WG*, 69). The Bible's one and only concern is God. Barth refers to Otto's use of the *mysterium tremendum* to talk about God, commenting, "He is not a thing among other things, but the Wholly Other, the infinite aggregate of all merely relative others" (*WG*, 74). Barth explains this Wholly Other God in a passage that nicely summarizes his new position:

> The affirmation of God, man and the world given in the New Testament is based exclusively upon the possibility of a new order absolutely beyond human thought; and therefore, as prerequisite to that order, there must come a crisis that denies all human thought (*WG*, 80).

With this article, then, the crisis has begun.

THE SUPPORTING CAST

The second edition of *Romans,* in which Barth's crisis thinking climaxes, was written in eleven months between autumn 1920 and summer 1921. It was finished by September 1921 and published in 1922. With this book Barth found his own theological voice, a voice that also spoke for many others: "All unaware, I had been allowed to take a step which many people had been waiting for and to do things for which many people were prepared" (*B,* 120).[40] While he was working on this commentary, several thinkers had a special influence on him.[41] These are the pieces Barth synthesized into his own unique version of the puzzle—the crisis—of the gospel. These are the voices—Blumhardt, Overbeck, Feuerbach, Dostoevsky, and Kierkegaard—Barth made his own:

Christoph Blumhardt   Barth grew to appreciate Blumhardt in 1915, although he met him as early as 1907 at Blumhardt's physical and spiritual health retreat center in Bad Boll. Barth thought he was a man who took God seriously; he taught his followers to expect God's activity and to overcome individualism and egotism, which were the great barriers to both physical and spiritual health. Blumhardt preached an eschatological version of Christianity, which was at one time biblical, realistic, and socialistic; his nonpietistic outlook could be even more critical of the established order than socialism. Connecting knowledge of God with the Christian's hope for the future, he helped Barth solve the problem of history: the Kingdom of God is a decisive action that breaks through time, transforming the present from the beyond. From Blumhardt, Barth learned to appreciate God as the radical renewer of the world who is always and ever completely new and unpredictably active. Blumhardt's influence was not limited to theology; Barth also admired Blumhardt's political convictions. Blumhardt had not only joined the Social Democratic Party, but he became a deputy for that party, a bold step for a religious leader at that time.[42]

Franz Overbeck   A professor of New Testament in Basel and a friend of Nietzsche,[43] Overbeck was a controversial figure, regarded by some as a curiosity and by others as a pariah of the modern theological scene. Barth was one of the few to defend him. In 1920 Barth wrote, "Unsettled Questions for Theology Today," a review of Overbeck's *Christentum und Kultur,* published posthumously. Barth expressed disappointment that Overbeck was ignored by his contemporaries; many theologians, in fact, thought that Overbeck was an atheist who simply had nothing positive to contribute to Christianity. What did Overbeck write that caused such strong reactions? "If it is read and understood," Barth surmised, "the normal effect would be that 99 percent of us all will remain caught in its net and will make the discovery that it is impossible for anyone really to be such a thing as a theologian" (*TC,* 57). It is true that Overbeck thought the theology of his day was totally corrupt and false; Christianity, he believed, had reached a dead end. However, Barth sensed a positive message here; he compared Overbeck to Blumhardt, suggesting that what one said in a positive way the other said negatively. They present the same message—that Christianity is essentially eschatological—in very different forms. Overbeck confronts the world with a great either-or: either history or Christianity. Christianity, he argued, cannot be based on history; history cannot tell us anything about Christianity. Christianity is not of this world; it stands in contradiction to the world. The only possible abode of Christianity lies in what Overbeck called the *Urgeschichte,* which is super or primal history, denoting a time of ever-new beginnings, which transcends ordinary or historical time. History cannot judge or understand this realm, which lies above and beyond it. In fact, Overbeck argued, and this is where he was often misunderstood or rejected, church history is by necessity a degenerative process simply because it is involved in history. True Christianity consists of the expectation of the Kingdom of God while church history is based on a compromise with the vicissitudes of time. This position, however, is ambiguous, and that accounts for some of the difficulties of Overbeck's reception; unlike Kierkegaard, Overbeck did not count himself a Christian. He did not advocate reform. He merely expected Christianity to continue to fade away. Yet Barth, in this article, defends him, perhaps ironically, as somehow a heroic Christian: Overbeck is a reluctant theologian who, by destroying church history, actually provides possibilities for the liberation of true Christianity. Overbeck was sufficiently courageous to proclaim that there were really few true Christians left in the world, and this is not the fault of individuals: the mechanism which functions to dissolve Christianity is theology. Modern theology conforms Christianity to the world and erases any trace of original Christianity. Although Barth was not to accept this position completely, he was very influenced by Overbeck's notion of time and by his hyperbolic critique of theology.[44] He concludes his article by asking the question: Was Overbeck a theologian? Barth writes, as much to himself as about Overbeck, that, "A theologian who is determined *not* to be a theologian might perhaps — if the impossible is to become possible — be a very good theologian" (*TC,* 71). Here Barth begins to understand theology ironically: only by going against theology can theology become itself.

Ludwig Feuerbach   Feuerbach was similar to Overbeck in that he relentlessly criticized Christianity, yet he was totally dedicated to the study of theology. In an article he wrote in 1920, Barth said of him that "among the philosophers of modern times there is perhaps no other who occupied himself so intensively and so exclusively with the problem of theology" (*TC,* 217).[45] Feuerbach did not want to say many things but only one thing with a relentless tenacity. Barth does not think that this one message, the projection theory of religion, is necessarily very profound or provocative. True, there is more to Feuerbach than the projection theory: he contributed to socialist thought, which Barth appreciates, and he developed a distinctive sensuous philosophy, which sought to affirm humanity in its complete fullness. What Barth likes most about Feuerbach is that his insistent reduction of theology to anthropology is really a description of the state of theology itself. For a long time, Barth argues, at least since Luther and Kant, theology had been becoming increasingly interested in humanity instead of God; Feuerbach both furthers that process and discloses its final destination. Feuerbach was, Barth claims, a spy within the camp of theology, reporting to the world the true secret of theology. To counter this insidious criticism, theologians need to get their priorities straight. "To repulse Feuerbach's attack effectively one must be certain that man's relation with God is in every respect, in principle, an irreversible relation" (*TC*, 231). Feuerbach could have understood this relation better, Barth suggests, if he had better understood the facts of death and evil; with that knowledge, nobody could possibly think of equating the being of God with the being of humanity. From Feuerbach Barth learns that theology cannot, as he would later put it in a famous phrase, speak about God by talking about humanity in a loud voice.

Fyodor Dostoevsky   Barth's good friend Eduard Thurneysen first introduced him to the works of this author; in fact, Thurneysen would later write a book about Dostoevsky, which Barth deeply appreciated.[46] Barth was especially struck by Dostoevsky's "The Grand Inquisitor," a central chapter in his novel, *The Brothers Karamazov*. It could be said that this is a literary presentation of the argument which Overbeck threw against church history. Dostoevsky's Inquisitor is more interested in making people happy—in improving the course of history—than in being true to Jesus Christ. He wants to give the people miracle, mystery, and authority in order to placate them and to keep the peace. In fact, when Jesus does appear to the Inquisitor, the old church leader cannot stand the sight of him, arguing that Jesus only cared for those few individuals who were brave enough to make the free decision of faith, while the church has had to care for the masses, who need not freedom but peace and security. Indeed, the Inquisitor interprets the three temptations Jesus overcame as precisely the three tasks that the church has had to accomplish: giving the people reasons to believe, physical sustenance first before spiritual teaching, and political structure. The impact of this short story is due to the extremity with which it pits the church against Jesus. The conflict does not consist of the church against the world, but Jesus against the very institution that professes to honor his name and further his cause. Religion, then, does not preserve but rather undermines the teachings of Jesus in an effort to save this world rather than to point to the salvation that is yet to come. Barth basically accepts this portrayal of the church, but whereas in the story Jesus responds to the Inquisitor with a silent kiss, Barth takes up the sword in a hyperbolic denouncement of religion in his own work, *Romans*.[47]

Søren Kierkegaard   Much has been written about Barth's dependence on Kierkegaard. I will only make a brief note of this influence because, first, I will argue that Barth's ironic method of theology actually keeps him from being as committed to a kind of Kierkegaardian dialectics as many have thought, and second, I will suggest, again in the chapter on irony, that perhaps Kierkegaard's real influence on Barth can be discerned precisely in that very trope, which both used so effectively.[48] However, the influence of Kierkegaard is ever present in *Romans,* and so it cannot be ignored. Especially important is Barth's use of Kierkegaard's category of the "moment" to denote the time that is not in history in which God breaks into history in a salvific act. Moreover, Barth also agreed with Kierkegaard on the reasons for the need to speak of the moment as a kind of condensation point of grace: "If I have a system it is limited to a recognition of what Kierkegaard called the 'infinite qualitative distinction' between time and eternity" (*R,* 10). This infinite gulf between the human and the divine—which Barth so effectively exploits in *Romans*—also provides a basis for a devastating critique of the church; in this regard, too, Barth notes his debts, saying that "we have heard what Kierkegaard said about it all, and we agree with him" (*R,* 392). Many have read passages like these and assumed that Barth's system must consist, therefore, of an adoption of Kierkegaard's thought. This does justice to neither Barth nor Kierkegaard: Kierkegaard was too gloomy, individualistic and human-centered for Barth, even at this early stage in Barth's development. Kierkegaard, for example, could not help Barth in his attempt to embrace socialism or in his search for some way to let God speak anew. Moreover, Kierkegaard's critique of the aesthetic does not bear much resemblance to Barth's critique of the church. In chapter five I will argue that their similarities are more evident in style than in content: both thinkers were more figurative than systematic, and their reliance on indirect discourse, especially irony, constitutes an unsystematic qualification on everything they said.

Traveling in such company, Barth could not help but to radicalize and intensify his dissatisfaction with liberal theology. Yet he still needed a way to make all of these distinctive voices blend into his own. He found this organizing motif, I want to argue, in the metaphor of crisis. I have already argued that Barth lost confidence not only in the progress of history—morally, politically, and religiously—but he also thought that the possibilities for basing theology on a historical analysis of the Bible were spent and exhausted. Nevertheless, as I have tried to show, Barth's notion of crisis was not merely provoked by the war and its aftermath. As Berkouwer has noted, "it was plain from the very beginning that this crisis did not find its center in doubt and despair."[49] Busch tells us, for example, that Barth did not like Spengler's *The Decline of the West* and did not want his work to be mistaken as mere pessimism (*B,* 120). He also did not want his work to be interpreted as a rebellion between the younger and the older generation of scholars (*RTM,* 53).

For Barth, the crisis is not the result of some interpretation of the present situation; it is not a reaction against some prior school or movement. Instead, the crisis goes deeper than that: it is a lens through which Barth has come to view every theological and cultural problem. It is related to grace and salvation as well as to the problem of time. Salvation is only possible when the crisis is recognized in its fullest form. History stands under the crisis because of the ever troubling presence of eternity which judges it.

The crisis, then, is permanent and universal. The war had lifted the veil of history to give us a better glimpse of it, but it has always been there. Perhaps Berkouwer overstates his case when he suggests, "This crisis does not have an independent function as an isolated motif occasioned by the negativism and disillusionment obtaining in Europe after World War I."[50] As I have shown in chapter one, there is some connection between Barth and his cultural peers. The general collapse of confidence in history is the impetus behind Barth's concentration on crisis. However, Berkouwer's remark is basically correct; Barth has radicalized and intensified the notion of crisis already present in his situation. In fact, Barth argues that crisis is nothing that can be discovered in an examination of humanity or history. The crisis comes from God, but even that statement must be carefully made, because every attempt to attribute something to God also stands under the crisis. Even dialectical language, which many have thought to be the most characteristic feature of Barth's theology, stands under the crisis. Crisis, then, is so pervasive in Barth's thought, coloring everything he says, that the only way to explain it is to suggest that it is Barth's root metaphor. It is the presupposition that directs his discourse, governing and formulating all of his arguments. Its origin, like that of any good metaphor, cannot be completely uncovered; it is the flash of insight that allows Barth to launch a terrific barrage of criticisms and exclamations. While many of his contemporaries had seen the crisis, for Barth the crisis becomes decisive in a distinctive way. It is the bomb, which Barth drops on his fellow theologians, but ultimately — and ironically — I will argue, it explodes also in Barth's own hands, necessitating further figurative strategies and ploys.

THE INDIRECTION OF THEOLOGY

Barth's *Romans* is a very figurative work, a vast and feverish swamp across which one can easily lose all sense of direction. In fact, Barth recognizes, even in this book, that rhetorical language is essential to what he has to say. Due to the otherness of God and the sinfulness of humanity, Barth does not think that theologians or preachers can use direct language about

God any more. "We think we know what we are about when we dare to use this direct language . . . Broken men, we dare to use unbroken language. We must not forget that we are speaking in parables and after the manner of men" (R, 221). Such a dare is unwarranted by God's condemnation of human pretensions and desires. This theme, that human sinfulness condemns humanity to a language separated from its origin of truth, is actually recurrent in theological and philosophical literature.[51] Derrida even uses it, arguing that theories of language that regret the split between the signifier and the signified are covertly longing for reunion with God; the sign freed from its real world constraints is a result of the fall. "The sign," he writes, "is always a sign of the Fall. Absence always relates to distancing from God."[52] For Barth, too, figuration is the result of the fall, but he neither laments this fact nor does he try to free language, as does Derrida, from any nostalgia for its prelapsarian state. He does, however, use figurative language in an excessive way in order to draw attention to the inability of direct discourse to say anything about God.

Thus, Barth argues that the Gospel can be "neither directly communicated nor directly apprehended" (R, 38). Theology has lost its object, and at best the theologian can use language against itself to keep theology honest about its own inabilities. This is necessary because Barth connects direct communication to and from God with the desire to possess and know God in the present, that is, in history. History is the realm of humanity's own creativity, and so a God known in history would be subject to humanity's inventiveness and manipulations. Such a God would not be God, says Barth. Indirect or broken language, by contrast, is able to talk about God because it does not pretend to know more than it says. But indirect language is not only a good strategy for avoiding idolatry; it is also a reflection of God's speech itself. God speaks to humanity outside of history, indirectly: "Direct communication from God is not divine communication. If Christianity be not altogether thoroughgoing eschatology, there remains in it no relationship whatever with Christ" (R, 314). Indirect language, then, does justice to both the human situation and to the nature of the futural God. Only in this medium can theology take place. "To those who have abandoned direct communication, the communication [of God] is made" (R, 41).

There are many examples of the figures that Barth uses to communicate indirectly about God. Perhaps the most famous one is the geometrical image of the tangent and the circle.

> In the Resurrection the new world of the Holy Spirit touches the old world of the flesh, but touches it as a tangent touches a circle, that is, without touching it. And, precisely because it does not touch it, it touches it as its frontier—as the new world (R, 30).[53]

This is an odd metaphor. A tangent is a line that meets another surface at one single point. Yet Barth, as soon as he offers this image, takes it away again, saying that the divine never really touches this world at all, at any point, perhaps playing on the ambiguity of the word tangent: the divine is tangential to this world, that is, irrelevant to it, diverging from it altogether. This metaphor is, therefore, ironic: while it seems to say something about God, it really says nothing at all.

Many of Barth's images are like this.[54] For example, a similar figure that Barth often uses is the image of the void. The impact of grace, the evidence that the new world has collided with this world, is the void. Barth does say that Jesus Christ is the point where the unknown world intersects the known, but this point is not extended onto the known plane for all to see. Instead, it is "the effulgence, or, rather, the crater made at the percussion point of an exploding shell, the void by which the point on the line of intersection makes itself known . . . " (R, 29). Here Barth uses an image drawn from the war—the explosion of a shell—to show not only how dramatic and real God's grace is, but also to demonstrate the problem of trying to point to that grace. After the explosion, there is nothing left. The only sign of God's activity is this emptiness or nothingness that unveils the essence of human activity. "Genuine faith is a void," Barth explains (R, 88). Using other favorite metaphors, Barth writes, "The empty canal speaks of the water which does not flow through it. The sign-post points to a destination which is precisely where the sign-post is not" (R, 88). The best metaphor for the divine, then, is a metaphor that does not make any "as if" identification at all, but dissolves itself or points to absolutely nothing. Thus, Barth talks about the intersection of planes, the algebra of a minus sign before brackets, a signpost, tangents, frontiers, prison bars, die Todeslinie (the line of death), the stamped impress, all of which point to the impersonality and incomprehensibility of divine grace. These metaphors are themselves like empty canals, appearing to direct our thought about the divine but actually carrying nothing and pointing nowhere.

As this language makes clear, grace leaves its mark on this world without becoming a part of the world; it accomplishes a negative work without leaving behind any positive trace that humanity could then manipulate or claim for itself. However, the impact of grace is not, therefore, insignificant. Barth uses a whole set of exaggerated military or war metaphors to express the collision of grace and nature. Like the war itself, grace is "a shattering disturbance, an assault which brings everything into question" (R, 225). Moreover, "The man under grace is engaged unconditionally in a conflict. This conflict is a war of life and death, a war in which there can be no armistice, no agreement—and no peace" (R, 225). True religion is a fight from which there can be no flight: "Religion spells disruption, discord, and the

absence of peace" (*R*, 266). Religion, in fact, is like a bomb which somebody has "so carefully decked out with flowers, [but it] will sooner or later
explode. Religion breaks men into two halves" (*R*, 168). For Barth, the relationship between humanity and the divine is a conflict between two completely irreconcilable powers; only one power can win, and the winning
power must conquer completely and unconditionally. There can be no compromise or negotiation between the two enemies. In the meantime, history
takes on the appearance of a battlefield in which God's grace is the aggres-
sor: "Explosions are the inevitable consequences of our bringing infinity
within the range of concepts fitted only for the apprehension of what is finite" (*R*, 290). The impact of grace is an explosion; the aftermath is the void.

This dizzying array of metaphors can be confusing: they are both exaggerated in a whirlwind of repetition and radicalization, and qualified by
ironically not saying what their metaphorical form would have them do. A
good metaphor should allow us to picture an unknown in a concrete way by
letting us imagine it according to a known. But how can we imagine the void,
the crater, the empty canal? What does that tell us about God? To make
sense of these metaphors, it is important to understand the notion of crisis
as their ruling or governing presupposition. Crisis is the prefigurative act
that makes possible all of the metaphors calling into question the relationship between humanity and the divine. Because of the crisis, the most extreme and contradictory things can be said about God and humanity; the crisis makes Barth's language undecidable and paradoxical. It is a metaphor
that threatens to run out of control. This trope, thus, must be the first to be
analyzed in a rhetorical reading of Barth. It is also a model of discourse that
is problematic: it makes all of the metaphors it spawns something less than
what they seem to be. As I will argue, because of the crisis, metaphors are
ultimately an inadequate expression of the religious and cultural situation.
Under the sign of crisis, a metaphor—like the image of the tangent and the
circle—cannot make a representation of the divine, portraying it as something else, without itself being subject to the very crisis it tries to express.
This paradoxical nature of crisis in *Romans* is due to the intensity and consistency with which Barth develops this root metaphor. Thus, I want systematically to discuss this metaphor in *Romans* under three headings: first,
an analysis of the term itself; second, its origin in Barth's approach to history; and third, its application to the concept of God.

THE CRISIS DEFINED?

First, then, it is important to see how Barth uses the term crisis. In the
German original Barth always uses the word *Krisis,* transliterated from the
Greek, not the German *die Krise,* which makes this crucial term even more

prominent. (Note that Edwyn Hoskyns, the translator, prints "KRISIS" in the translation.) The word, which does not appear in Paul's letter, means a decisive turning point, and *Krisis* is still used in Germany in medical discourse to denote that point in an illness at which a dramatic change takes place. For Barth, though, the turning point does not take place at a particular point in history but at every point. This rather unhistorical use of the term is evident in the very first chapter of *Romans*, where Barth introduces the crisis by announcing his intention to focus not on Paul but on what Paul himself was interested in. "However great and important a man Paul may have been, the essential theme of his mission is not within but above him — unapproachably distant and unutterably strange" (*R*, 27). Paul's theme, variously described as the Gospel, the Kingdom of God, grace, or simply God, is strange because in an unexpected way it does not let itself be known. In fact, Barth says that the apostle does not have a positive theme at all but instead makes visible the void (*R*, 33). "The Gospel is therefore not an event, nor an experience, nor an emotion — however delicate! Rather, it is the clear and objective perception of what eye hath not seen nor ear heard" (*R*, 28). More explicitly, the Gospel, the proclamation of God's righteousness and the resurrection of Jesus Christ, introduces the crisis (*R*, 32). The Gospel is "the signal, the fire-alarm of a coming, new world" (*R*, 38). Paul's theme, then, and this is Barth's theme too, must be treated in a special way; it is not an object for reflection but in fact calls into question all such reflection.

This is why it is the crisis: it fundamentally undermines the human capacity to understand and react and know. It is the deepest metaphorical reality that cannot be adequately explained or examined. It is the night which Barth discusses in his first chapter, and which I discussed in the context of Beckmann's painting in my first chapter. Drawn from Romans 13:12, the night is an oddly illuminating metaphor for Barth: in the night nothing can be seen, not even the night itself. What then is the crisis if its origin cannot be known and its impact cannot be felt or understood? Surely, this is no ordinary crisis that Barth is talking about! How can he talk about it at all? He himself admits that it is "both something and — nothing, nothing and — something" (*R*, 36). What is this phenomenon whose very existence is troubled and questioned, whose essence will not yield to the power of reflection?

At times Barth talks about the crisis as an objective reality, which has little to do with human activity. "The judgement under which we stand is a fact, quite apart from our attitude to it. Indeed it is the fact most characteristic of our life" (*R*, 42). Crisis, then, is something Barth presupposes as the most basic reality of existence. Barth, however, also wants his readers to come to feel the subjective weight of the crisis, to let the crisis transform their lives. After all, even in the above quotation, the crisis is discussed as an aspect or attribute of human life; it must, then, affect our life in some way. Barth frequently refers to Kierkegaard's analysis of the human situation of despair to support his understanding of crisis, and he often speaks as if he wants people to come to know and feel the crisis that they so far have only avoided.

> If we do not ourselves hinder it, nothing can prevent our being translated into a most wholesome Krisis . . . And indeed, we stand already in this Krisis if we would but see clearly. And what is clearly seen to be indisputable reality is the invisibility of God . . . (*R*, 46).

This is a difficult passage. How can we come to see what is invisible? And how can something that is not be so disruptive and painful for us?

Barth ends chapter one, and his discussion of the night, with a reflection on human forgetfulness. In a passage reminiscent of the more Platonic first edition, he asks why we have forgotten the crisis, and answers this question with the topic of death. "But why is it so difficult to remember what has been forgotten, though it is quite clear that the operation of this forgetfulness and the end of our wandering in the night is—Death?" (*R*, 54). This chapter thus ends, appropriately enough, with a question mark. Is death the crisis itself, or does it just put an end to the crisis? Do we try to avoid the crisis just like we try to evade death? In a later chapter Barth writes a crucial passage on death:

> Death is the supreme law of the world in which we live. Of death we know nothing except that it is denial and corruption, the destroyer and destruction, creatureliness and naturalness. Death is engraved inexorably and indelibly upon our life (*R*, 166).

Moreover, "even that which, in this world, points to the overcoming and renewal of this world, takes the form of death" (*R*, 167). Death is not, then, the end of crisis but one of its most vivid forms. But death itself—the unknown law—is not the crisis; in fact, in the end, we still do not know what the crisis really is. The question of the crisis remains.

Perhaps the crisis metaphor is overused by Barth in this text, extended in so many directions and mixed in so many ways that it threatens to become a knot too tangled ever to neatly untie. At one point Barth does suggest that crisis is at least in part ambiguous (*R*, 82). He even wonders if God is subject to crisis, a theme to which I will soon return. The problem is whether the crisis can be turned into an answer in itself: can it tell us how to live, who God is, what life should be? "Is it resignation following upon disillusionment, or enthusiasm born of pessimism? Is it violence offered to the riches of human life, a revolt against history, or the arrogance of some form of Gnostic radicalism?'' (*R*, 85). Here Barth is not only preempting his many critics by listing their very descriptions of his own work, but he is also asking if the crisis, which he is announcing, can become a way of life. Does the crisis imply a particular philosophy of history, whether gnostic or otherwise? His answer is an unequivocal no. Under the crisis we cannot understand history at all. The closest Barth does come to a definition is in saying that the crisis is, in the end, God's wrath against original sin: sin is the human tendency to try to play God, to try to usurp the role of judge and lawgiver from God, to create in history what only God can do in eternity. The crisis, then, infects all of life, including, it is important to note, the way in which people — and even Barth himself — understand the crisis. Barth thinks that even a quick overview of history will prove him right: ''The whole course of history *[Geschichte]* pronounces this indictment against itself'' (*R*, 85). But what is the crisis that it can turn history against itself?

THE CRISIS OF HISTORY AND THE HISTORY OF CRISIS

One of the best ways to try to grasp this elusive metaphor is to examine Barth's philosophy of history as presented in *Romans,* for here the nature of the crisis is, at times, clearly formulated. Barth's first full statement on history appears at the beginning of chapter three, where he describes history as an inane struggle for power that is hypocritically defended by different ideologies as a movement toward justice and freedom. History consists of the ebb and flow of various forms of human righteousness, vying with each other in mock solemnity and banal triviality. ''Yet one drop of eternity is of greater weight than a vast ocean of finite things'' (*R*, 77).[55] History, then, stands — or rather collapses — under the unbearable pressure of eternity. I should note that Barth often uses the term eternity to denote all aspects and activities of the divine; his position is that eternity and time are related in a perpetual and absolute contradiction, which never can be resolved or muted. This is a shift from the first edition of this book, which argued that the new world transforms the old world; in the second edition the Kingdom of God does not gradually supercede and then replace the kingdom of humanity. ''The judgement of God is the end of history *[Geschichte]*, not the beginning of a new, a second, epoch. By it history is not prolonged, but done away with'' (*R*, 77). The crisis, then, announces itself not just as a critique of this world—and certainly not this world's fulfillment or culmination—but as the end of the world. The crisis is nothing that history can respond to and try to overcome because the crisis stands absolutely and completely apart from and over against history.

The question immediately arises as to what Barth means by the end of history. Is history now, at this time, coming to a literal end? What will come after it? Or is the end of history just another metaphorical corollary to the metaphor of crisis? Again, due to the troubling status of the crisis metaphor, Barth finds it difficult to talk about the relationship between eternity and time. Is the crisis the meaning of history? Barth wonders: "If the meaninglessness of history be the revelation of its meaning, must it not follow of necessity that its meaning is also meaningless?" (R, 82). In other words, if the crisis is the manifestation by eternity that time is nothing, then what can this nothing mean to time? Can the meaninglessness of history be made meaningful? Perhaps it is helpful to see that Barth fluctuates between two positions: either crisis is the deepest truth of history that history can know (the subjective meaning of crisis) or crisis so transcends history that its power and activity are unknown and unknowable (the objectivity of crisis). Put another way, either history is the story of crisis, or crisis marks the end of history.

For example, in this same chapter Barth can say, "When history points beyond itself and discovers in itself its own inadequacy, when there emerges in history a horror at history, then its high places are made known" (R, 90). Here, clearly, Barth is speaking from and to the post-war situation, hoping that the terrors of the period will urge people to look beyond their own particular time for some higher truth. However, Barth can also say that the crisis dissolves time, making any such recognition impossible. "The whole course of this world participates in true existence when its nonexistence is recognized" (R, 91). How can history learn something by acknowledging its own nonexistence? If history does not exist, it certainly cannot overcome itself to try to know God. Barth's analysis of history at this point seems hopelessly confusing. The crisis destroys history, and yet history knows it not; history must face its own horror and thus glimpse the truth of God, and yet history does not even exist. True, it is possible that more sense can be made from Barth's position than I have allowed here, but really to read Barth is to refuse to resist his endless perplexities and contradictions. To repeat and clarify a claim I made earlier, the crisis is so pervasive that even Barth's own language about it is in crisis. The crisis is the root metaphor, which itself cannot be spoken or explained. It is a model that defeats itself and, therefore, necessitates further elaboration.

Barth does go some distance toward making his position on history more consistent and clear in chapter four, "The Voice of History." What history speaks is the negation that God has already pronounced on all human existence. This negation, Barth argues, must be absolute.

> A negation which remains side by side with the position it negates must itself be negated, and is therefore no truly radical negation. Resurrection ceases to be resurrection if it be some abnormal event side by side with other events (*R*, 115).

The negative power of the crisis must reside completely outside of the history realm in order for it to be absolute. What does this mean for the possibility of meaningful action within history? How can such a negation be identified and acted upon within the confines of history? I will turn to this theme more fully in the next chapter where I will focus on Barth's critique of religion. However, in the present context, that of history, Barth makes some very interesting comments on the possibilities of religious meaning that should be noted.

Take, for example, his discussion of Abraham. Barth does not interpret the Old Testament on its own terms; he thinks the light of Jesus Christ shines throughout all of history, so that Old Testament figures function as types for New Testament lessons. The question to be asked about Abraham is whether he was righteous, as the Bible implies. Barth suggests that Abraham does have a kind of righteousness of which he can boast — but not before God.

> The works which a man does in his concrete and visible life are no more identical with his work which is righteous before God than are the fetters with which a prisoner is tightly bound and by which he is led hither and thither against his will identical with the real limbs of his body (*R*, 119).

In fact, the only good work that a person could do before God would be repentance, but even that must come from God. What Abraham teaches us, then, is that even he, a seemingly righteous man, lives under the sign of crisis. All of his works belong on the side of death, says Barth, not on the side of life and eternity. But this is not all; Barth goes so far as to read into Abraham his own understanding of crisis. "That he awoke to his position and was aware of the Krisis, that in this Krisis he feared God, that he heard the 'No' of God and understood it as His 'Yes' — this is Abraham's faith" (*R*, 123). Abraham has indeed heard God, but he has not been given "some new, deep, positive religious experience" (*R*, 125). Instead, he has simply been told 'No.'

From Barth's reading of the Old Testament, it is easy to see that he does not treat history with the eye of a professional historian. Indeed, he suggests that history, objectively understood, tells us nothing religiously useful about Abraham. History seen through the metaphor of crisis, however, can say a lot: because the contradiction of eternity and time is constant throughout all of history, the same patterns, the same exact lesson, can be learned no matter where one looks. The particular events of history serve as parables of timeless truths. This is why Barth can read Paul as a contemporary, speaking directly into Barth's ear and not across countless stretches of cultural and religious differences.

> Particular episodes in history can be of universal importance. The past can speak to the present; for there is between them a simultaneity which heals the past of its dumbness and the present of its deafness, which enables the past to speak and the present to hear. This simultaneity makes possible an intercourse in which time is at once dissolved and fulfilled, for its theme is the non-historical, the invisible, the incomprehensible (*R*, 145).

This passage is not as clear as it might at first appear. What unites history is the 'Moment' in which history is overcome, set apart from itself, and dissolved into eternity. This moment, however, does not lie in history itself. It cannot be read from history by, say, an objective historian, but it is there, undeniable and unavoidable, the moment in which truth is made known in an act of unknowing, when our attempts to understand the truth are thoroughly crushed and destroyed.

At the very least Barth is fighting against charges that his theology leads to skepticism and relativism. Earlier, in chapter three, Barth had confronted this very problem in a typical act of self-scrutiny. Does the crisis mean, he asked, that there are no advantages in history, that everything is ever the same? "Are there in history any high points which are more than large waves upon the stream of transitoriness, thick shadows where all is shadow?" (*R*, 78).[56] These mixed metaphors serve their point: is history one long night? In chapter four Barth asks this same question, wondering if history is "merely a sequence of epochs and a series of civilizations" (*R*, 145), dumb and speechless, perhaps interesting but certainly meaningless and trivial. Barth refuses to accept this as a consequence of his position. In fact, in a passage surely influenced by Nietzsche, he argues that,

> History is a synthetic work of art. History emerges from what has occurred and has one single, unified theme. If this work of art, this occurrence, this one theme, be not engraved upon the historian, there can be no writing of history (*R*, 146).

Like Nietzsche (and Hayden White), Barth thinks that history can only be understood from the perspective of the prejudices of the present. In fact, he suggests that the scientific method of historical inquiry is only adopted in times of spiritual poverty (R, 147). Simply put, history is not an object of study but the product of a struggle of interpretations, and Barth wants to assert a religious perspective, which will be strong enough to reappropriate history religiously. He even makes the bold claim: "Thus there is open to us no way of writing history otherwise than as it is written in the Book of Genesis" (R, 147).

To understand history according to the present, and to face the present as a religious moment, which obliterates our understanding—this is Barth's task. The method of critical analysis, so different from the outlook represented in the Book of Genesis, is open, Barth claims, only to those who do not believe.

> We have no desire to fetter or cast suspicions upon the critical method. But it also cannot in the end survive the Krisis, the sickness unto death, under which we stand. Indeed, in its own fashion it hastens the process. For it inevitably shows that the historical [*historiche*] Abraham really does not concern us. And just in so far as it comes to this conclusion, it opens the road to the understanding of the non-historical Abraham of the Genesis story, to the necessary synthesis, and finally to the impossible possibility of which we must sooner or later dare to take stock, namely—our faith (R, 148).

Only our faith makes sense of history.[57] It is a faith, though, of which history itself does not make sense. In fact, faith is nonsense; it is the impossible possibility, born and bound to a crisis, which is the only unity history has. This crisis is a strange model for historical understanding; what it says is that we cannot understand history except as we see it being dissolved and overcome by eternity. Barth has had difficulty in talking about history because he had to make his talk figurative and indirect; his talk was governed by a metaphor, which made all of his talk metaphorical. Clearly, the unity of history is understood only through an interpretive act. At best it is a biblical unity; at worst it is based on a metaphor that is disruptive and fragmentary, hardly able, like any good concept, to unify a phenomenal field. Sooner or later, Barth says, we must dare to take stock of this unity itself, the object of faith. What does it tell us about the crisis? It is with an analysis of crisis and God, then, that I will close this chapter.

THE CRISIS OF CRISIS

In a pointed statement, Barth writes, "He who says 'God' says 'miracle' " (*R*, 120). This is the best summary of Barth's understanding of God. God can only be spoken of, really, by God. In fact, this is the miracle to which Christianity witnesses: through Jesus Christ, God speaks about Godself. Otherwise, God is the Wholly Other, the eternal one who is in complete contradiction to time. I will have to discuss Barth's concept of revelation and his understanding of the appropriate theological response to revelation in later chapters. Here I want to talk about the furthest reaches of Barth's metaphor of crisis, which actually includes the idea of God. Often we do not have a miracle, we do not hear God talking about Godself, and so we must venture to talk about God ourselves. Such talk, Barth wants to argue, is subject to the crisis. In fact, such talk is part of the essence of the crisis, for the crisis means that we want to say God, but we really end up saying No-God. Barth's use of the term No-God is one of his most interesting rhetorical ploys. It allows him to exercise some of his most fantastic dialectical deliberations by playing off these two contradictory notions, God and No-God. In the midst of his paradoxical flourishes, I want to argue, is to be found the essence — or the crisis — of the crisis.[58]

The idea of the No-God is introduced in the first chapter. What people call God, Barth asserts, is really the No-God. We never know God, in fact, but only the No-God. This is the God that Feuerbach criticizes in his projection theory of religion. This God is created by humanity out of boredom because people lack the courage to despair. The No-God, then, is Barth's term for the reduction of God to the status of an idol. It serves the important function of allowing Barth to accept fully the critique of secular atheism. When people either praise or reject God, they are talking about the No-God; therefore, rejection is better than praise. "The cry of revolt against such a god is nearer the truth than is the sophistry with which men attempt to justify him" (*R*, 40). The true God is known by the crisis God brings. People will continue to prefer, therefore, the false god of their own creation as long as they seek to avoid the crisis.

Not only is the No-God not God, Barth continues, but also we cannot know God. This is because God says 'No' to us in the judgment of wrath against our sin, which constitutes the crisis. The true God, then, is also the No-God in the sense that God says No to all of our attempts to both understand and imitate God. This 'No' from the true God, which is basically a no against the No-God, is also God's 'Yes.' God's 'Yes' is not a separate statement, which God makes after uttering God's 'No.' God's 'No' *is* God's 'Yes.' Only through a negation of the No-God can God be understood, and such a negation comes only from God saying 'No.' We experience this no-saying of God as the void, as a negation, which says yes only indirectly by the means of destruction and demolition. If we give the name God to the No-God, we only force God to say 'No' louder and stronger. Thus Barth can say, quite simply, that God breaks us to pieces (*R*, 43).

The No-God, it must be explained, is not an object that is *prima facie* evil. On the contrary, the God that humanity creates is usually a beautiful and noble object, an example of all that is good in the world. Nevertheless, Barth suspects our motives in making such moving idols.

> We assign to Him the highest place in our world and in so doing we place Him fundamentally on one line with ourselves and with things. We assume that He needs something, and so we assume that we are able to arrange our relation to Him as we arrange our other relationships ...
> (*R*, 44).

We want to be in control of God, and so we treat God as a companion or friend. In fact, we desire to be God's patrons or advisers. The result is—and here Barth echoes Feuerbach—that in worshipping God we are really worshipping ourselves. "Men fall prey first to themselves and then to the No-God" (*R*, 44). This is the limitation of the No-God; we are unable to think of this god more highly than we think of ourselves. "Being to ourselves what God ought to be to us, He is no more to us than we are to ourselves" (*R*, 45).

A significant problem arises when a criterion is sought to distinguish between the No-God and God. Once we think that we have overcome the No-God, we are certainly not dealing with God. All of our most strenuous attempts to see through our idols to God's own self are nothing more than highly refined modifications of the No-God. God is not, in fact, one possibility among others that we can actualize, given the right conditions. God is the impossible possibility. God is Wholly Other: "Only when the all-embracing contrast between God and men is perceived can there emerge the knowledge of God, a new communion with Him, and a new worship" (*R*, 80). This is the paradox: God can only be known when God's unknowability is confronted and accepted. To know God we must see that in history there is no God. But this, to return to Barth's equation of Godtalk and miracles, can only be the work of God. God, then, is the origin of the crisis which makes God known by showing how God is completely unknown: "The true God, Himself removed from all concretion, is the Origin of the Krisis of every concrete thing, the Judge, the negation of this world in which is included also the god of human logic" (*R*, 82).[59] There is, therefore, no criteria for our talk about God because *all* such talk is conducted under the sign of the crisis. Moreover, it is just such talk that is the high point of the crisis: here God's wrath is the most extreme and our confusion the most intense. Whenever we try to say God, we say No-God, and God says 'No,' a no which we can never really hear even though it tears through history like an earthquake.

This is the furthest reach but also the final limitation of the metaphor of crisis: it paralyzes all of our talk about God. What positive assertion can be made about God who is "pure negation?" (*R*, 141). This God is "the Stranger, the Other, whom we finally encounter along the whole frontier of our knowledge. Our world is the world, within which God is finally and everywhere — outside" (*R*, 318). God is the source of the crisis, but God is not the answer to the crisis because God lies outside of every answer. At best Barth is left with the tautology, "God is God" (*RF*, 88). This tautology, borrowed from Luther, often serves as a banner Barth repeatedly uses: "Let God be God." This is an odd maxim, not one from which any inferences can be readily drawn. It seemingly stands alone, incapable of further explication. It is both a stubborn understatement and a careless overstatement, giving us both too little information and too much. Looked at in different ways it says alternatively nothing and everything. God is so great that God can only be identified with — God. But if we do not know who God is, how can that identification mean anything at all to us? This theological tautology is, in fact, the major consequence of Barth's crisis position. Because we literally cannot speak of God, to speak metaphorically of God is to speak literally of nothing. All that can be said about God is that God is God, and humanity is humanity and never, as in a good metaphor, should these two disparate strands of discourse intertwine.

The only positive implication of this position is that it guards the fact of God's freedom. God is utterly new, strange and wild because God is totally different from anything we already know. The other implications are negative. Liberal theology, which for Barth is the culmination of the tendencies inherent in all of religion, is especially confused in reference to God's freedom. It errs in attempting to impose an agenda on God's free and mysterious activity. Theology cannot communicate about God; it can only communicate its readiness to listen and respond to God's initiatives, and even that willingness must, of course, come from God. Theology, then, is sinful to the extent that it tries to build bridges up to God rather than let God speak for Godself. In sum, the metaphorical model of theology — as represented in this chapter by Soskice and McFague among others — the attempt to reach up to God by beginning with knowledge about humanity or the world, is for Barth the model of sin. No metaphor, not even the metaphor of crisis, can do justice to God. The attempt to encompass God in theology — to make metaphors of God — is a sign of the anxiety that flows from a fundamental lack of faith. It is the attempt to replace a miracle with frail and fallible human activity. The best that theology can do is to make failed metaphors, figures, which, by not connecting disparate elements in order to make a coherent image, indicate the discontinuity between God and humanity.

Barth's metaphor of crisis has thus turned against itself. As a model, it has shown that no models are permitted in this arena of discourse.[60] The most that Barth can do is to show that his own failed language prefigures the failure of humanity to know God. Yet Barth is still a theologian, and he must write about God somehow. That is, he has chosen to write, to say something, and not merely to wait in silence upon God. The metaphor of crisis is the root metaphor of Barth's work, but it is not the only figure operative here. In fact, this metaphor necessitates further figurative elaboration. In the midst of such a crisis, what can be said, if anything at all? I will argue in the next two chapters that this crisis of metaphor forces Barth to other tropes, namely, hyperbole and irony, which avoid the extension of knowledge implied by metaphor. Hyperbole allows him repeatedly to announce and exploit the crisis, to foretell the end of theology, without speaking about the crisis in either a literal or metaphorical fashion. Irony lets him exist within the crisis, writing and yet not writing in a space that cannot really be. These tropes are attempts to re-figure a theology whose basic presupposition has called itself into question.

MAGIC OF THE EXTREME

A LESSER TROPE?

Hyperbole is the poor relation of the tropes family, treated like a distant relative whose family ties are questionable at best. Often discounted or disregarded in discussions of figures, hyperbole seems to be an embarrassment to those who want to take tropes seriously. How could exaggeration, that frequently irritating, too often foolish and always transparent speech event, stake a claim to philosophical consideration? After all, Aristotle argued that the construction of a good metaphor is one sign of genius, but anybody can make an exaggeration. When we hear an exaggeration (for it seems part of the plight of exaggeration to be connected more often to oral rather than to written language), we are quick to see through it and put it in its proper place. If metaphors are difficult or impossible to summarize or paraphrase, nobody will admit to this problem with exaggerations. Perhaps this is the most significant defect of exaggeration, that it is simply too obvious. There is a moral tone to this judgment: exaggerations are thought to be attempts at manipulation by claiming something greater than the situation allows. As Aristotle noted in a rare comment on this trope, "Hyperboles are for young men to use; they show vehemence of character."[1] An exaggeration is a sly but easily discernible attempt — or better, bluff — to obtain more (more sympathy, more attention, more audience) than is morally permissable. Surely this is why children are taught to avoid especially this one trope. Exaggeration is so simple that children learn it first among the figures by being warned against it: "Now, now, don't exaggerate." It just might be that metaphor has a positive relation to truth, but not exaggeration; the latter is merely a fancy way of telling a lie.

All of these considerations argue for the illegitimacy of exaggeration. In fact, Robert Evans, in his article, "Hyperbole," for the *Princeton Encyclopedia of Poetry and Poetics,* summarizes the rhetorical tradition on this particular figure, concluding that hyperbole is usually assigned to the second order of tropes, along with such minor persuasive ploys as amplification, examples, and images. Indeed, Aristotle subordinates hyperbole to metaphor (*Rhetoric,* 1413a20), and Evans notes that hyperbole is sometimes classified as a form of irony.[2] Rarely is it allowed to stand with the other tropes as a significant mode of communication in its own right. Such classificatory schemes, although illuminating for the way that they treat (or mistreat) hyperbole, are less important than attempts at a definition because hyperbole must first be fully understood before it is situated in the tropical field. I will examine two attempts at a definition, one from the field of communication theory and the other from the field of aesthetics and literary criticism.

One of the most sustained and systematic treatments of hyperbole can be found in the encyclopedic work by Chaim Perelman and L. Olbrechts-Tyteca, *The New Rhetoric, A Treatise on Argumentation.*[3] The subtitle of this book indicates its main focus, which is argumentation and not figuration. Thus, the authors discuss hyperbole as an adjunct to a specific type of argument, which they call "unlimited development," a structure or pattern of persuasion that insists "on the possibility of always going further in a certain direction without being able to foresee a limit to this direction, and this progress is accompanied by a continuous increase of value" (*NR,* 287). This argument refers to a "something more," a protraction of a line of thought that is already approved or admired. The two authors suggest that often the intent of unlimited development is to define certain purified notions or to provide for the conception of an ideal that is unrealizable. The mechanism of this idealization, they contend, is the work of hyperbole (along with its counterpart, the litotes, or the understatement).

Hyperbole, they state, "is an extreme form of expression" (*NR,* 290). Its character resides in the fact that "it is not justified or prepared, but fired with brutality," and its justification consists in its capacity to "give a direction to thought, to guide it toward a favorable evaluation of this direction, and only by a return shock is it intended to give an indication of the significant term" (*NR,* 290). By this I think the authors mean that hyperbole takes the reader or listener by surprise, leading her further in one direction than she ever thought possible. The impact of the hyperbole occurs when the reader or listener realizes just how far the hyperbole has gone; the result is a shocking jolt, which upsets the easygoing moderation of everyday language. To effect this shock the hyperbole does not try to create a coherent image, as does the metaphor. Instead, its "role is to provide a reference which draws the mind in a certain direction only to force it later to retreat a little" (*NR,* 291). This comment by the authors, although intriguing, suggests their limited taste for this trope; in fact, they argue that hyperbole is easily susceptible to ridicule if it goes too far. Indeed, hyperbole "is often involuntarily funny" (NR, 292). In the final analysis, then, hyperbole is acceptable only to the extent that it serves the structure of the argument of unlimited development, and even then it should not violate the standards of good taste. Otherwise, hyperbole might not make good sense; in a passage that seems written for my purposes, they argue that "the theologian who asserts that the ways of God are inscrutable is obliged to modify this assertion in one way or another, or theology becomes impossible" (NR, 290). Coincidentally, this is one of Barth's primary uses of hyperbole; however, he is not afraid to enter into the realm of the impossible. He does not hesitate to go too far.

Another systematic attempt to define hyperbole has been made by Louis Wirth Marvick, who connects this trope to the sublime.[4] Unfortunately, the sublime is just as difficult to define as is hyperbole. This does not mean, though, that there is no consistency in its use: from Longinus's notion of the sublime as an heroic work of genius, which carries intense and lofty appeal, to Burke's emphasis on the terror and danger in the sublime moment, and to Johnson's more controlled notion of style in the grand manner, Marvick suggests that in the sublime the "artist tries to render the quality of an ideal which, despite his best efforts, remains more or less aloof" (MS, 19). The sublime is an ideal that does not exist, or at best exists only ideally. We desire that which we know we cannot obtain. The language of the sublime is, therefore, both a bitter and an exalting task, and Marvick offers many rich readings of the various exponents of the sublime; especially interesting is his description of the transference of the sublime object from God to nature in the eighteenth century. However, one thing Marvick says is particularly helpful for my purposes. There are, he suggests, certain conditions for the recognition and expression of the sublime, and these conditions are, at heart, rhetorical. That is, two principles regulate — or provide the pivot for — the sublime moment: irony and hyperbole (which he often calls enthusiasm).

Marvick equates hyperbole with faith and irony with disbelief. Hyperbole not only believes in the sublime but acts as a discharge of enthusiasm; it locates the ideal and pays it tribute. Such enthusiasm can become wild and fanatical, of course; to be specific, its dangers are twofold. First, we can never overshoot or exaggerate the ideal, so hyperbole does not really describe the ideal itself but rather what it would wish the ideal to be. Marvick argues that hyperbole works, then, by passing off a lie, "by injecting so heavy a dose of idealism into his [the reader's] fare, that the resistance of his faculties is overcome, and he gives himself up to the enjoyment of the illusion" (MS, 51). Second, the enthusiasm of hyperbole must be shared by the audience or else it will look pretentious and ridiculous. This is why "the presence of irony is required as a complement or corrective to hyperbole, in order for justice to be done to the ideal" (*MS*, 51). Derrida, of course, would argue that any literary text can be deflated by irony by showing that it means something other than what it says. Marvick argues that in rhetoric about the sublime hyperbole, which is deceptive and credulous—it means what it literally says—gives irony its material on which to work, while irony, by contributing reflective criticism to a naive discourse, manifests the real truth in hyberbole. Both must work together to establish the sublime. To what extent one will dominate the other depends on whether a given writer thinks the ideal can be sequestered by language: the greater the disbelief, the greater the use of irony. An example of the failure of this combination of tropes is the Romantics, Marvick argues, who took their hyperbole too literally, and thus needed a stronger dose of irony. Though Marvick does not suggest this, we could think of deconstructionism as an ironic discourse, which is bereft of the counterbalance of hyperbole.

The conclusion to Marvick's provocative analysis of hyperbole is that this trope is really not a figure of speech at all. Indeed, hyperbolic exclamations about the sublime are too simple or direct to demand interpretation:

> Unlike the stylistic facts of a text, which require to be interpreted as departures from the norm of liberal communication (i.e. as variations or comments upon the message conveyed by the linguistic facts of the text), the structure of hyperbole requires the reader to credit unreal assertions as literal truth. In other words, hyperbole does not function by affording the reader an appreciation of the difference between what is stressed and what is expressed, but by blinding him to that difference (*MS*, 57).

It is not a rhetorical device because it literally means what it says; in other words, it does not announce itself as what it is not. Moreover, what it says is a lie; it deceptively tries to get the audience to believe in the incredible. The deceit of hyperbole can only work in the case of prior agreement; hyperbolists must make their own enthusiasm contagious. Hyperbole is so passionate and naive that only an audience that wants to be uplifted and overcome will take it seriously. Otherwise, hyperbole will appear to be what it really is, that is, ridiculous. It really belongs more to the field of psychology—perhaps in the phenomenon of mass hallucinations — than to rhetoric. Therefore, Marvick argues that hyperbolic discourse about the sublime must be cut with irony in order for it to seem credible, let alone palatable. Yet, perhaps Marvick has gone too far in his analysis of hyperbole, because a question remains: If hyperbole is so easy to see through, to domesticate or normalize, then how could it ever pretend to be literally true? Who would ever use it? Marvick, no doubt, would answer this query by suggesting that that is why hyperbole is so often found (solely) in the Romantics; only those who are enthusiastic can speak in an enthusiastic form.

This detour through Marvick's work is helpful for its comments on both hyperbole and the sublime. I want to argue that Barth's use of hyperbole does not fit neatly into Marvick's analysis, even though he too, it can be argued, is dealing with the sublime. For Barth God is a sublime other, inspiring awe and terror and causing cognitive dissonance. After all, Barth did approve of Rudolf Otto's description of God as the "Wholly Other" *(das ganz Andere* or *totaliter aliter)* — a term upon which he was to increasingly depend after he read *The Idea of the Holy* in 1919.[5] Barth does talk about God as being unimaginably great, of such magnitude and dynamic breadth that to try to speak into this otherness is to whisper hollow words into an infinite void without even the hope of an echo. He also talks about the terror of God, comparing grace to the flash of lightning or an uncontrollable flood. However, for Otto, God is not just Wholly Other; God is also *mysterium tremendum,* inspiring a distinctive mixture of feelings of fear and fascination. In *Romans,* Barth's God is more frightening than fascinating, and so he could not agree with Otto's emphasis on mysticism as one proper response to this ultimate mystery. Indeed, Barth uses hyperbole, as I will argue, not to exaggerate the greatness of God but to emphasize God's absence and to exaggerate the inability of humanity ever to grasp this absence properly. Barth reverses Marvick's tropical map: he uses hyperbole in a negative way, as a sign of disbelief, while irony is positive in that it allows him to speak in the midst of the hyperbolic critique.

For my analysis, then, neither of these approaches to hyperbole is satisfactory. Perelman and Olbrechts-Tyteca subordinate hyperbole to a certain argument, thus unnecessarily limiting its range. Marvick offers a subjective definition of hyperbole as a discharge of enthusiasm, thus connecting the excess of this trope to the trope maker. Moreover, all three of these writers connect hyperbole to the search for the ideal. This constraint strikes me as artificial and forced. All three authors seem to think that outside of this containment hyperbole threatens to become too wild and unrestrained, but this is exactly the kind of hyperbole I want to discuss. It should be accepted as a strange feat of language; residing on the border of both the sublime and the ridiculous, it can shout the most extreme and jubilant ecstacies or utter the most crude and provocative denouncements. Hyperbole, therefore, does not necessarily serve an elusive but impossible ideal. It can also be destructive, affirming negations and magnifying the lack of an ideal. In this

role hyperbole often does not further an argument of unlimited development; instead it can serve to end all arguments, to freeze all developments.
This negative and antiargumentative use of hyperbole is the one I find most
often in Barth. Perhaps to accommodate this kind of hyperbole only a general definition can be posited: hyperbole allows one to say more than is
strictly appropriate to the expectations set by the subject matter, the
speaker, and the situation. This definition, though, must be qualified by a
statement about the cognitive worth of hyperbole. Hyperbole does not
merely say the "something more"; it does so for a purpose. That purpose,
however, is best defined in more general terms than those of one specific argument. As one writer has argued, "Hyperbole is an exaggeration on the
side of truth."[6]

Still, this definition of hyperbole is too broad to be used in practical
analysis. Moreover, the question of its relation to the other tropes remains
unresolved. In a way, hyperbole is the easiest of the tropes to recognize because it always draws attention to itself. By its nature it is the least subtle of
the tropes, but this does not mean that it is easy to define or simple to use. It
resembles the form of metaphor in that it creates a new meaning by taking
language to a new extreme. However, it does this not by drawing together
two disparate realms but by extending one realm as far as it will go. In other
words, hyperbole can be considered a vertical trope, while metaphor is hor-
izontal: metaphor reaches out to fuse together separate items on the horizon, while hyperbole reaches up or down to push one item further out of the
horizon. Hyperbole thus stretches language not to make a new identification
(the metaphorical "as if") but to see how far an observation can be taken
when stripped of all reservation and qualification. It abstracts an observation from its context, its horizon, in order to see, when it is being positive,
how high it can fly or, when it is being negative, how deeply it can be buried.

The single-mindedness, or what I have called "verticality," of the hyperbole means that its shock value is more readily apparent than the metaphor; there is little desire that it be taken literally. The metaphor's basic
work is positive in that it extends meaning by joining together two meaning
systems into a higher synthesis; the hyperbole's work is more negative in
that it stretches one meaning system to the point where that meaning threatens to snap or break. One way to put this difference is to say that the metaphor tends to be naive, while the hyperbole is a more critical trope. Perhaps
this is why some authors, Perelman and Obrechts-Tyteca among them, connect hyperbole to irony (NR, 292). Both of these tropes exercise a negation
or destruction through a seemingly positive statement. This negative aspect
of hyperbole, though, should not be taken to imply that it has no positive
cognitive content: hyperbole cannot be reduced to simple declarative state-

ments just as metaphor cannot be reduced to mere comparison or simile. Both have cognitive content—they say something new, and their saying cannot be said in any other way—even though they function differently. In fact, it is not always easy to discern the difference between metaphor and hyperbole. Why, for example, is "God is love" considered to be a metaphor — drawing together two different realms of discourse, rather than a hyperbole — making an absolute affirmation when all the evidence supports a more modest and qualified viewpoint?

Although in chapter two I pointed out that Voltaire considered hyperbole to be the form of figuration, rhetorical tradition, following Aristotle, has more consistently regarded metaphor as the prototype of all tropes. Perhaps one reason is its multifaceted subtlety. Hyperbole, by comparison, often is blunt and forceful. While a good metaphor quietly insinuates, a good hyperbole arrogantly demands. Marvick blames the low standing of hyperbole on this trait. "If twentieth century critics have not appreciated the full meaning of hyperbole, it is doubtless because they have clung too tenaciously to their ability to see through it" (MS, 60). Hyperbole is thus too easy; in other words, it does not give rise to a sufficient amount of interpretive complexity, the kind of thing upon which criticism rests. Certainly this could be true of everyday exaggerations. When a host says, "The army is coming over for dinner tonight," a critic would be too bored to point out that "army" represents (or distorts) a group of friends; the host has violated the context of the situation in order to focus on the number—in a complaining or prideful tone?—of the dinner companions. Of course, if later a small battalion did show up for dinner, the statement would have proved to be literally, not hyperbolically, true. Moreover, the interpretation becomes even more complex when we realize that army itself can mean merely "a great multitude." The fact that language is inherently flexible makes the stretch of a hyperbole difficult to measure at times.

As even this basic example demonstrates, surely one of the mysteries of hyperbole is that it often feigns enthusiasm, and thus it invites speculation as to why it goes so far. As I have tried to show, hyperbole is a more critical trope than the naive metaphor; it has more than a touch of irony in its structure. This, at least, is the case with Barth. Yet Marvick is right in emphasizing the hyperbole's literalness (although the same could be said of the other tropes, especially metaphor). However, that literalness does not mean, to return to my example, that the reader will immediately imagine a lot of people in uniforms eating in a mess hall. Instead, the hyperbole's literalness is its strength; because it really wants to mean what it says, it cannot easily be reduced to a more tame equivalent. Its stubborn intensity does refuse paraphrase, and thus it does demand interpretation just like the metaphor. Good hyperboles and metaphors stand on their own. They both recognize the literal untruth of their claims and yet boldly make their claims anyway. Hyperbole knows that it is not literally true, and yet it pursues its own logic of extremity in spite of this knowledge—for the sake of a different kind of truth. Perhaps Marvick's analysis goes awry because he assumes that hyperbole always seeks the ideal. Hyperbole not only offers too much of a good thing; it also negates, criticizes, and destroys. In this role it does not require the agreement of the audience because it sets out to show that the audience does not really agree with itself.

In sum, Marvick's contention that hyperbole requires the identification of speaker and audience goes too far; all hyperbole requires is that the audience acquiesce to its plausibility. Agreement or disagreement can come later. This rule of plausibility, by the way, applies equally to all the tropes. A metaphor, because it fuses together two separate elements, also must appear acceptable and plausible to its audience. Barth's metaphor of crisis, for example, seemed to many of his contemporaries to be an unreliable figure, to be, in fact, an exaggeration. What makes Barth's hyperbole plausible, the context within which it works (if it does work), is that very metaphor. The point I am making is a very simple one: Barth's style is an interconnected whole. Because crisis is the primary configuration of Barth's discourse, the devastation of culture, the emptiness of religion and the otherness of God can be repeatedly announced in increasingly intense forms without fear of ridicule. This does not mean that, given the metaphor of crisis, Barth's exaggerations are literally true; rather, they are figuratively true. That is, only hyperbole can develop and exploit the truth of the crisis situation. In this context, nothing less will do; this means that hyperbole cannot be summarized or paraphrased without suffering irrevocable cognitive loss. To read Barth is to accept his sometimes outrageous exaggerations as necessary to his theological scheme. All other figures at this point would be sterile, insufficient, weak, and irrelevant.

Even given this analysis of hyperbole, it is still difficult to pinpoint a hyperbolic statement. More so than metaphor, hyperbole operates on the level of discourse as a whole rather than at the level of the individual utterance. Usually, one sentence is enough to signal the presence of a specific metaphor. Hyperbole, on the other hand, often involves a series of sentences marching to an ever increasing and noisier beat. It functions like a root metaphor, structuring the whole range of a discourse rather than appearing in a particular sentence. Perhaps the reason for this is that an isolated hyperbole stands out too much, while a series of hyperboles—or rather, a series of sentences making a hyperbole — can force its way onto the reader in a much more dramatic fashion. The *Oxford English Dictionary* makes this point when it defines exaggeration as "to heap or pile up; accumulate." In chapter one I noted that repetition and accumulation were characteristics of expressionism in general, and Barth is no exception. This means, though, that showing exaggeration at work in a text is not as easy as isolating specific metaphorical utterances. A repetition can occur — sporadically or consistently — throughout all of the phases of an entire text. The problem here is similar to my task in the last chapter where I tried to show that Barth's entire discourse, not just his particular use of metaphors, is structured by crisis. Perhaps the difficulty of this kind of reading accounts for the many commentators who note Barth's hyperbole with general descriptive terms like volcanic and explosive, but fail to specify where the eruption actually occurs. My own analysis of Barth's hyperbole will have to follow several routes in order to show the excesses of his argument. I will argue that hyperbole functions to assert a complete critique, a criticism which knows no bounds outside of its own sharp points and uneven edges. Before I turn to Barth, though, it might be helpful to understand how another author's hyperbole works, a philosopher whose influence on Barth is unquestionable.

NIETZSCHE AS EXAGGERATOR

Barth certainly read Nietzsche; he refers to him several times in *Romans*. He notes the idea of the "overman," compares the felt need for forgiveness with Dionysiac enthusiasm, contrasts Nietzsche's antireligiosity with Overbeck's, commends Nietzsche for his wild and passionate rejection of "god," and approves of his "fulminations" against the alleged right of some people to establish themselves in power over and against other people (*R*, 80, 101, 137, 349 and 479). In one passage he even argues that Nietzsche knew the truth, but the disturbances of his life show that the truth is intolerable (*R*, 354). Nietzsche's greater influence on Barth, however, is indirect, mediated by the work of Overbeck. Both Nietzsche and Overbeck taught at the University of Basel — where Barth would later teach — and Overbeck's denouncements of liberal theology were largely the result of their friendship. Perhaps Barth liked Overbeck more because he dealt more directly and almost solely with theology; in addition, Overbeck did not have a well-developed constructive position of his own, restricting his thoughts to criticisms, which Barth could easily appropriate. Nietzsche's more positive position, to the extent that he did have one, could not have influenced Barth much. Barth was not interested in philosophical speculation about the will, the eternal return of time or a post-theological anthropology and morality. In addition, Barth was writing at a time when Nietzsche's views were still obscured by those, most notably his sister, who either did not understand him or wanted to use him for their own purposes.

What Nietzsche's real views were is still a subject of a vast and lively debate. First connected to a crude kind of Darwinism, then usurped by the Nazis, a rehabilitating — and more accurate — interpretation of this philosopher began fairly recently with the works of Kaufmann and Heidegger.[7] Even more recently, however, Nietzsche's style, his rhetoric, has come under increasing scrutiny.[8] I want to argue that it is a style that bears an uncanny resemblance to Barth's, qualifying as one of the rhetorical precedents for *Romans*. Allan Megill, for example, has argued that Nietzsche's prophetic style is an example of the use of hyperbole, suggesting that one would have to be "either a madman or a fool" to believe literally in Nietzsche's position.[9] This is, in fact, Nietzsche's problem, according to Megill, for "the rhetorical effectiveness of these assertions very much depends on their being taken literally."[10] I have argued that hyperbole's strained literalness should give rise to interpretation instead of either literal acceptance or rejection. Unfortunately, hyperbole often does offend rather than educate. Alexander Nehamas, who also has argued that Nietzsche's writing is irreducibly hyperbolic, suggests that this, "the most unscholarly of tropes," accounts for the reactions of indignation to Nietzsche and for his own occasional buffoonery.[11] Hyperbole attracts some readers with the same intensity and power with which it repels others — or leaves yet others alternating between comprehension and confusion.

Perhaps this shared trope is one reason many readers try to resist the rhetoric of both Barth and Nietzsche. In Nietzsche's case, he has long been acknowledged as a great German stylist, but this is usually taken to mean that how he writes is more important than what he has to say. This attitude naturally leads to the attempt to separate style from content. One recent critic, for example, commendably tries to distinguish Nietzsche's philosophy from the many incrustations of myths and speculations that have covered his thought from the very beginning, lamenting that his philosophy has been "eclipsed by his flamboyant style."[12] Does this mean, though, that hyperbole is one of Nietzsche's tools, which the critic can afford to neglect? Arthur Danto seems to think so. In a groundbreaking study, which seeks to show the significance of Nietzsche's philosophy from an analytical perspective, he has this to say about Nietzsche's flamboyancy:

> His language would have been less colorful had he known what he was trying to say, but then he would not have been the original thinker he was, working through a set of problems which had hardly ever been charted before. Small wonder his maps are illustrated, so to speak, with all sorts of monsters and fearful indications and boastful cartographic embellishments.[13]

Thus, Nietzsche's style would have been more manageable if he had only understood his own content better. Because "we know a good deal more philosophy today,"[14] our maps can be both more modest and more exact. So Danto sets out to recast Nietzsche's writing into a more usable form. Against such interpretations it might not be malicious to recall Nietzsche's frequent — and appropriately hyperbolic — comment that his critics simply do not know how to read.

Others have argued that Nietzsche's most distinctive trait is his insistent transgression of the usual boundary between poetry and philosophy, thus necessitating a rhetorical approach. Indeed, I have already shown in chapter two that Nietzsche thinks language creates reality; truth is a style that is credited as literal or realistic. Nehamas argues that hyperbole is Nietzsche's own preferred style; it is the form that his philosophy most often takes. His early work, written as a young professor of classical philology, was brilliantly rebellious, but it was restrained by the domination of his chosen discipline, his attachment to Wagner and Schopenhauer, and his romantic idealization of the Greeks. Yet even in *The Birth of Tragedy*, hyperbole is already playing its role: Nietzsche claims that Euripides literally killed tragedy by introducing a rational element into a sacred and frenzied rite. This is no ordinary account of the evolution of drama; life and death are said to be literally at stake. Socrates, who polishes the seductive mirrors of reason at the expense of instinct and the affirmation of reality, is portrayed as a world-historical villain. Moreover, here Nietzsche develops the idea of the power of the Dionysian, which, as opposed to Apollonian reason that always seeks to construct a merely mental world, wants to destroy the illusions of culture in order to become truly creative.[15] The Dionysian could be considered the historical power of hyperbole; as a disruptive force it is also present in Nietzsche's later work. After he resigns from the university and begins to experiment with his writing style, he becomes even more extreme and destructive. His denunciations of Christianity, for example, are surely prime examples of hyperbole. His use of this troublesome trope climaxes with megalomaniacal claims, which, near the end of his life, are difficult to separate from the symptoms of his oncoming insanity. Statements like this become common in his letters: "I hold, quite literally, the future of mankind in the palm of my hand."[16]

Two genres are especially exploited by Nietzsche for their hyperbolic potential. It is easy to argue that Nietzsche's famous use of aphorisms, which marks the middle of his career, is a species of hyperbole. An aphorism is a brief, startling statement that reveals unexpected connections. Because aphorisms are usually terse, condensed, agitated, and yet elegant, this genre is especially suited to statements that tend toward an unqualified extreme.

Nehamas notes, though, that the spaces that separate aphorisms "act as frames that magnify the power of exaggeration within them but don't allow it to penetrate beyond their confines."[17] The aphorism form thus serves simultaneously to foreground and neutralize the hyperbole it contains. Outside of this genre Nietzsche's language is ordinarily even less restrained. This is evident in Nietzsche's polemical writings, another favorite form and one which he shares with Barth. The strategy of denouncing an opponent usually involves an exaggeration of both the distance separating the two writers and the deficiencies of the other party. A good example of Nietzsche's polemical style can be found in the first of his "untimely meditations," which devastated a popular book on religion, David Friedrich Strauss's *Der alte und der neue Glaube.* Indeed, in 1874, after the death of Strauss, Nietzsche privately expressed the hope that his essay had not made the end of Strauss's life miserable and that Strauss had died without even hearing of him.[18] Nietzsche's late criticisms of Wagner, after an early adulation of the composer, can also be counted as hyperbolic in form.

Whatever the form, Nietzsche's tendency is toward bombast and rant. Nehamas locates this hyperbole compulsion in relation to Nietzsche's reaction against Socrates, his great nemesis: if Socratic irony is manifested in his saying too little, then in Nietzsche we find only excess and extreme. Socrates' usual rhetorical ploy is a feigned humility of self-effacement while Nietzsche's strained arrogance serves his aggrandizing, aristocratic, and esoteric manner. Both strategies are complementary in that they provoke and disorient, forcing the reader to think through traditional problems anew. Yet Nietzsche did not always want himself to be taken so seriously, or literally; his rhetoric was self-consciously employed. In a letter he admits that his work is "radical to a criminal extreme."[19] In an illuminating passage from *The Will to Power,* Nietzsche recognizes that extremity is the ultimate form of his position:

> The princes of Europe should consider carefully whether they can do without our support. We immoralists—we are today the only power that needs no allies in order to conquer: thus we are by far the strongest of the strong. We do not even need to tell lies: what other power can dispense with that? A powerful seduction fights on our behalf, the most powerful perhaps that there has ever been — the seduction of truth — "Truth"? Who has forced this word on me? But I repudiate it; but I disdain this proud word: no, we do not need even this; we shall conquer and come to power even without truth. The spell that fights on our behalf, the eye of Venus that charms and blinds even our opponents, is *the magic of the extreme,* the seduction that everything extreme exercises: we immoralists—we are the most extreme.[20]

This is a fascinating and troubling passage. He begins by arguing that the strength of immorality lies in its autonomy. Perhaps because the immoralist does not need to make the many compromises that sociability entails, the immoralist does not need to lie. The immoralist, then, is honest and has the attraction of truth; yet in mock surprise Nietzsche asks why that word, truth, has entered the discussion. The real seduction of the immoralist is, in fact, not truth but hyperbole, the magic of the extreme, which is the immoralist's trademark because he stands alone, unencumbered by the constraints of social convention. Yet this passage leaves us with an unanswered question: this extremity, is it magic, or is it truth? Or could it be that truth, which is also a kind of seduction, is itself a kind of magic?

Even if this passage does not explicitly tell us what kind of magic extremity is, it does suggest that extremity has deep roots in Nietzsche's philosophy. In fact, Nietzsche's own philosophy invites speculation about the reasons for his stylistic strategies. His epistemology, a genealogy that traces reason back to its nonrational origins as opposed to Kant's critiques, which sought the rational presuppositions for various phenomena, does not allow for a separation of argument from intention or content from style. For Nietzsche, reason cannot justify itself; justifications are merely masks for deeper and usually unfounded purposes. Even the most rigorous discourse is, therefore, a dramatic fiction; it is the task of philosophical psychology to uncover the reasons that reason does not want to know. Nietzsche applies this theory to Christian morality by arguing that apparently compassionate maxims really reflect the resentment of weak-willed people against those who are morally superior. Nietzsche's analysis of Christianity is sometimes preposterous, often insightful, and always provocative, but his method can be turned against his very own work: What are the purposes which fuel his various exclamations and denouncements? Why hyperbole?

Of course, to suggest that Nietzsche's work should be traced back to his own personality, perhaps connected to the physique of a depressed, frail, and sick man, is absurd, even though Nietzsche himself toys with this kind of autobiographical criticism in *Ecce Homo*[21] and, furthermore, this is how he often explains or rather reduces the position of Christian morality. However, a plausible case could be made for the origin of Nietzsche's style that is strikingly similar to the context of Barth's rhetoric: Nietzsche's hyperbole is intended because he thought he was responding to a crisis, which could only be overcome in the most extreme terms. Megill puts this point simply: "The style of Nietzsche's thought finds its justification in the conviction of crisis."[22] Nietzsche knew he had a purpose; he was driven by the mission to foresee and announce a rift in history, a collapse of culture, which had not yet occurred. His attempt to re-evaluate all values, to both diagnose and cure the nihilism of a post-Christian culture, is a philosophical agenda for the future, and he often wrote that he was glad nobody in the present understood him, thus proving how great he really was. Nietzsche's real audience could only be a culture that knew, without any doubt, it had been destabilized and was tottering on the edge of the abyss. This prophetic stance was necessarily hyperbolic because Nietzsche was speaking across his own contemporaries and to the future. Nietzsche was trying to speak loud enough so future generations could hear him; his contemporaries, however, for the most part were only offended and confused by all the noise. Not until Barth's age, and in Barth himself, could much of Nietzsche's work make sense in all of its unbounded madness.[23]

Nietzsche was aware of all of this. In *Human, All Too Human* he suggests that in the case of an emergency, exaggeration is helpful because it will lead otherwise unmotivated people into action. "To that extent, it is useful to exaggerate when describing emergencies."[24] It is easy to read this inoccuous passage as merely another observation about the herd mentality. Yet Nietzsche's own description of contemporary culture fits that of an emergency. Could it be that he once hoped his own exaggerations would lead to some action? Later in this same work he does offer a hint about his own position: "He who is forced to speak more loudly than is his habit (as in front of someone hard of hearing, or before a large audience) generally exaggerates what he has to communicate. Some people become conspirators, malicious slanderers, or schemers, merely because their voice is best suited to a whisper."[25] Here he again makes an innocent observation about exaggeration, but he follows it with a statement linking whispering, the opposite of exaggeration, with manipulation and deception. Exaggeration, therefore, is by implication not just a tool of the lecturer's trade. It is a sign of strength, the necessary form of the prophet's tirade, a gesture that is essential to a philosophy ruled by an exclusive concern for that which cannot yet be understood. Of course, one is forced to suspect that hyperbole itself must take some of the blame for the inability of Nietzsche's contemporaries to understand him. However that may be, near the end of his life Nietzsche's tirades became more blatant and strident; the more he was misunderstood, the louder he wrote.

This vicious cycle climaxes in *Ecce Homo*.[26] Written in the apparent form of an autobiography, at the very end of his productive career, this last testament is Nietzsche's most uninhibited and fantastic work. He does not try to narrate the facts of his life, because he knows that the meaning of his life has little to do with objective observation. Instead, he announces with sheer exuberance his own hitherto unnoticed greatness. If the hyperbole of his earlier works is often ignored, here the trope of excess and extremity cannot be avoided. He writes that he is approaching humanity with "the heaviest demand that has ever been made on it" (*EH,* 33). That demand is that he be, someday, understood. But how could he possibly ever be understood? "I am by nature warlike," he writes, and he defends his sense of honor by suggesting that he only attacks causes that are already victorious and that have given him no reason to be vengeful (*EH,* 47). Indeed, there seems to be no limit to what he could attack, or to the value he places on his own unrecognized victories. Because he was "born posthumously" (*EH,* p. 69), the world does not yet realize how wise and clever he is, why he writes such excellent books (an understatement, given what else he says about his works), and why he is destiny (these are all titles to some of the chapters of this book). Zarathustra, for instance, is "the most exalted book that exists" (*EH,* 35). In a reflection on his style, he suggests that "no one has ever had more of the new, the unheard-of, the really new-created in artistic means to squander" (*EH,* 74). In fact, "before me one did not know what can be done with the German language" (*EH,* 75). These are wild claims, but in the last chapter, Nietzsche connects these hyperboles not only to his own personality but also to the situation that he has had the courage to confront:

> I know my fate. One day there will be associated with my name the recollection of something frightful — of a crisis like no other before on earth, of the profoundest collision of conscience, of a decision evoked *against* everything that until then had been believed in, demanded, sanctified. I am not a man I am dynamite . . . I am by far the most terrible human being there has ever been; this does not mean I shall not be the most beneficent (*EH,* 127).

Because of the rocklike hardness of his culture's ignorances and prejudices, Nietzsche has had to philosophize with the hammer of hyperbole.

What is perhaps most distinctive about this book is that its hyperbole becomes almost indistinguishable from irony. The title itself is both exaggeration and irony; the phrase, "Behold, the man!" was originally Pilate's appellation for Jesus Christ, with whom Nietzsche (assuming the guise of Dionysus) is evidently competing. Nietzsche is not praising himself in this work only because others have failed to do so; his self-congratulations really mask a critique of the culture that could not understand him. The chapters that describe his previous books read at times like the adolescent adulations of a fanatical disciple — or a parody of what should have been written about his books, even if he would not have liked such praise. Some of his comments, it should be understood, are not meant to be taken literally. Instead,

Nietzsche is turning his obscurity into a sign of his greatness. That, in the end, is the great irony that he exploits. His hyperbole depends for its very magic on a lack of recognition, or correspondingly, on his ability to be offensive and disturbing. If he had been accepted as a philosopher of some importance, he could not have said what he wanted—or how he wanted to say it. Nietzsche's whole style depends on the misunderstandings that he hyperbolically initiates and then denounces. Perhaps this is why the hyperboles in this book often seem funny, irreverent, and good-natured. They are not spoken out of bitterness or resentment. They are not a cry for better interpretations, more journal articles, more sensitive reviews. They are spoken because this is the logic within which Nietzsche thinks, and he thinks it is a healthy logic: "A big meal is easier to digest than one too small" (*EH*, 53).

I want to argue that Barth, too, is a hyperbolic thinker, although he only rarely turns his hyperbole onto himself as Nietzsche did. Nevertheless, there are striking similarities between these two. Barth, too, is speaking from a crisis and to the future; but he is not speaking to a hoped-for human destiny but the future that lies only with God, the future that is always present in history as eternity. Because his audience does not know or understand this eternity, he, too, must speak with the sword of hyperbole. Barth also denounces religion, Christian morality, and the God of human creation in extreme terms. He, too, alienates his audience with hyperbole so that the urgency of his message will not be mistaken. All of these points will be better made, I think, with the example of Nietzsche's style hovering in the background. I will note one final similarity here: Barth too knows that he will be misunderstood, not because nobody will listen to premature judgments but because his age is ripe for crisis, and people will think that he has all the answers. Therefore, Barth will cut his hyperbole with a heavy dose of irony; to argue that, though, will be the task of the next chapter, where I will have to leave behind Nietzsche's hyperbole and turn to Kierkegaard's irony.

A NECESSARY EXCESS

Theology, for Barth, is conducted in a temporal disruption, under the sign of an eschatological provision, which allows for something to be said only indirectly, because the object of theology is utterly absent. Theologians, therefore, cannot have direct rapports with their audiences; to the extent that the theologian really wants to speak about God, no common ground can be found that might enable such a discussion to take place. God is of eternity, which in history is understood at best as the coming future of judgment and redemption or as a present all-encompassing crisis. Barth, then, cannot make of theology a civil discourse, a discipline that resides on the same level as the many other discourses of everyday life. Theology will not be able to speak as if it could be understood simply. "So long as we endeavor to speak about grace," Barth explains, "our speech must labour under a necessary obscurity" (*R*, 224). Many of Barth's readers, however, did not understand this key point and accused him of acting irresponsibly. In the preface to the second edition of *Romans* Barth responds to this charge by suggesting that "theologians serve the layman best when we refuse to have him especially in mind" (*R*, 5). Theology must not cater to contemporary ideas and attitudes. This passage is more than a defense of Barth's intellectual integrity; it signals his entire methodology. "Thirty years hence," he notes, "one may perhaps speak of simplicity, but now let us speak the truth" (*R*, 5). For the present — in the midst of crisis — the truth can only be grasped by obscurity itself: "Those who claim to speak simply seem to me to be — simply speaking about something else" (*R*, 6). Near the end of *Romans*, he again pauses to defend the excess and obscurity of his language:

> It is not 'complicated' thinking which is doctrinaire, but that much-praised 'simplicity.' Men think simply when they pretend to know what they do not know. The straight-moving thought which we so earnestly desire is not genuine thought at all. Genuine thinking is always strange to the world and unsympathetic (*R*, 425).

Only in language that does not pretend to be what it is, which knows that it is what it is not, can religious thinking begin.

Given the metaphor of crisis, Barth has no choice but to write in a style many will perceive as being too turbulent, profuse and distorted—in a word, exaggerated. Jülicher, for example, accused Barth of proceeding from the "arrogance of spiritual enthusiasm" (*R*, 20). Jülicher mistakes the tone of Barth's work for an indication of Barth's desire to be the only theologian to possess the whole truth. Barth does make grandiose and enthusiastic claims —and I will return to the problem of absolutist claims at the end of this chapter — but this is not one of them. The only place where truth can be found, Barth clearly states, is in fact a single point: where God and the world intersect in Jesus Christ. Because this intersection is a contradiction, however, it cannot point to any other truths. It is, in fact, an explosion which destroys all other truths. This is why Barth is so strident in his criticisms of, literally, everything. "To him that is not sufficiently mature to accept a contradiction and rest in it, it becomes a scandal—to him that is unable to escape the necessity of contradiction, it becomes a matter for faith" (*R*, 39). Because truth is a contradiction, Barth's discourse is limited to two options: he can show how truly other God really is, and he can show how attempts to speak about God, to deny this otherness, must inevitably fail. Barth hyperbolizes both of these themes throughout his text: with one and the same force he pushes God further and further away from any possible human understanding, and he condemns any attempt to ignore this implacable inability of fathoming the divine.

AN OTHER OTHERNESS

I have already discussed Barth's use of the No-God concept to show that all language about God is in crisis. At the end of chapter three I suggested that the interplay of God and No-God drove Barth to admit that nothing can be said about God at all. This is not a very satisfactory position for a theologian, and it is not Barth's final word on God. The one positive thing Barth can say about God is that God is unknown, not only untouched by humanity but beyond human reach. Barth says this repeatedly in *Romans,* in a vociferous manner, with certainty and passion. The question immediately arises: How can Barth say this about God when he has just said that language can say nothing about God at all? True, these pronouncements are about God's otherness, so they do not try to control or contain God as do the statements of most other theologies. However, they are still statements that imply a knowledge of God's nature, even if that nature is said to entail an essential inaccessibility. How can Barth pretend to know so much about God, given his critique of all such knowledge as directed toward the No-God?

The full answer to this question can only be completed in the next chapter, where I will discuss irony. Here I can begin the answer by suggesting that Barth's blatant statements about God's otherness should not be taken literally but instead as examples of hyperbole. Barth does not know the unknowability of God. All he knows is that religions claim to know something about an otherwise unknown God. He knows that the effect of revelation is to destroy this knowledge. Barth sets out, then, to critique religion by taking the first step of exaggerating the unknown aspects of the deity. He takes what has long been a staple of theology and makes it the only word theology can speak. He distorts theology by turning one of its main principles against it: if God is so difficult to know, so mysterious, so infinite, then let us be honest with ourselves, and admit that God is simply unknown altogether. This is a dangerous, perhaps self-destructive position. It is a sweeping, tumultuous claim, which could only lead to misunderstanding, resentment, and confusion. Few theologians would want to take this step with Barth because it leads to the abolition of religion. Barth was willing to

take this step—or better, leap—because that is precisely where he wanted
to land.

Barth exceeds the normal decorum of theology by repeatedly prolif-
erating the absence of God throughout *Romans*. Ordinarily, however, critics
reduce this clamor to the theme of the Wholly Other God, and analyze it
without regard to its rhetorical construction. This is unfortunate: For Barth,
the Wholly Other God is not a doctrine, a rule in propositional form that can
be debated according to its implications and inferences. The Wholly Other
God is a hyperbolic power, which forces the reader into the shock of recognizing that there cannot be any doctrine of God at all. Barth makes this point
in as many vivid ways as possible. The distance between God and humanity,
he emphasizes, has an "essential, sharp, acid and disintegrating ultimate
significance" (*R*, 49). Humanity cannot afford to be indifferent to this infinite distance; although it extends away from the world, it is also a terrible
force that can smother humanity with confusion and ignorance. Indeed, if
we do know God at all, it is only through God's wrath and God's utter
strangeness. Even that knowledge, however, cannot be coherently formulated; those who think they understand the judgment of God will have that
judgment turned against themselves.

From the human perspective, Barth admits, God does seem to be one
among many possibilities in the world, but humanity should know better.
God is actually, and Barth relishes the contradiction, the impossible possibility. God is so impossible that even God's otherness is not really known;
God's otherness is also other than anything that humanity can experience
in this world. "This 'otherness' cuts sharply through all human sense of
possession and semi-possession, even through all sense of not-possessing"
(*R*, 92). Yet Barth continues to speak of this otherness, using it as a critique
of everything human. On this point Barth's discourse cannot entail any constructive content, although it can play a destructive role. Thus, God's impossibility becomes a very real possibility. True, it is a force that cannot be
contained in language: "But we know, when we pronounce this, that we are
speaking of a possibility of which we are ignorant; a possibility which—and
we must repeat it again and again!—can only be believed in" (*R*, 114). Indeed, he does repeat again and again that his language is ignorant, and yet
his statements continue to be bold and profligate. The impossibility of God
transcends language, but its power still must be expressed: "For impossibility is, as such, nigh at hand, ready at our elbow, possible. Impossibility
presses upon us, breaks over us, is indeed already present. Impossibility is
more possible than everything which we hold to be possible" (*R*, 381). Here
the contradiction of the impossible possibility ignites, breaking apart any attempt to contain God.

Sometimes it must be admitted that the result of this position is a language that appears to be confused and out of control. Note, for example, this passage:

> God is pure negation. He is both 'here' and 'there.' He is the negation of the negation in which the other world contradicts this world and this world the other world. He is the death of our death and the non-existence of our non-existence (*R*, 142).

This passage contradicts itself with an excess of negations in order to disclose that God is an impossibility whose possibility we cannot avoid. Yet once we think that we know God's otherness, that we can simply say it, then we are speaking about something other than God. How we talk about God, then, must reflect who God is. "We must therefore never allow this dialectical presupposition to be hardened or petrified into a concrete and direct occurrence" (*R*, 164). Once the tensions in language about God are relaxed, giving it the appearance of being an ordinary cognitive discourse, then such language becomes worse than silence; it becomes idolatrous. Language that does not exaggerate God's otherness is literally about No-God. This is one of Barth's central teachings, and he exaggerates the consequences of ignoring it:

> So far as human possibility is concerned, prophets and priests, theologians and philosophers, men of faith, hope and charity, break in pieces on the impossibility of God. They have laboured in vain and spent their strength for nought (*R*, 185).

This is a harsh judgment, which must include Barth himself. Yet there is no other way if the obscurity of language is taken seriously.

> All our answers, all our attempts at consolation, are but deceitful short-circuits, for from this vast ambiguity we ourselves emerge; we cannot escape from it, not even if we evoke in our imaginings an infinite divine harmony beyond this world of ours (*R*, 303).

One way that Barth avoids—or better, suspends—the debilitating implications of this position is by the use of rhetorical questions.[27] If no answers can be given to the human predicament, then perhaps at least questions can be asked. Barth uses this rhetorical ploy throughout *Romans,* and his interrogations take a hyperbolic form. He piles questions onto each other in elongated sequences in order to accentuate the impossibility of any rebuttal. This allows him to write without making any positive claims. Notice this rather typical passage:

.How are we to provide any further elucidation, explanation, and interpretation, of the words of God to those who love Him — words which only He can utter at the place where He wills that men should seek and find Him? Is it not inevitable that anything we say must be said 'about' or 'in addition to' or 'contrary' to what God has said? Must not our silence also, quite as much as our speech, obscure the truth concerning the knowledge of love? Do we not do equally wrong, whether, in answer to these things, we burst into speech or relapse into silence? (*R*, 326)

Do we not do wrong, it is tempting to add, even if we just continually ask unanswerable questions? Barth has stretched his language past the point where it threatens to break. By stringing together a series of questions he produces the illusion that he has made progress toward some point when he really has no answers at all. Thus, these questions are not "rhetorical" in the ordinary sense of a question whose answer is already known.

What else can be done in the midst of crisis? In a gloss on a passage from Paul's letter, Barth offers some insight into his own situation: "These words are not spoken from the security of the shore, or from the safe refuge of a lifeboat as it approaches, or pulls away from, a wreck. These words are spoken from the deck of a ship — as it sinks" (*R*, 393). Barth's frustrating questions and tumultuous cries are those of a drowning man. It is no wonder, then, that they sound so frantic and fraught with anxiety. Barth continues in the very next sentence of that passage to write, "Only one who is himself a Churchman knows what it is to sin against God, to betray Him and to deny Him" (*R*, 393). The ship that is sinking, then, is nothing else but the church. This adds the agitated dimension to Barth's discourse that he is lambasting the very platform on which he is standing, as it sinks away into destruction.

A CHURCH DESTROYED

Indeed, Barth's entire discourse on the otherness of God serves as the groundwork for his critique of the church, to which he nonetheless belongs.[28] The irony of this situation will be explored in the next chapter. Here it is important to understand Barth's denunciations of the church as a form of hyperbole. Because God is unknown, everything the church does and believes is utterly wrong. The otherness of God contrasts with this miserable sameness of the church. Yet Barth stands with the church, so how should this "everything" be interpreted? This becomes clear when Barth writes, "The desperate situation of the Church cannot be exaggerated" (*R*, 394).[29] This disclaimer should not be taken literally. It is itself an exaggeration: the church is in such terrible trouble that no matter how harshly Barth criticizes it, it still deserves even harder words. However, it is hard to imagine how any situation could not be exaggerated; by denying that his discourse is exaggeration, Barth only makes the sting of his remarks a little sharper. Barth makes this clear when he comments, a little later, "Nor is it possible to 'exaggerate' *[ubertreibung]* a single failure [of the church], for it does but remind us of the vast ambiguity of our whole situation" (*R*, 395). It is possible to exaggerate the importance of one failure if its significance resides in the context of a whole pattern of failures. Indeed, a single failure would remind us of a whole structure of failures only if it were to be exaggerated. Barth is saying that the form of his discourse is such that he only needs one failure in order to demonstrate that the church's failure is complete and irreversible.

The church's failure has nothing to do with the drama of individuals not reaching their goals, of moral decline, or limited visions; it is a necessary failure, mandated by the nature of God. As a failure, the church does make some claim to validity. Indeed, Barth speaks of the true church in terms of the military metaphors that I analyzed in chapter three in connection with the focus of the crisis. Members of the true church are described as victims of a successful surprise attack. Barth uses images of strife to make the point that not only has the church failed but—like its very own God—it does not even exist: "But the activity of the community is related to the Gospel only in so far as it is no more than a crater formed by the explosion of a shell and seeks to be no more than a void in which the Gospel reveals itself" (*R*, 36). Elsewhere he says that religion is a bomb hypocritically decked out with flowers (*R*, 268). Religion is only acceptable when it explodes.

There is another church, though, whose existence is only too obvious: the church that does try to understand God, which does work in the world, which does not want to be a void—the flowers that cover the bomb. Barth is relentlessly critical of this, the false church. In one passage he echoes and twists Nietzsche's image of truth as an effaced coin (which I quoted in chapter two) in order to make his point: "Just as genuine coins are open to suspicion so long as false coins are in circulation, so the perception which proceeds outward from God cannot have free course until the arrogance of religion be done away with" (*R*, 37). Religion, every religion, is a counterfeit; the only true currency comes from God. "God alone is the merchant who can pay in the currency of eternity. He alone can make a valuation which is eternally valid" (*R*, 62).

These two themes, then, govern Barth's discourse about the church: the true church is the void; the false church is anything that tries to rise out of the void. Their combination is potent, as can be seen in chapter two of *Romans,* ironically entitled, "The Righteousness of Man." Here Barth's consideration of religion begins with an emphasis on human depravity and inability. "Does not an island of the blest rise from the ocean of the unfortunate?" Barth asks, rhetorically (*R*, 55). At times Barth's discussion merely repeats Luther's doctrine of the two kingdoms. However, he pushes the two kingdoms even further apart than Luther intended; there is no traveling from one to the other because war has been declared. Not even those who understand their sinful situation — who want to surrender — are any closer to the Kingdom of God. "Everything human swims with the stream either with vehement protest or with easy accommodation, even when it appears to hover above it or to engage in conflict with it" (R, 57). Thus, even Barth's protests against the human kingdom do not allow him to rise above the earth and toward God. Being a believer is something that only God decides. "He who has been chosen by God cannot say that he has chosen God" (R, 59). To misunderstand all of this is to make room for religion.

> Misunderstanding such as this immediately condenses, solidifies, hardens, into a solid mass of misunderstanding. For the initial misunderstanding causes every human thought and word and action, however pure and delicate, to unite as elements in the composition of one hard and solid lump. There comes into being what is known as the 'religious' life, which is regarded as something peculiar, which is contrasted with the life of the generality of men, and which, because it is nothing more than romantic unbelief, has no protection against the enmity of those who despise it (R, 60).

Religion is born of misunderstanding. Those who think they can know God set aside a special sphere, a compartment of human activity devoted to this pursuit. Thus, the world is divided into religious and nonreligious people. This is a lie; nobody is truly religious because nobody knows God. Because of its impudence, then, religion cannot understand this truth: we scale the summit of religion, only to find ourselves the furthest removed from God.

In this chapter Barth makes it clear that righteousness comes only from God's self-revelation, which is a miracle, but this righteousness is invisible. What marks human righteousness is never some ethical program. Barth does argue that the Law is "the impression of divine revelation left behind in time, in history, and in the lives of men" (R, 65). Its function is to point to the crisis by demonstrating the unrighteousness of humanity. Unfortunately, people try to preserve, protect, and expand the Law, with the best intentions. This merely prolongs the crisis and distorts the human situation. It would be better if there were no Law at all:

> The Gentile world no doubt lies in wickedness; but it may be a world so disintegrated, so disorganized, and so undermined, that the mercy of God seems closer and more credible than where the 'Kingdom of God' is displayed in full bloom (R, 67).

Not only does the ethical life fail to establish righteousness, but Barth even denies to humanity the act of repentance: it is not a noble and refined act, he claims, an achievement in the service of God, but rather it is an act of God. There is, then, no observable righteousness in this world, no visible company of saints. "And yet, there is a claim to salvation from the wrath of God: the claim is where every claim is surrendered and broken down by God Himself; where His negation is final and His wrath unavoidable; when God is recognized as God" (*R*, 19).

Only in its very destruction, therefore, can the church be said to exist. This might sound like a fairly simple, even if perverse, theological program: wherever destruction occurs, there God may be found. In this chapter, for example, Barth makes of God's judgment an observable and predictable — as well as terrible — event: "For in the radical dissolution of all physical, intellectual, and spiritual achievements of men, in the all-embracing 'relativization' of all human distinctions and human dignities, their true and eternal meaning is made known" (*R*, 78). When human meaning is destroyed by God, then that is a sure sign that God's meaning is at work. Barth infers from this that the way to know God is by accepting the contradiction of the divine judgment: "No road to the eternal meaning of the created world has ever existed, save the road of negation. This is the lesson of history" (*R*, 87). This is a fairly positive statement, for Barth. Perhaps by the process of recognizing negations, God can become known. This, after all, is the lesson that Luther, during one phase of his spiritual journey, learned from the crucifixion: the theology of the cross finds grace in the opposite of what would be expected; life is found in death, righteousness in unrighteousness.

However, there is another strand of discourse in this text in which Barth rejects a simple one-to-one correlation between negation and grace. In chapter three, where he discusses "The Righteousness of God," he makes it clear that God's judgment is mysterious and lies, in fact, outside of history altogether. Furthermore, in God's wrath God becomes known only as the Unknown God. In fact, God can be known not if negations are recognized, but if negation is absolutized: "The whole course of this world participates in true existence when its nonexistence is recognized" (*R*, 91). Here Barth has exaggerated the significance of negation to the point of absurdity, in order to show that negation, too, is not a sign of God but a pointer to an infinite distance along which there are no signs. "No work, be it most delicately spiritual, or be it even a work of self-negation, is worthy of serious attention" (*R*, 110). In another chapter he says, almost insensibly, that, "We believers stand in the negation of the negation of the suffering of Christ" (*R*, 156). Barth is negating his own negative theology. His superlative discourse has led him to imagine the end of everything.

To some extent Barth's critique of the church is not based on any peculiarities of that institution. God judges everything and finds everything to be lacking. However, religion in general, and the church specifically, is a special province which deserves careful consideration. Barth thinks that religion, for example, is a natural aspect of human existence: "There is a disposition and manner of thought and action which is characteristically religious" (R, 183). In fact, "As men living in the world, and being what we are, we cannot hope to escape the possibility of religion" (R, 230). Barth even thinks that this tendency toward religion is not completely lacking in positive value, for "it is in religion that human capacity appears most pure, most strong, most penetrating, most adaptable" (R, 183). Elsewhere Barth can say that, "In religion the supreme competence of human possibilities attains its consummation and final realization" (R, 236).

Yet precisely because religion is humanity's greatest achievement, it is also in need of the greatest criticism. In its institutional form, the fault of religion becomes obvious: the church makes the audacious attempt to understand God, to rise above the leveling effects of God's judgment, and to pass judgment on who God really is. "Instead of pointing beyond itself, it may be erected, like some great pyramid, as an immense sepulchre within which the truth lies mummified in wood and stone" (R, 129). This insolence marks the church for special criticism from Barth; it also means that the church stubbornly refuses to cease existing, and that it cannot be eradicated. "Religion is neither a thing to be enjoyed or a thing to be celebrated: it must be borne as a yoke which cannot be removed" (R, 258). That is false religion; as for true religion, "Rightly understood, there are no Christians; there is only the eternal opportunity of becoming Christians — an opportunity at once accessible and inaccessible to all men" (R, 321). The church, in an act of self-protection, refuses to understand this, and so it makes explicit the fundamental human traits of pride and arrogance. Religion, thus, "stands within the bracket which is defined by the all-embracing word, *sin*" (R, 235 – 6). Not only is it sinful, but it is also dangerous; it organizes and gives direction to humanity's sinful impulse to be in control, to know the divine. Thus, Barth can say, "Apart from God, it is the most dangerous enemy a man has on this side of the grave" (R, 268). He can also suggest that, "Happy are those mature and superior humanists who know nothing of the arrogance and tragedy of religion, who seem to be spared the illusions and disillusionments of Israel" (R, 187). With that statement, his argument has reached the peak of its "unlimited development."

This critique of the church is repeated and clarified in chapter nine, "The Tribulation of the Church," where Barth inquires into the conditions which make possible his criticisms. Here he tries to correct a possible mis-

perception which his discussion could have caused. From what point of
view is he attacking the church? How has he earned the right to make such
declamations? Barth wants to say that his criticims are not based on any of
his own observations, no matter how acute. Instead, the church is attacked
because it is itself an attack on God; that is, the church can be criticized only
from God's viewpoint. "The Church confronts the Gospel as the last human
possibility confronts the impossibility of God" (*R,* 332). It seeks to transform the eternal into the historical. Returning to his image of grace as a destructive force, Barth writes, "In the Church, the lightning from heaven becomes a slow-burning, earth-made oven . . . " (*R,* 332). It blunts the sharp
edge of truth, making simple what should be kept obscure: "To sum up: the
Church is the endeavor to make the incomprehensible and unavoidable Way
intelligible to men" (*R,* 332). Because the nature of the church is clarity and
organization, it can never represent the strange and excessive ways of God;
it strains after the literal when the only path to truth is indirect and uncanny.

Does this mean that Barth stands outside the church as he passes judgment on it? The answer to this question is, of course, no. Barth's massive
critique is the privilege of an insider. Only by understanding the failure of the
church with God, not the failure of the church with humanity, can a properly
hyperbolic attack be announced; otherwise, somebody could always point
to various successes the church has had in the world to counteract this critique. Judged according to human standards, the church is neither better nor
worse than many institutions.

> Nothing but the honour of God can make sense of anti-clerical propa-
> ganda. Attacks on the Church which proceed upon the assumption that
> its enemies possess some superior knowledge or some superior method
> of justifying and saving themselves are—non-sense (*R,* 337).

In fact, from the human perspective the church is necessary and valuable
because it makes visible the invisibility of God; without its magnificent failure, all other failures might look too much like successes. Barth is interested
in ultimate questions here; his assault is aggressive because it assumes
God's perspective, and it is directed at an institution that continues to pros-
per and grow. Only from this divine perspective does Barth's discourse
make complete sense. Thus, although the church serves the positive function of displaying both God's absence and God's wrath, Barth can say that
from God's perspective the church does not even exist: "God does not belong to the Church . . . Seen from God—as God—the Church is even now
already done away" (*R,* 339).

Perhaps Barth's clarification in this chapter of the distinction between the true or invisible and the false or visible church can make some sense of the dilemma of a necessary church that, nevertheless, should not exist. He calls the visible church the Church of Esau and the invisible church that of Jacob. To explain their relationship Barth advocates the doctrine of double predestination. The Church of Esau tries to take salvation into its own hands; the Church of Jacob is not an outgrowth of Esau but is completely hidden in the mysterious will of God. This act of predestination is God's greatest secret, the furthest extent of God's otherness:

> Only as free, regal, sovereign, unbounded and incomprehensible, can we comprehend God and do Him honour. Only because He elects and rejects, loves and hates, makes alive and puts to death, can He be apprehended and worshipped by men of this world (*R*, 347).

Here Barth displays his Calvinist heritage. His interpretation of predestination is certainly not original, at this point in his career, although the way in which he relishes this doctrine is distinctive: "God would not be God, were He not liable to such accusations [of injustice]" (*R*, 349). What is original is the way he uses this doctrine not only to humble the church and accentuate the majesty of God, but to call, hyperbolically, for the very end of the Church of Esau. In the end, predestination is the tribulation of the church, the one doctrine that renders it dispensable and impudent.

> And yet the Church seeks to live: it struggles to preserve its life by turning its back on its veritable tribulation, by engaging in a tenacious defense of its traditions and customs, by attempting to galvanize itself into life or by setting out to erect new religious societies. This unwillingness-to-die is the real tragedy of the Church'' (*R*, 344).[30]

Of course, once Barth has accepted the doctrine of predestination, he must immediately stress its unknowability; as an action of the Wholly Other God, it too is wholly other. "We must abide humbly by the recognition that His procedure is altogether beyond our powers of observation" (*R*, 351). In a discussion of Moses and the Pharaoh he admits, "Our definition of the man Moses as elected and of the man Pharaoh as rejected is repellent, meaningless, and utterly incapable of proof" (*R*, 352). In this discussion Barth approves of Nietzsche's insight that truth is intolerable. For Barth truth also has the perplexing characteristic of being utterly unknown. This hiddenness of predestination contrasts with the tenth chapter, "The Guilt of the

Church," where Barth wants to suggest that the tribulation is felt even if it is unknown, the result of guilt and the cause of misery. Salvation is decided independently of the actions of humanity due to the sinfulness for which humanity is responsible. This guilt is not isolated in the church, but Barth does make the church its special location. Everyone, however, shares in the church's guilt. Not much can be done about this situation; certainly, "an exchange of compliments between men and men is totally irrelevant" (R, 372). This last comment shows that even in the midst of this very serious discussion, Barth has not lost his sense of humor. Yet a mood of submission pervades this chapter in the way that Barth refuses to make any recommendations or advocate any action to resolve the pervasiveness of guilt.

In the end, after the hyperbolic storm has passed and clear skies allow for some sober reflection, Barth refuses to make of his torrential downpour of criticism the ground for new growth and expansion. In fact, Barth states that "we are not demanding some new 'reformation' . . . " (R, 379). His hyperbole is not to be taken literally and acted upon; it should lead not to the burning of churches, which would not accomplish much, but to something more radical, to changed ways of thinking and living. Yet in a passage where Barth relaxes his tensive voice even this effect of hyperbole is called into question:

> The children of God present nothing peculiar, nothing new, nothing that exercises a compelling power. And so after standing for a moment in amazement before the comedy of an unreal communion with God, the children of the world turn away supported and confirmed in their knowledge that, after all, the world is the world (R, 73).

Here Barth mixes contradiction (the children of God have nothing to offer, and yet their comedy holds the attention of the children of the world) and tautology (the children of the world conclude from this little scene a completely vacuous statement, that the world is the world) to completely strip religion of any significance. On a first reading this might sound like Nietzsche talking about the fatigue of tragedy after Euripides. However, there is a resignation in this passage that betrays its apparently critical structure: tragedy survives Euripides, no matter how impoverished and attenuated, just as religion survives Barth's massive critique, no matter how transformed.[31] Just as I noted in chapter three that Barth's critique of metaphorical Godtalk eventuated in the simple declaration, "God is God," here Barth's exaggerations are defused by another tautology, "the world is the world." And, I might add, religion is religion, for this passage shows that religion, too, is unchanged, unaffected by the cynical stare of the world. Ironically, the culmination of all of Barth's ranting against the church is that these three spheres, God, world, and church, lie so far apart that nothing at all can be said about their interconnection. No metaphor can grasp a similarity within such excessive otherness. Hyperbole has led directly — and ironically — to understatement.

Perhaps this ambiguity is inherent in the tropical gesture with which Barth swept through liberal theology. Hyperbole does rise above ordinary discourse, but it is forced to breathe very thin air. It is a momentary ascendancy, stretching language to the point where, if there is no snap, language will be stretched out of shape. Rene Girard has noted the risk of a complete critique: "A work that is against everything in general is really against nothing in particular and no one actually feels disturbed by it."[32] Hyperbole is a view from a peak which does not exist.

THE LIMITS OF EXTREMITY

This blast against the church is potentially self-defeating; it could lead to a religious cynicism, indifferent to the churches' plight, instead of empathic critique. Barth does push his language as close to cynicism as it can possibly go, without going over the edge. Only the vivid and terrible presence of God's absence keeps his discourse from sputtering into a vapid skepticism. Perhaps this is why Barth included a word of warning in the preface to the second edition

> to those who are babes in the study of theology, that is, to any undergraduates who may chance to read this book . . . Above all, do not be 'enthusiastic.' This is a critical work in the full and most serious meaning of the word 'critical' (R, 13).

Barth knew that the enthusiasm of hyperbole is contagious, and he wanted to emphasize its critical function. He repeats this warning a bit later, this time directed to his reviewers, asking them not to write about this book with "enthusiasm or with peevishness" (R, 14), realizing that his foreceful and relentless exaggerations could be both exciting and irritating, thus accounting for a wide variation in reader response. From the perspective of hyperbole, though, these concerns for his audience are marginal to Barth's project; like Nietzsche, Barth was writing to the reader of the future. At the end of his preface to the first edition, he makes this clear. After stating his hope that others will join his work, he writes, "However, should I be mistaken in this hope of a new, questioning investigation of the Biblical Message, well, this book must — wait. The Epistle to the Romans waits also" (R, 2). Some reviewers thought that this passage was especially arrogant; certainly the identification of his own situation, the delayed recognition of the prophet, with Paul's letter itself, is extravagant.

In later works, Barth was to modify and refine this critique. Instead of proclaiming the Wholly Other God, he would talk of the humanity of God, and instead of condemning the church, he would criticize one strand of theology, what is called natural theology, which tries to ground statements about God in observations about human nature and the structure of the world. As I will point out in chapter six, the later Barth thought theology should begin and end with God, not with humanity or the world, a rule he certainly violated in *Romans*. This later position was classically formulated in a controversial exchange with Emil Brunner first published in 1934.[33] It was provoked by an essay in which Brunner tries to establish some common ground between himself and Barth. Brunner argues that Barth's "genius of one-sidedness" (*NT*, 59)—which is one way to put the verticality of hyperbole—needs to be supplemented with a reappraisal of natural theology. Surely, he suggests, Barth goes too far in rejecting any "point of contact" *(Anknüpfungspunkt)* between revelation and human nature and in eradicating any sign of the image of God in fallen humanity. Brunner wants to argue that the differences between him and Barth are really due to different interests: Barth is concerned with special revelation, which is biblical and unique, while Brunner wants to focus on general revelation, which is the image of God's creativity in nature and the human conscience. Without general revelation, Brunner asks, how can the theologian demonstrate the relevance and importance of special revelation?

Barth's response, his famous "No!" is the best example of his masterful use of the genre of polemics. I have already suggested, in connection with Nietzsche, that this genre is essentially hyperbolic, and Barth's essay shows that *Romans* was not his last outburst in this trope. Indeed, Brunner anticipates Barth's response by complaining about the treatment he has already received:

> Barth appeared to me like a loyal soldier on sentry duty at night, who shoots every one who does not give him the password as he has been commanded, and who therefore from time to time also annihilates a good friend whose password he does not hear or misunderstands in his eagerness (*NT*, 16).

Barth goes too far, Brunner suggests, in his attempt to purify theology of its anthropological elements. For Barth, however, one can never go too far in clearing away the subjective tendencies of theology. Such tendencies, Barth claims, are signs of the anti-christ and if untreated, will become a disease, which will eventually kill the Evangelical Church (*NT,* 128).[34]

This weighty response actually begins with an ironic understatement: "I am by nature a gentle being and entirely averse to all unnecessary disputes" (*NT,* 67). This nearly comical opening is an attempt to defuse the vituperative attack that follows. Part of Barth's attack is justified by the way in which Brunner portrays Barth as only recently and unreasonably betraying a unified front; Barth claims that he has long been opposed to natural theology — and he regrets any contrary indications in *Romans*[35] — and that it is Brunner who is going a separate way. Brunner, therefore, is being unfair in implying that Barth is a "wicked man . . . lacking all communal spirit and stubbornly refusing to allow even the least correction" (*NT,* 72). Barth blames Brunner for the impossibility of conversation between these two different camps. For Barth, natural theology is an "abyss into which it is inadvisable to step if one does not want to fall" (*NT,* 75). He depicts natural theology and evangelical theology as two bitterly opposed enemies that cannot afford any compromise, and it is not easy, reading this text, to take this description figuratively. One can talk about either God or humanity; there are no degrees that gradually mark off the differences between these two discourses. Theology can only do one task or the other; otherwise, its divided loyalties will result in confused priorities. Indeed, "Real rejection of natural theology can come about only in the fear of God and hence only be a complete lack of interest in this matter" (*NT,* 76). Barth's own lack of indifference, though, makes this a rather strange comment.

Both authors misread each other in this exchange, although Brunner's careful attempt to formulate Barth's position is not equally reciprocated by Barth's caustic and harsh remarks. However, Barth does manage a penetrating insight into Brunner's program. He claims that its basis is a concern for pastoral care. He thus recognizes Brunner's desire to find a common ground on which communication between the church and the world can rest. Brunner is following one of the oldest rules in rhetoric: you must know your audience and meet it on its own level in order to persuade it to act or change beliefs. This is the same rule that guides his interpretation of Barth himself. Barth, in contrast, both practices and defends a rhetoric of confrontation: he does not want the theologian to identify with any human audience. As he puts it, the "what" of theology should decide the "how." Theology's loyalty to its own peculiar object, God, should dictate matters of communication and strategies of persuasion.

> In my experience the best way of dealing with 'unbelievers' and modern youth is not to try to bring out their 'capacity for revelation' but to treat them quietly, simply (remembering that Christ has died and risen also

for them), as if their rejection of 'Christianity' was not to be taken seriously. It is only then that they can understand you, since they really see you where you maintain that you are standing as an evangelical theologian: on the ground of justification by faith alone (*NT*, 127).

This is a fascinating passage; its implications for theological apologetics have never been fully explored. Apologetics, for Barth, has an essentially ironic structure: if the Christian tries to reach out to the non-Christian, nothing of any importance will have been exchanged; if the Christian turns away from the world and to the Word of God, then a real dialogue will have been initiated. Whatever the other implications of this position, Barth thinks that it allows him to avoid the problem of rhetoric. Indeed, he says that "my sermons reach and 'interest' my audience most . . . when I least rely on my ability to 'reach' people by my rhetoric, when on the contrary I *allow* my language to be formed and shaped and adapted as much as possible by what the text seems to be saying" (*NT*, 127). I will explore the implications of this remark in chapter six, where I will examine Barth's turn to realism as an attempt to evade his earlier — and quite successful — rhetoric. For now I merely want to note that "No!" is an odd text. At one and the same time, Barth advocates a theology that speaks only the objective Word of God and practices a hyperbolic discourse which extends beyond that Word in a startlingly vivid, even brutal — hardly indifferent — polemic. Perhaps this essay can be best understood as a transition from the use of hyperbole in polemics to a more objective, realistic discourse in which his earlier figures would have a limited role at best.

Later Barth does relax his hyperbole in order to restore a more rounded and comprehensive view of God and the church.[36] In a biographical reflection in the *Church Dogmatics*, for example, he could look back at his "reduction of God's eternity to the denominator of post-temporality, the eternally future,"[37] and the corresponding reduction of true religion to an invisible hope as unfortunate "concentrations." He thought that his early theology risked making God supratemporal, and that in God's place he had substituted a philosophical idea of crisis.[38] In a later volume of the *Church Dogmatics*, Barth acknowledges that his critique of the church was a necessary "counterblast to the general subjectivist trend of modern Protestantism," and he goes on to say that it is "obvious from the presence of the I-Psalms in the Bible, it can only be a relative and not an absolute criticism."[39] Yet, such relative criticism, undoubtedly more accurate, would not have had the same impact as Barth's exaggerations. Barth recognized this, because even with his misgivings he could say of *Romans*, "Well roared, lion!"[40]

Barth's lionlike roars were effective, perhaps too successful. In fact, I want to suggest that it is the forcefulness of these exaggerations that constitutes their problematic status in Barth's *Romans*. I argued earlier that the metaphor of crisis necessitated a hyperbolic discourse. Now I want to argue that hyperbole, too, has its limits. Barth's hyperbolic enunciation of God's otherness and denunciation of the church and religion make claims to absolute knowledge. Statements about God's hidden nature and about the absolute failure of the church are made, in fact, from an ultimate, that is God's, viewpoint. In the end, these prophetic statements function to expose and transform human sinfulness, and so they threaten to take the place of the Word of God itself. In other words, the more effective Barth's words were, the more closely he could be seen as speaking for and not just about the Word of God. Note this passage where he establishes a criterion of offense for theology, a criterion for which his exaggerations were especially suited:

> Do we desire a test as to whether we have spoken rightly of the mission
> of the Son? Well, if we have not offended every possible human method
> of investigation, and offended it at its most particularly tender spot, then
> assuredly we have spoken about—something else (*R,* 277–8).

Barth's hyperboles serve to make the judgments that should be reserved to God alone. Thus, even though they exploit the metaphor of crisis, they betray the crisis of metaphor. They claim too much, go too far, to be part of a discourse that is itself subject to the crisis. To counteract the strident claims of hyperbole, then, Barth is led inevitably to his most fundamental figuration, the trope that allows him to keep from taking his own hyperbole literally, namely, irony.

CHAPTER 5

WEB OF IRONY

THE VARIETIES OF IRONY

If this analysis were to end with the last chapter, the charge that Barth's prose is too arrogant, aggressive, and confrontational would be at least in part justified. Indeed, many commentators limit their observations about Barth's style to its volcanic, explosive, and destructive aspects.[1] *Romans* is supposed to be some sort of earthquake whose tremors can still be felt, but which should be avoided at all costs or at best admired from a safe distance. It is no wonder, then, that so many people have ambivalent attitudes about Barth; especially in an age of feminism, when readers are taught to be suspicious of thinkers who exemplify and valorize what are considered to be male traits, Barth can appear to represent all that is wrong with the *man* of the church: quick to draw lines and make judgments, reluctant to reach consensus and promote harmony, willing to stand alone, and always ready to turn the quest for truth into a struggle, even a fight. I want to argue that such a portrait of Barth in the *Romans* period, although it undoubtedly carries some insight, is really a caricature. I have already shown that Barth's use of the central theme of crisis makes some of his images and claims unstable and undecidable, and in my discussion of hyperbole I have shown that Barth's prose often drifts into understatement and tautology in order to counter its own thrust. Now I want to make it clear that Barth's final figuration is in fact irony, which allows him to put into question his entire enterprise. As Barth himself puts it, theology should be both an exclamation point and a question mark (*RF,* 531). The most apt image of *Romans*, then, is not a volcano or an earthquake but a bomb—which explodes in the very hands of the person who lights the fuse.

In an ironic statement, the dictionaries tell us, something is said when its opposite is meant, and in an ironic action the result is the opposite of the intent. Or in Kenneth Burke's more elegant formula, what goes forth as A returns as non-A.[2] Take for an example, "Hail, King of the Jews!" which the

Gospel of Mark reports as a mockery of Jesus Christ. The crowd is being ironic because it really thinks that Jesus is the opposite of a king: he is a criminal, being punished for his pretensions. However, there is another level of irony here: from Mark's perspective what was intended as sarcasm is actually literally true, so that the real victims of this irony are those who reject Jesus Christ. One could go even further and say that the basis for these reversals is, from the Christian perspective, an even greater irony: that God has chosen the form of a suffering and humble person for God's self-revelation. As this example shows, irony, once located, has a tendency to multiply. This example should also show that the definitions I have offered are themselves too simple to be of much use: irony can consist of contrast, incongruity, even plain discrepancy as well as contradiction. This has led one ironologist, D. C. Muecke, to suggest, "Its forms and functions are so diverse as to seem scarcely amenable to a single definition."[3] Wayne Booth has echoed this claim: "There is no agreement among critics about what irony is, and many would hold to the romantic claim ... that its very spirit and value are violated by the effort to be clear about it."[4]

What makes irony so difficult to discuss? The problem is that irony does not just denote a figure of speech; it can also represent an attitude, a philosophy, a general way of life. This has been true of irony from its very beginning: it is impossible to imagine Socrates, both his philosophy and his personality, without his irony. Irony allows him to appear weak and foolish, a modest seeker of wisdom, who in the end dramatically exposes the ignorance of his opponents. In Voltaire and Swift irony merges with satire as it is directed against the complacencies and superstitions of their times. With Hegel, irony becomes a philosophical category, implying an infinite negativity,[5] and with Schlegel and the German Romantics, irony expresses the paradoxical nature that lies at the heart of reality. In our own day Cleanth Brooks can suggest that all good poetry is ironic,[6] Umberto Eco has recently defined postmodernism in terms of irony,[7] and Richard Rorty equates irony with philosophical relativism.[8] Irony has thus grown from a literary quality to a description of art, reality or the modern world. Indeed, any event or text can be interpreted ironically, so it is hard to know where to stop. Yet, precisely because it means so many different things, it runs the danger of meaning nothing at all.

As Wayne Booth's comment indicates, the conceptual fogginess surrounding irony can be considered one of its strengths. It is a many-edged tool: it can be a weapon in a satirical attack or it can conceal a sudden retreat. It can unmask ignorance and innocence, or it can certify the superiority of a higher vantage point. It can turn the world upside down, or ironists can turn it against themselves in displays of genuine or feigned humility.

There seems to be no limit to its uses. Muecke has compiled a partial cata-
logue of its various permutations over the centuries: tragic irony, comic
irony, irony of manner, irony of situation, philosophical irony, practical
irony, dramatic irony, verbal irony, double irony, rhetorical irony, self-irony,
Socratic irony, Romantic irony, cosmic irony, sentimental irony, irony of
fate, irony of chance, irony of character, and the list could go on. In terms of
genre it has been closely connected to satire, the comic, the grotesque, the
humorous, and the absurd. It gains these effects by its ability to turn reality
against appearance. In doing this it displays similarities to jokes: mistaking
irony for literal speech is like listening to a joke with a straight face, and it is
as difficult to explain an irony as it is to explain a joke. You either get it or
you don't.

Irony is the only trope that has received as much attention as metaphor, and it is not surprising that it is the contemporary trope of choice. Perhaps its capacity to see through the appearances of things—while metaphor
tries to extend one's vision of reality by arranging elements in new ways—
makes it especially suitable to modern sensibilities. Many people today have
a view of the world as fragmented, unstable, ambiguous and unfriendly;
therefore, it is only natural that irony has come to dominate the arts. Irony
is able to discern the tangle of contradiction that hangs behind appearances,
and it is always ready to reverse the direction of the flow of things. It creates
a new reality, which can only be imaginatively construed and which lies at
odd angles to what people ordinarily accept as true. For Thomas Mann, one
of the most consistently ironic writers, this trope was the only way to make
sense of the world while maintaining one's composure and perspective:
"Irony and radicalism—this is an alternative and an Either-Or. An intelli-
gent man has the choice (if he has it) to be either ironical or radical. There
is, in all decency, no third possibility."[9] Mann's commitment to irony might
have been distinctive in his time, but today irony is a prerequisite for any
entry into the cultural realm. In fact, Muecke can say as an aside that,
"Nowadays only popular literature is predominantly non-ironical" (CI, 10).

Of course, for such an important and complex concept, which ranges
across so many fields, many definitions have been presented. A representative example comes from John Searle:

> Stated very crudely, the mechanism by which irony works is that the ut-
> terance, if taken literally, is obviously inappropriate to the situation.
> Since it is grossly inappropriate, the hearer is compelled to reinterpret
> it in such a way as to render it appropriate, and the most natural way to
> interpret it is as meaning the opposite of its literal form.[10]

The problem with this definition, besides its limitation of irony to contradiction, is that it reduces this trope to its effect. Irony should be so obvious that it results in a corrective judgment. But what about ironies that are subtle and complex, which cannot be immediately translated into their opposite meaning? Some ironies have a purely negative effect, so that their opposite meaning would be hard to specify. And what about ironies that are not meant to be understood by everyone? After all, some ironies, like some jokes, are about a person or group of people, and so presuppose a victim who will not be able to understand the ironic intent. Searle's definition, although clear and concise, applies only to the simplest of ironies, like the response of a lazy person asked to take part in a difficult project, "Oh sure, I'd be glad to help!"

A better attempt at a definition, indeed one of the best surveys of the whole scope of irony, can be found in Muecke's work. He argues that there are two basic kinds of irony, situational, in which an event or action is called ironic, and verbal, which involves a speaker or writer saying something in an ironic way. In an ironic situation the outcome of an event or action does not merely contradict the expected result; it is such that it reveals the true meaning of the event or action. A person expecting a raise, for example, actually receives a demotion, and so his whole career is put into a different, perhaps truer, perspective. In ironic actions, then, people get what they no longer desire, or people meet what they set out to avoid. This kind of irony has long been used in theater, in both tragedy and comedy, although it was not named as such until the eighteenth century. It is not difficult to see that with one step all of life, not just specific situations, can be understood as ironic. Muecke calls this world or general irony, and Wayne Booth calls it unstable irony. This irony is not meant to be corrective; unlike simple or stable irony, its meaning cannot be reconstructed by appeals to the context of the utterance and the author's real intention. In general or unstable irony, life is at odds with itself, revealing fundamental and irremediable contradictions. Perhaps the most interesting feature of this irony is that the ironist is both the detached observer and a fellow victim.

Muecke and Booth both offer several examples of the kinds of predicaments general or unstable irony depicts. The world could be seen as open, infinite, and dynamic, and yet human knowledge could be understood as necessarily limited, unable to grasp reality. Human power could be seen as apprehending the world, but the world is understood as chaotic and absurd. Human longings could be represented as both unlimited and insatiable, thus binding humanity to an endless cycle of thwarted desires. The future could be envisioned as something we both must and must not trust. In any case, general irony both unmasks these deep contradictions and enables the ironist to live with them; it does not resolve the conflicts, but it can encompass these paradoxes in a ceaseless movement of transcending reflections. The question immediately arises, however, if irony is enough. Can the continual recognition of the endless irony of things serve as the basis for a healthy, happy existence? What kind of life would this be? Booth at least believes that at the heart of all infinitely negative ironies lies an affirmation, even if it is only an affirmation of nothingness.

Verbal irony is usually a much simpler affair. Booth suggests that it can be reconstructed by looking for clues from the author. Muecke, on the other hand, argues that it displays a basic structure: in verbal irony, he observes, there are two levels, that of the victim and that of the observer, and there exists an opposition or tension between these two levels. For example, what the victim thinks or does is contradicted by what the observer knows. The victim, it is important to note, is characterized by an element of innocence or ignorance. Often the victim is confidently unaware of the level of the observer. In what Muecke calls self-irony, there is a splitting of the ironist's ego and hence an ability to present oneself as both innocent and as overcoming that innocence. Although Muecke is aware that not all irony involves an obvious victim, he suggests that it is useful to think in these terms. To ironize something is to place it in a context that will invalidate or correct it; inside that context there is, indeed, a victim who does not realize the invalidity of a belief or action or situation.

The victim, however, is not necessarily directly attacked, as in sarcasm. Irony is more indirect than sarcasm because ironists pretend to be unaware of their true intentions. This gives irony its humorous form, and invites the listener or reader to try to discern the speaker's true meaning. The result, however, is the same as satire: confident innocence and pretentious ignorance are unmasked. "For one of the odd things about irony is that it regards assumptions as presumptions and therefore innocence as guilt. Simple ignorance is safe from irony, but ignorance compounded with the least degree of confidence counts as intellectual hubris and is a punishable offence" (CI, 30). To the extent that everyone makes confident assertions, which are not completely protected and defended by a rational examination of all of the alternatives, everyone is a potential victim of irony. "The only shield against irony, therefore, is absolute circumspection, a shield no man can lift" (CI, 31).

Does this give the ironist an unfair advantage? Certainly the ironist often displays a dispassionate and urbane manner. Even in general or world irony the ironist can seem detached, an unobserved observer, practicing an almost scientific ability to pass judgment on situations. This gives ironists their freedom and joy: "To see someone as a victim of irony is to see him as

being, relative to oneself, still submerged in unreflective subjectivity'' (*CI*,
219). Many writers, however, have noted the other side of this objectivity,
that the ironist risks appearing arrogant and conceited, aloof and, possibly,
alone. Moreover, Muecke points out that ironists are also vulnerable to the
very force they unleash: knowledge of the situation is the ironist's only advantage, yet by focusing on the victim, the position of the ironist is exposed
to an ironic attack from behind. Mark's ironic reporting of ''Hail, King of
the Jews!'' for example, can be turned against him; if Jesus were just a fanatic visionary, then Mark's attempt to be ironic would really show him to
be deluded instead. Such reversals of reversals make irony an enchanting
maze to some and a chaotic nightmare to others. Moralists in particular have
been troubled by irony; note Jacques Barzun's warning, ''To admire nothing at all, for fear of being duped, is a progressive disease of the spirit''
(*CI*, 241). Muecke, however, argues that much of the discussion of general
irony exaggerates the significance of this trope. He modestly suggests that
the virtue of irony is mental alertness and agility. Likewise, Wayne Booth
has argued that irony only appears elitist. It actually invites everyone to join
in the deceit, thus forming a community of those who are ''in the know.''
Irony creates a solidarity because the author has revealed a secret or hidden
perspective. ''Often the predominant emotion when reading stable ironies is
that of joining, of finding and communing which kindred spirits'' (*RI*, 28).

   This discussion has been necessary because, I will argue, Barth used
many different kinds of irony. Indeed, his theology runs the whole range of
irony, from simple ironic comments to an ironic conception of God and the
church and, finally, an ironic understanding of theology which can only be
called, in Booth's sense of the term, unstable. This contention should not be
surprising; any theologian who stresses God's hiddenness is inevitably
lured into a web of ironies. Note this reflection from Augustine:

> Have we spoken or announced anything worthy of God? Rather I feel
> that I have done nothing but wish to speak: if I have spoken, I have not
> said what I wished to say. Whence do I know this, except because God
> is ineffable? If what I said were ineffable, it would not be said. And for
> this reason God should not be said to be ineffable, for when this is said
> something is said. And a contradiction in terms is created, since if that
> is ineffable which cannot be spoken, then that is not ineffable which can
> be called ineffable.[11]

This is a fascinating and contorted passage. Augustine admits that the result
of his theology has not been the meaning he intended. This irony is itself the
product of a deeper paradox: to name God as ineffable is to say that which

cannot be said. Augustine decides that this contradiction must be passed over in silence, and yet, ironically, God asks that people continue to name and praise the divine. Christians are expected to do what they cannot do, and Augustine concludes, somewhat hastily, that this must be for human, not divine, benefit.

Barth's theology is located in a similar bind. Hyperbole has named God as unknowable and the church as impossible. Irony serves to counter the inability of theology; it allows theology both to speak and not speak about a reality that it does not know. It is a corrective to Barth's hyperbole, but not in Marvick's sense. Irony does qualify and modify hyperbole, but in a positive not a negative way, serving to create possibilities where hyperbole left only negations. Irony allows Barth to write theology in spite of his hyperbolic denunciations. Barth has reversed, therefore, the relationship between these two tropes as outlined by Marvick. Irony gives Barth, as with Mann, the composure and perspective that hyperbole — and the metaphor of crisis — render impossible. However, in the final analysis irony, too, is a trope that cannot do what it sets out to accomplish: it turns against itself and leaves only a trail of ambiguity. Irony thus closes the circle of Barth's unique style.

The circle, once drawn, never meets itself in a spiral of incompletion. As Barth himself says, "The point from which the circle is seen to be closed cannot be situated within the circle" (R, 271). Barth's prose can venture no closure. This can be seen from a survey of Barth's entire tropical strategy. Wayne Booth has argued that metaphor is an additive trope while irony is subtractive, and continuing these mathematical metaphors, I would want to add that hyperbole, which Booth does not mention, is a multiplier. In Barth, metaphor adds up the crisis without limit and hyperbole multiplies its impact, while irony subtracts any permanent damage. But what does irony subtract? Does it simply eliminate everything that has gone before it? This was the picture White left us: irony as the last trope negates all others. However, there is another way of looking at the relationships among these tropes: metaphor synthesizes, hyperbole intensifies, and irony dissolves, or better, suspends.[12] For Barth, the synthesis of the metaphor of crisis never quite congeals, the intensity of hyperbole threatens to explode, and the dissolution of irony is itself suspended. Irony leaves theology a mixture of elements, which cannot be passed into solution. Theology keeps decomposing, but it never disappears. This is meant to be difficult to understand: theology repeats the tensions and anxieties that plague the Christian's relationship to God. It puts itself into question, just as the individual believer must doubt the efficacy of belief. Perhaps this would be easier to explain if I put Barth in a rhetorical context. Just as Nietzsche helped to frame Barth's hyperbole, I want to use Kierkegaard to situate and clarify Barth's irony, for Kierkegaard, too, uses irony to keep theology questioning its own answers.

THE IRONOLOGY OF KIERKEGAARD

Kierkegaard's connection to Barth has been discussed from the very beginning of Barth's revolutionary theology. Kierkegaard has been hailed as a herald of crisis theology, and Barth himself has contributed to this reading of Kierkegaard, as I noted in chapter three. The Danish writer, this argument goes, developed a theology of contradiction—the infinite distance between God and humanity results in crisis and necessitates an existential decision—in opposition to Hegel's theology of identity, where in the realm of thought or spirit God and the world coexist in an evolving but complete harmony. However, recently there has been a growing attempt to do justice to the literary and rhetorical aspects of Kierkegaard's authorship, an endeavor that parallels current Nietzsche scholarship. The title of the best work of this new kind of criticism, *Kierkegaard: A Kind of Poet,* by Louis Mackey, indicates the intentions of this position: Kierkegaard's use of pseudonyms means that his writings cannot be reduced to some sort of system. The pseudonyms are not mere names, meant to hide the real identity of the author; instead they are whole persons, imaginative constructions. Kierkegaard created fictitious worlds in order to present his views indirectly, so that he is best studied with the tools of literary criticism. Thus Mackey can claim that, "His writing, even the most ostensibly theoretical, is not syllogistic but figural."[13] This Kierkegaard, I want to argue, serves as the true precedent for Barth's theology.

One explanation of Kierkegaard's use of pseudonyms can be found in his *The Point of View for My Work as an Author: A Report to History.*[14] Here Kierkegaard argues that the whole course of his work has been religious from the very beginning, and most discussions of this text focus on the trustworthiness of that claim. Walter Lowrie, for example, suggests that it "falls short of being a biography" (*PV,* xxiii), explaining that "here he is solely intent upon emphasizing the religious categories (*PV,* xxiv). I do not intend to enter this complicated biographical debate; what I find most interesting in this book is something frequently overlooked, its reflections on rhetoric. Kierkegaard does not explain his authorship only according to a religious orientation. He also traces his indirect discourse to a tropical matrix. His main concern, he claims, is the problem of becoming a Christian. This is a problem because most people think they are Christians simply because they live in a society that considers itself Christian. Thus, most people count

themselves Christians by a kind of argument of association. For Kierkegaard, this is a prodigious illusion, a tremendous and frightful confusion.
How, then, can he set out to talk about Christian training? Kierkegaard's answer to this question has to do not only with irony, but also—and this makes
it especially valuable for my purposes—with hyperbole.

In an age when so many people think that they are such good Christians that they do not need to think about Christianity any more, religious
communication becomes a difficult matter. How can Kierkegaard communicate the true seriousness, perhaps even impossibility, of becoming a
Christian? Could he simply propose to reintroduce Christianity into ...
Christendom? Kierkegaard considers, and rejects, this strategy, which he
understands as a species of hyperbole: "Once in a while there appears a religious enthusiast: he storms against Christendom, he vociferates and
makes a loud noise, denouncing almost all as not being Christians—and accomplishes nothing" (PV, 24). Such an enthusiast will not succeed in stirring
Christians form their slumber; in fact, she or he will be called "a fanatic, his
Christianity an exaggeration—in the end he remains the only one, or one of
the few, who is not seriously a Christian (for exaggeration is surely a lack of
seriousness), whereas the others are all serious Christians" (PV, 24). Ironically, the exaggerator will not be taken seriously; extremity will beget only
extremity. Members of Christendom will harden their attitudes and turn
away, all the more convinced that they are in the right. As Kierkegaard explains, an illusion is not the same as ignorance; the latter can be corrected
with the communication of the lacking information. An illusion is not so easily dispelled. "A direct attack only strengthens a person in his illusion, and
at the same time embitters him" (PV, 25). An illusion must be handled
gently, indirectly; "If anything prompts the prospective captive to set his
will in opposition, all is lost" (PV, 25). What is needed is a more ambiguous
and duplicitous—an ironic—approach.

This rejection of hyperbole almost sounds like a warning against
Barth. It is also a kind of anticipation of Kierkegaard's own later attack on
the church, a hyperbolic discourse whose similarities with Barth make it
worthy of examination. Kierkegaard's blast against the church took place at
the end of his life, in 1854 and 1855, and it was nothing but exaggerated. Walter Lowrie realizes this, commenting with what is surely understatement
that, "One-sidedness, he thought, and even a dose of exaggeration was necessary for the effect he desired to produce."[15] Lowrie calls this last stage of
Kierkegaard's career an explosion. In newspaper articles and pamphlets
Kierkegaard abandons the poetic indirectness that had marked his previous
work. The result is an agitation, which is too direct and serious to be called
satire. It is, Lowrie notes, extravagant; "And yet I dare not denounce it as

untrue merely because it asserts something more than the truth.''[16] I have already noted in chapter three that Barth accepts Kierkegaard's exclamations as reasonable and agreeable (see *R*, 392), and much of Kierkegaard's discourse resonates in Barth's. Both writers display an urgency and anxiety and unleash a barrage of criticism that cannot be easily summarized or explained.

Although Kierkegaard names two individuals for particular incrimination, his one-time advisor and then-deceased Bishop Mynster and the Hegelian Professor and later Bishop Martensen, he is really reacting against two classes rather than two specific persons. Like Nietzsche, he did not want to attack Christianity at its weakest points, but at its strongest, and like both Nietzsche and Barth, he was a master of polemical writing. These two individuals represented the best aspects of the Established Church, but for Kierkegaard, all priests and professors (that is, theologians) have betrayed the original impulse and the paradoxical essence of Christianity. Christendom, in fact, is a conspiracy against the Christianity of the New Testament: by trying to extend Christianity into the world as a political and moral power and a form of social organization, it has betrayed the intensity of the Christian message. Many people thought these charges, especially when directed against Mynster and Martensen, were monstrously unfair. For Kierkegaard —who even near the end of his life would have become a minister if he had been able—being a Christian had to mean following Jesus Christ, not conforming oneself to some general idea of what Christianity might mean.

Kierkegaard knew his diatribes were extreme and excessive; in them his usual ability to see every side of every situation comes to an end. He himself once referred to his final discharge as the ''irrational method,''[17] but there was more reason to this discourse than that remark might imply. Although his contemporaries thought that Kierkegaard was being too direct, too personal, even this discourse, I would like to suggest, is indirect, thus consistent with his previous work.[18] His contemporaries were confused by the attack, not knowing how to read it. People were unsure of Kierkegaard's commitment to Christianity: was he attacking it from within or from without? Kierkegaard knew that the purest impact of hyperbole could only be achieved if his broadsides were left unqualified, unexplained. He wanted to disorient his readers, to leave them without their usual props of ready answers and easy rationalizations. Hyperbole, then, was his last pseudonym, and like every good trope, it had to stand on its own.

> If I dared to accompany my action with a commentary, throwing light upon the ingenious purposefulness of the whole, I should have a brilliant success — but totally fail to accomplish my task. One would get no

impression, no sting, of the decisive character of the action, but would be enchanted by the interesting character of the reflection by which the action was supported.[19]

On his deathbed he was enjoined by Pastor Boesen, a longtime friend, to "alter his statements because they did not correspond to reality." Kierkegaard patiently replied,

> It must be thus, otherwise it cannot accomplish the purpose. It is clear enough to me that when a bomb explodes it must be thus! Do you mean to say that I should tone it down, first speak to produce an awakening, and then to put people at their ease? Why will you disturb me in this way?[20]

So Kierkegaard, too, had his bomb, and it explodes in much the same way as Barth's. What is more difficult to show is that Kierkegaard's irony also serves as a rhetorical precedent for Barth. To make that argument I need to return to the *Point of View*, where I left Kierkegaard after he had rejected the path of hyperbole. In this book he claims that the illusion of Christendom can be confronted "not by one who vociferously proclaims himself as extraodinary Christian, but by one who, better instructed, is ready to declare that he is not a Christian at all" (*PV*, 24). Kierkegaard claims that this is a truly Christian invention of discourse: the writer practices self-denial and makes all the effort, without condemnation or denunciation, in order to bring the other person to the truth. Whether this method is Christian is a matter for debate; its rhetorical structure, however, is easy to identify: assume the opposite of what you want to prove, in order to show that what people say is not what they really mean. Thus irony, not hyperbole, must be the trope of Christian apologetics. The religious writer must pretend to be what the alleged Christian really is, that is, an aesthetic. Once this common ground is established, then the writer can introduce true religion into the discussion, thus reversing roles: Christendom is shown to be un-Christian, while the aesthetic writer is revealed as a serious Christian. Kierkegaard describes his method as humble, loving, gentle, not coercive, but it is really just as compelling and aggressive, let alone deceitful, as the hyperbolic form, which he later adopted.

Deception is an ugly thing, Kierkegaard admits, but he does it for the sake of truth, and so it is, he thinks, acceptable — if not in the eyes of humanity, then at least in the eyes of God. The risk this irony runs, of course, is that it will be taken literally; that is, the aesthetic mask of the religious writer will be perceived as a face and not a disguise at all. That this happened to Kierkegaard gives him great pleasure; he relishes the irony that the people of Copenhagen thought he was an idler, a frivolous and perhaps brilliant man who "represented a worldly irony" (*PV,* 50). The Danes did not know that Kierkegaard's irony was actually of the utmost seriousness, and he admits that he drew "a certain sort of satisfaction in this life, in this inverse deception . . . " (*PV,* 52). As a great ironist, Kierkegaard could take his own failure ironically. Indeed, Kierkegaard calls himself "the Magister of Irony" (*PV,* 57 and 58), and he hints that this is why his books are often dedicated to The Individual: "Irony tends essentially towards one person at its limit" (*PV,* 55). Here Kierkegaard is playing on the alleged elitism of this trope. He even suggests that he is "like a spy in a higher service, the service of the idea" (*PV,* 87). There is no other way: in a mediocre age, when all great truths have been trivialized, "in the eyes of the world the truth is a ludicrous exaggeration" (*PV,* 88). The truth, then, both cannot be and must be spoken, or in other words, it can only be spoken ironically.

It should not be surprising that Kierkegaard was a master of irony. His second book, *The Concept of Irony,*[21] which was the publication of his masters of arts thesis submitted in 1841, is still considered one of the most profound works on this trope in any language. Not even mentioned in *The Point of View,* it has been variously interpreted over the years: first considered a youthful effort not worthy of serious attention; then examined as evidence that the young Kierkegaard was still captivated by Hegel, so that it should not be included among a list of Kierkegaard's original productions; often read for its brilliant comments on irony, which are usually taken out of context; now some scholars have suggested that it is itself an ironic work, an observation that can either increase its value or make it even less trustworthy.[22] Booth and Muecke both agree that it is one of the boldest and most comprehensive statements on both the power and the corruptive effect of this trope, and so for my purposes it can help to put Barth's irony in context. The outline of Kierkegaard's position can be readily summarized: irony is not a matter of words or situations; it marks the beginning of subjectivity, the birth of the personal life. But it is also something that must be overcome if true personhood is to be achieved.

The first part of this work focuses on Socrates because he introduced the concept of irony into the world. Kierkegaard argues that Socrates was not like a philosopher lecturing on his own views, presenting a body of beliefs or propositions. Instead, Socrates meant something other than what he said. The essence and the appearance of his thought were not in harmony, "for the outer was in opposition to the inner, and only through this refracted angle is he to be apprehended" (*KCI,* 50). Socratic irony means, therefore, that Socrates did not have a positive philosophical position of his own; he was not really ignorant, but he was not knowledgeable either — he was ironic. In fact, Kierkegaard likes Aristophanes' satirical portrait of Socrates better than Plato's or Hegel's, both of which tried to make Socrates into a serious and constructive thinker. Socratic irony, according to Kierkegaard, is directed against everything; it is not an instrument that he employed in the service of an idea, as Hegel suggests. This gives Socrates an infinite freedom, but it also effectively alienates him from the whole world; Kierkegaard is thus not surprised that the Athenian government pressed charges against him. Like many good ironists, Socrates did not know when to stop: unlike scepticism, which always really believes in something, irony, "constantly makes the tantalizing attempt first to devour everything in sight, then to devour itself too, or, as in the case of the old witch, her own stomach" (*KCI*, 92).

The second part of this book maps the development of post-Socratic irony, but it also extends the implications of this portrait of Socrates. Kierkegaard argues that irony is a dangerous trap. The ironist takes pleasure in appearing to be ensnared by the same prejudices that imprison the ironist's victim. Irony thus preys on weakness and innocence; it tries to get the world to reveal itself, without saying anything about its own self. The result is that irony "directs itself not against this or that particular existence but against the whole given actuality of a certain time and situation" (*KCI*, 271). Irony, then, and here Kierkegaard is borrowing from Hegel, is the "infinite absolute negativity." Irony's only purpose is more irony; it never tries to take a position or reaches any conclusions, and thus Kierkegaard can say that it is always only beginning. To some extent, Kierkegaard wants to argue, this is a positive and necessary move: "when subjectivity asserts itself, irony appears" (*KCI*, 280). Irony is in fact the furthest reach of subjective freedom. Irony's ability to turn against everything, however, inevitably turns against the ironist, too; it is a trap, which can shut on the hunter as well as the victim. "The more vain everything becomes, so much the lighter, more vacuous, more evanescent becomes subjectivity" (*KCI*, 275). The ironist is never constrained by reality because a phenomenon always conceals its opposite. Reality is made empty: the ironist destroys it by turning it against itself and leaves nothing in its place.

The result is estrangement and alienation not only from the world but also from the ironist's own self because ironists are not bound to what they say. Kierkegaard's main target in these remarks is Schlegel, whom he mistakenly thinks defends a view of irony as totally destructive.[23] The justice of his reading of Schlegel can be bracketed because his reading of irony is very clear. What is particularly troubling is that the ironist becomes removed from history, trying to live in an eternal moment of freeplay and manipulation; "all historical actuality was negated to make room for a self-created actuality" (*KCI*, 292). Irony is free from all obligation and responsibility; in a word, it knows nothing of ethics. It is purely poetic; all things are possible for its boundless creativity. Yet its limits are obvious: the ironist, finally, loses all sense of continuity, and so in addition to the world the self too is lost. "With this he wholly lapses under the sway of his moods and feelings. His life is sheer emotion" (*KCI*, 301). The ironist's eternity is void of any content: "he is a ball for the irony of the world to sport with" (*KCI*, 301). Boredom is the ironist's only continuity, and freedom is really a mask, for the ironist is bound to the terrible law of irony itself.

The truth of irony, Kierkegaard concludes in this work, can only come from irony as a mastered moment. This is the most Hegelian part of Kierkegaard's discussion. When irony is mastered, phenomenon and essence or idea are equated. Reality is what it appears to be, and the self must become responsive to as well as creative of reality. To become a true individual, then, to live in history with obligations and to act with commitment, irony must be overcome; it can then be used by the self without fear that it will rule the self. Irony should be only the beginning of subjectivity; otherwise it will also be its end. Unfortunately, Kierkegaard's remarks here are brief and rather vague. How can such an overwhelmingly negative trope ever be mastered? What about the dangers of trying to recruit such a powerful tool for the solidification of the self? With these questions this early work must be left behind and the world of the pseudonymous writings entered, but they are so ambiguous and ironic that there are no easy answers there as to what irony is and how it should be overcome.

The pseudonymous works are ironical because in them Kierkegaard creates fictitious characters who say things which he, Kierkegaard, does not really mean. This has given scholarship the complex and seemingly endless task of trying to figure out what Kierkegaard himself really meant. These works are also ironic on another level; as Louis Mackey has argued, Kierkegaard conceives of the aesthetic type of person as an ironist. This is clear in the first volume of *Either/Or,* where the aesthetic stage of existence is not described but portrayed through a series of papers from a person labeled "A."[24] The aesthetic person thinks that everything is possible, but he cannot make commitments or take responsibility for life. The aesthetic person above all wants freedom, but in the pursuit of pleasure the aestheticist becomes a victim of the frantic efforts necessary to repel boredom. This can be seen in Kierkegaard's humorous depiction of the rotation method as a means for maximizing pleasure while minimizing both boredom and responsibility. In the end, as with the diary of the seducer, the aestheticist becomes completely estranged from other people, able only to manipulate the appearances of things. By trying to live a life of immediacy, the aestheticist ironically falls into the trap of reflection, always thinking about how to withstand boredom, and so carries out what can only be called an abstract existence.

How Kierkegaard advances beyond the ironical in his own writings — how and to what extent the ethical and then the religious stages of existence transform and overcome the ironic — cannot be my concern here. For my purposes, Kierkegaard has developed one of the most fascinating positions on irony, which, although intrinsically interesting for its contributions to the discussion of this trope, also serves to provide a framework for understanding Barth. This is especially true because the ironic also pervades Kierkegaard's explicit discussions about theology. I will offer only one example. In the *Concluding Unscientific Postscript,* which *The Point of View* terms the turning point of Kierkegaard's authorship due to its focus on the problem of becoming a Christian, Johannes Climacus, the narrator, sets out to understand Christianity. It is an ironic journey, and in a footnote Kierkegaard reveals his intentions:

> Because everybody knows it, the Christian truth has gradually become a triviality, of which it is difficult to secure a primitive impression. This being the case, the art of communication at last becomes the art of taking away, of luring something away from someone. This seems very strange and ironical, and yet I believe that I have succeeded in expressing precisely what I mean. When a man has his mouth so full of food that he is prevented from eating, and is like to starve in consequence, does giving him food consist in stuffing still more of it in his mouth, or does it consist in taking some of it away, so that he can begin to eat?[25]

In his attempt to subtract from the accepted truths about Christianity, Kierkegaard leads Climacus along a tortuous path of investigation. After deciding that Christianity teaches the subjectivity of truth, Climacus inquires into the possibility of subjectively appropriating the Christian faith. Before he can reach any conclusions, however, he takes — or rather, imagines — a detour through Deer Park, a sidestep I want to follow briefly.

This detour through Deer Park takes many pages to describe, and the reader must be very patient because the trip really never takes place but itself leads to a maze of excursions on a wide range of topics. Near the beginning of this story (for lack of a better term), Climacus remarks, "Everything dissolves itself into contradiction," and the reader should be grateful for the warning.[26] Climacus has just heard in a sermon that people are nothing in themselves but must always depend on God alone. He thinks that he under-

stands what this means, but he is not sure how such a belief could be practiced. So he sends out a spy to find out if people really are dependent on God,
and the results are predictably absurd: God is nowhere to be found. Climacus then tries a thought experiment: suppose one wanted to visit Deer Park
while maintaining an absolute relationship to the absolute. Can the religious
person make this journey? After all, if the religious life is completely inward,
it should appear to be nothing special in its external manifestation, so that
such a trip would be quite simple. Unfortunately, the more Climacus thinks
about it, the more confusing the possibility becomes. How can the infinite
be held together with the finite during a brief pleasure trip? This question is
never really answered, just as the trip to Deer Park is never really made. If
there is a moral to this story, it seems to be that, "It is easy enough to talk
about it, to do it is something else."[27] Dialectical deliberation can never resolve itself into action; and yet, such deliberation seems unavoidable. The
story of Deer Park, the attempt to put the act of faith into a narrative form,
is a story that has no development and no resolution, a story that cannot
really be told but once begun can hardly end.

Theology is thus ironically conceived; what it sets out to do it only distorts and delays. Yet there seems to be no escape from theology, just as there
is no end to the telling of the trip to Deer Park. Barth, too, I want to argue,
envisions theology ironically. A reading of Barth can actually benefit from
all of Kierkegaard's ironies: the relationship between irony and hyperbole,
the reflection on the limits of irony and its destructive consequences, the acknowledgement of the need to speak in an ironic voice, and the necessity of
thinking of theology as a species of irony. Barth uses both verbal and situational irony, and his irony ranges from stable to unstable. His irony has victims, who sometimes include himself. It will be helpful, then, to keep this
whole discussion in mind as I look at Barth's distinctive ironic style. What
I am hoping is that just as an interpretation of Nietzsche's rhetoric helped to
put Barth in a new light, so this reading of Kierkegaard's figures will be an
impetus to a new understanding of both their relationship and Barth's own
theological voice.

THE IRONY OF THEOLOGY

Barth often displayed an ironical attitude toward his own theology.
This is probably surprising to those who think of him as overly forceful and
ever confident. The fact is that Barth could take himself less seriously than
those who either praised or denounced him. Hans Frei explains this in psychological terms:

His protective device against his own, as well as others', pretensions
was frequent ironization, self-ironization and self-needling, sometimes
in mock-solemn, mock-elevated language ... People often try to exor-
cise their all too real demons by mocking them either in deliberate exaggeration or in transparently tongue-in-cheek denial.[28]

For an example of this from *Romans,* note the passage where he talks
about the flourishing business of sin creating not only frivolous literature,
but especially "the publication of books such as the one I am now writing"
(*R,* 174). In describing the impact of the *Romans* commentary, he compared
himself to someone groping up the dark stairs of a church tower, thinking he
is holding the handrail but instead finding that he is gripping the bell rope and
incredibly enough the great bell is ringing away.[29] This attitude is echoed in
an autobiographical reflection: "I did not know then what I was undertak-
ing, and now that I know this sphinx [theology] more closely, I do not think
that today I would have the courage to take the same step."[30] These ironical
comments about *Romans* should not be taken literally; Barth was certainly
not a theological innocent during that period, and he was aware that *Romans*
would create a storm of controversy, although how great a storm nobody
could have foreseen.

What these examples do indicate is that irony could serve several purposes for Barth: it could put his own work in perspective, serve as a humorous interlude to serious and weighty claims, show that Barth is more humble
than one might think, and add to the myth that *Romans* came out of nowhere, without any precedent, and took everybody, including the author, by
surprise. The result was that Barth could appear to be detached and free
even from his own theology, the essential characteristics of the ironist. For
example, he writes in the preface to the second edition, "I am in no way
bound to my book and to my theology" (*R,* 6), trying to preempt those who
would charge him with fanatic enthusiasm. His theology was an attempt to
overturn all other theologies; therefore, it certainly should not have been
well received, so Barth could say of his new fame that *Romans* "has gained
the applause by which it is condemned" (*R,* 22). Ironically, the revolutionary was accepted (by some) as a fine theologian, so something must have
gone wrong! These many uses of what Muecke would call verbal irony
should qualify Barth as a dedicated ironist. However, I want to argue that
irony is more important for Barth than these occasional examples might indicate. It was not merely a factor in his psychological makeup; indeed, Barth
conceives of the entire religious situation as ironic, and thus theology is and
must be ironically structured, if it is to do justice to a very ironic God.

Theology for Barth is essentially ironic because in trying to speak *about* God it inevitably ends by speaking *for* God. God's otherness creates the space for theology to exist, but that very same otherness ironically makes of theological space an emptiness, which denies theology any rightful existence. God's absolute otherness creates an absolute dilemma for theology, a "to be or not to be," which theology must try but will always fail to resolve. Thus, if theology is to speak at all, suspended in an empty space between God's total otherness and the foolish words of humanity, it must speak in an ironic voice: that is, it must raise its ironic situation to the level of a self-conscious practice. In other words, there must be a poetic resolution to this theological problem.

This position is made clear in an essay Barth delivered in 1922, during the time that he was revising his *Romans* commentary. In "The Word of God and the Task of the Ministry," Barth's ironic vision of theology—that it inevitably cannot do what it sets out to do—is focused on the task of preaching. Here, we can find a good example of Barth's basic agreement with Kierkegaard that religious communication must take an ironic form. Notice that he does not spend any time dealing with academic theology. Systematic theology, he suggests, is like "the turning over of a sick man in his bed for the sake of change" (*WG*, 184). What one generation finds interesting the next will reject as boring. Theology, because it must speak from the emptiness of human life, is always seeking something new to say, a newness that Barth suggests can only barely cover up its profound *ennui*. But what about preaching, which is theology practiced in the setting of the church? Can preaching communicate any truth about God?

Barth's initial answer to that question is an unequivocal no. People seem to get along quite well without the ministry: "The people do not need us to help them with the appurtenances of their daily life" (*WG*, 187). What they really want is assurance of their own worth and importance, even though what they really need is knowledge of God. This knowledge the minister cannot communicate: "We cannot speak of God. For to speak of God seriously would mean to speak in the realm of revelation. To speak of God would be to speak God's word, the word which can come only from Him, the word that God becomes man" (*WG*, 198–99). Indeed, Barth argues that to hold the word 'God' before someone—in an act of direct communication—is not to speak of God. The minister cannot communicate God as if God were some kind of information that people were lacking. What can be spoken, Barth suggests, is the negation of religion, but this is not enough. "We hear the imperative even from history: we ought to speak of God! It is an imperative which would give us perplexity enough even if we were in a position to obey it'' (*WG*, 197). The minister must also speak of God, must say the unsayable, but how can this be accomplished?

The solution to this contradiction can only involve the suspension of irony. Barth makes this painfully clear by sharpening his rhetorical flourishes to the fine point of paradox:

> As ministers we ought to speak of God. We are human, however, and so we cannot speak of God. We ought therefore to recognize both our obligation and our inability and by that very recognition give God the glory (*WG*, 186).

Barth does not really ''explain'' this aporia because he does not want to blunt its contradiction. He observes that people do cry out for God, and so something seemingly needs to be said. However, Barth suggests, because these cries come from humanity, humanity itself is inevitably given as their answer. Theology is only theology if and only if it is constituted by God. The newness that theology as a form of human satisfaction seeks is only satiable in the absolute newness of the event of Jesus Christ. Thus, truly to speak of God would be to speak God's word; unfortunately for theology, that is the Word Jesus Christ, which only God can speak and which God has already spoken. All theological discourse, then, is limited—or worse, preempted— by the language always already spoken by God.[31]

This limitation constitutes an insurmountable barrier for all three of the basic kinds of theology that Barth examines. Orthodox dogmatism tries to describe God, and thus treats God as an object; instead of doing justice to God's language, it substitutes human for divine discourse. The self-criticism of mysticism does not turn God into an object; it treats God as pure being and puts the soul onto the path of negation in order to achieve unity with God. Mysticism, however, is too certain in its negations; people cannot become divine, precisely because God had to become a person. Barth does privilege his own use of dialectics, saying that it is the best theological option of the three. Indeed, his theology is often called dialectical, but here Barth makes it clear that his use of dialectics is distinctive. Dialectics cannot mean the elaboration of a position through the interplay of an ascending order of opposite but related viewpoints. Instead, dialectics must be a way of maintaining tensions, which cannot be resolved:

> On this narrow ridge of rock one can only walk: if he attempts to stand still, he will fall either to the right or left, but fall he must. There remains only to keep walking—an appalling performance for those who are not

> free from dizziness—looking from one side to the other, from positive
> to negative and from negative to positive (WG, 207).

Dialectics is a way of keeping one's balance, not a method for reaching any conclusions.

The problem with dialectics is that it seems like a good trick; by its very success it implies an ability to speak for and about God. This is misleading, because all theology obscures and usurps the authority of God's Word. What then can Barth, the theologian, do? Barth does consider the option of silence. If we cannot seriously speak about God, then why not keep silent on this one subject? This Barth himself could not do, but should he recommend it to others? In fact, often he does recommend silence to other theologians, but not as a matter of general policy. Somehow theology must both speak and not speak about God. This can only be done by recognizing the irony of all theology. Barth makes this explicit when he suggests that dialectics, by coming so close to true religious communication, is actually the most spectacular theological failure of all. Dialectics, then, must be practiced with the knowledge that it cannot do what it intends, and this very knowledge must be the ground upon which human discourse says God. Irony is thus the sign that God may be working in our midst. That we must speak of God but cannot so speak is evidence for the freedom of God's own voice, which, however, we cannot hear due to the clamor of our own contentions. Yet we must continue to speak, in full recognition of these ironies.

In sum, Barth's early position on religious communication takes this form: "Theologically speaking, theology is impossible." Theology says what cannot be said. To say anything more is to say nothing at all: "Can theology, should theology, pass beyond prolegomena to Christology? It may be that everything is said in the prolegomena" (WG, 217). Barth will later decide that theology must become constructive, but here theology says everything by saying nothing. This gives Barth's theology the feel of a riddle at times; the closest parallel, perhaps, is the notorious comment by the Cretan Epimenides that, "All Cretans are liars." Epimenides' self-cancelling proposition is an ideal paradox, a circular self-contradiction, which cannot be reduced to a consistent argument. In much the same way, Barth's vision of theology turns against itself: he is a theologian who must write against theology, but who is, nonetheless, a theologian. What makes this ironic is that Barth must use theological discourse in order to displace that discourse. That is, the disruption of theology must occur from within theology, or else silence really is the only option. Only from within theology can the statement of theology's impossibility be made, and in fact that is the only statement that theology can make. Theology, therefore, cannot really mean what it says. Not by success or silence, then, can theology make God known; only by saying what cannot be said can the unknown be known as that which is present in its very absence, that which is revealed when language fails.

AN IRONIC GOD

In previous chapters I have noted Barth's frequent uses of irony in *Romans*. The entire discussion of God and the No-God, for example, can be interpreted as a form of irony: what people think is God is really the No-God, while God says no to everything that people want and expect. Now it is time to make explicit the irony of God, and the implications that follow from that irony. Many readers of *Romans* receive the impression that God is wrathful and judgmental, ever ready to condemn and destroy, more like the powerful and jealous figure who releases the flood in Genesis than the loving father of whom Jesus speaks. On the contrary, a close reading of *Romans* will show that God is not capricious and tyrannical — God operates on a strict logic that overturns human expectations and conceptions. "When He sits in judgement the all-embracing unrighteousness, caprice and arbitrariness of our world meet their contradiction, and in this contradiction their nature is disclosed" (*R*, 82). This definition of God's activity neatly coincides with the definition of irony. Irony is not a mere contradiction; it is an unexpected contradiction, which somehow reveals the nature of that which it contradicts. In this case, God's judgments reveal human pride and pretension for what they really are. God is the great reversal, not only defeating but also transforming human thoughts and desires. "God pronounces those who are awake to be asleep, believers to be unbelievers, the righteous to be unrighteous" (*R*, 70). Thus, Barth can say that the righteousness of God is a 'nevertheless' that contradicts every human logical 'consequently' (*R*, 93). If people could only look closely enough, they would see that God reflects a different kind of reality behind the appearance of things.

The mechanism that serves to upset human expectations is grace. Barth often speaks of grace in ironic terms. Redemption is not a state which humanity can achieve, nor is it a gift which humanity can receive. Redemption is the recognition of God's reversals: "Justification can be found only in the light of God's sincerity and of His irony" (*R*, 137).[32] God's irony is sincere: it is not purely destructive, but rather it is an objective response to the human predicament, giving people what they really need. "By dissolving us, He establishes us; by killing us, He gives us life" (*R*, 61). Yet because it is so radical, it is nothing that can be anticipated or finally understood. Like all good irony, God's devastation is unpredictable. Even when it is ex-

pected, it will appear in surprising ways. Thus, theological ignorance is a
condition for the efficacy of God's activity. This is the irony of the human
situation: we can best understand and experience God by not knowing who
God is and how God acts. "We know that God is He whom we do not know,
and that our ignorance is precisely the problem and the source of our knowledge" (R, 45). God's irony is truly an infinite absolute negativity; it is nothing that we can affirm or analyze. Grace is a mystery we can never touch or
feel, but that does not mean that it is totally absent from this world; it works
to undermine and overthrow human arrogance, just as all irony works
against an overly confident innocence. Just because the irony of grace is infinite and absolute, it can never be reduced to some kind of program or
agenda: "Only when grace is recognized to be incomprehensible is it grace"
(R, 31).

The state of human affairs is thus never quite what it seems. Devotion
to the truth may turn out to be disobedience, humility may become arrogance, those who mean well might be ripe for evil. Indeed, the entire pursuit
of ethics is a mask for hidden immoralities and deceit; the desire to do good
is one more manifestation of what Nietzsche calls the will to power.

> The possessors of the law are the idealists, the especially favored, those
> who have an experience of God or, at least, a remembrance of such ex-
> perience. Their impress of revelation, their religion and their piety, dem-
> onstrate and bear witness to God. Such men are directed to God; but for
> that very reason they are not directed by Him (R, 87–8).

God's ironies are directed most against those who think that they are on
God's side, those who think that they have nothing to hide. Yet this situation
is not the product of human disingenuousness, and it cannot be discerned by
human circumspection. God is the force that causes and reveals these contradictions and inconsistencies. The terrifying result is that those who think
they are saved often are not, and those who possess no revelation stand before God in full righteousness. This is a hard lesson to accept: "This strange
occurrence, this firm fragility, must be carefully considered by those who
trust in human righteousness" (R, 65).

God's irony, then, constitutes the crisis: its instability threatens the
meaning of all human thought and activity. At times, however, Barth does
suggest that some people are willing to confront the crisis. He describes
these people in terms which closely approximate the features of irony. People who acknowledge the crisis refuse to equate or identify appearance with
reality:

Those who lead this attack are moved neither by pessimism, nor by the desire of tormenting themselves, nor by any pleasure in mere negation; they are moved by a firm horror of illusion; by a determination to bow before no empty tabernacle; by a single-minded and earnest striving after what is real and essential; by a firm rejection of every attempt to escape from the veritable relation between God and man; by a genuine refusal to be deceived by those penultimate and antepenultimate truths with which human research has to be content both at the beginning and at the end of its investigations (*R*, 87).

The proper response to the crisis is not mere negation or pessimism, attitudes with which irony is often allied. The problem that needs to be faced is, as with Kierkegaard, one of illusion, and the strategy that is needed is an objective and even detached "striving after what is real." The Christian needs to develop an insight into the incongruity of human claims and contentions. Barth continues in this passage to outline the greatest irony of this strategy. The full rights of the materialistic, secular, skeptical view of the world should be granted, he argues. History is void of any transcendental meaning. Ironically, though, this embrace of the secular can lead to a new reverence for the divine: only by seeing through every human claim to know God can the path be cleared for God's revelation.

Like Kierkegaard's Socrates, then, Barth's God does not have any positive or constructive position to teach or expound. Even Jesus Christ appeared in an ironic form: "His greatest achievement is a negative achievement" (*R*, 97), that of self-sacrifice. God demands a transvaluation of human values, not the adoption of some higher form of wisdom; if God asked for anything else, then human obedience would be possible and people could prepare plans and systems that could fulfill God's requests. At times Barth explains this point by suggesting that God merely asks for the opposite of what people already are: "The Jews therefore must first become Gentiles, the religious irreligious, churchmen men of the world, rather than vice versa" (*R*, 132). People who want to become close to God must assume the opposite of what they want. But Barth, ever aware of the instability of God's ironies, realizes that this sounds too much like a ready-made program that people can master and practice. God's ironies cannot be interpreted so easily. Thus, he immediately adds, "And yet, this is a dangerous manner of expressing the truth; for the deprivation of the Gentiles no more provides the true Beginning than does the advancement of the Jews. Minus has no pre-eminence over plus" (*R*, 132). Thus Barth suggests that God's irony is such that there is quite literally nothing we can do about it. Indeed, "Through what they are not, men participate in what God is" (*R*, 121).

At best, all that we can do is summarized by the word hope. Jesus Christ is experienced only through his resurrection, which is a futural not an historical event, still waiting to happen. But it is a resurrection in which we can hope to participate, and its power is mediated to us by the Holy Spirit, which Barth, in a momentary lapse of optimism, once called the 'Yes' (R, 272). However, he goes on to say that in the phrase, "We have the Spirit," we means not we and have means not have. On the very same page Barth can write, "The Spirit is the truth," and "There is no objective observation of the truth" (R, 287). This puts us in a difficult situation; we must recognize the "ambiguity of our ambiguity" (R, 294). Hope is all that is left. "All that is not hope is wooden, hobbledehoy, blunt-edged, and sharp-pointed, like the word 'Reality'" (R, 314). There is no way to get across the gap, which irony opens, between reality and appearance; the best that we can do is hover in the midst of this opening and hope for some future closure. "Do we wish to be something more than men who hope? But to wait is the most profound truth of our normal, everyday life and work, quite apart from being Christians" (R, 314). Waiting is hard work, especially when there is no basis for one's expectations: "We must wait," Barth writes, "as though there were a God ... " (R, 314). All other strategies are based on a reality that is not what it appears to be.

Hoping for hope is the best that we can do; however, Barth is not always so confident about the human situation. Barth often hints that there is nothing we can do, not even hope. Every action people can take is limited by irony, especially religious actions. In fact, we only discover who we are when we realize that we cannot do what we think we can. "Stretching out to reach what they are not, men encounter what they are, and they are thereby fenced in and shut out" (R, 248). There is a double irony here: we reach out for God and find only ourselves; then we think that what we have found is indeed God. The result is obvious: "The more men seem to speak deeply and really about God, the more unreal is what they say" (R, 439). Even theology is only an eloquent illustration of "the universal struggle for existence; a struggle in which animals furnished with younger teeth and horns do to death those older and weaker than themselves, until their own time comes" (R, 372). Barth's irony is such that even he cannot accept his own critique of the church without qualification:

> To destroy temples is not better than to build them ... Amaziah *and* Amos, Martensen *and* Kierkegaard, all the protestations against religion from Nietzsche down to the most degraded and loud-voiced anti-clericals, the whole anti-theological romanticism of aestheticism, socialism, and the Youth Movement in its multifarious ramifications, are

without exception enveloped in haze, and incompetent to provide
security. And the haze solidifies into the cloud of the wrath of God
(*R*, 136).

Both antichurch and church are subject to the crisis, but Barth clearly prefers critique to construction. There is a certain horror in the way that the
church, oblivious to its situation, attempts to bring about the Kingdom of
God, and Barth lists the steps the church thinks it can take: it can refine its
liturgy; popularize its technical language; broaden the basis of the education
of its clergy; make its administration more efficient; yield hurriedly to the
demands of the laity, no matter how doubtful they might be; encourage theological journalism; and surrender to the spirit of the age, even to socialism
(*R*, 378). All of this, of course, is quite beside the point.

As these passages about theology and the church indicate, the furthest
reach of God's irony must finally include the ironist, that is, Barth himself.
Barth recognizes this: "He [the Prophet] knows the catastrophe of the
church to be inevitable; and he knows also that there is no friendly lifeboat
into which he can clamber and row clear of the imminent disaster. He knows
that he must remain at his post in the engine-room or, maybe, on the bridge"
(*R*, 336). The one who understands God must communicate that understanding through a sinking vessel. In fact, the church is born in irony, because when people think that they are on the road toward discovering God,
they are really only building the church, a structure that sits apart from that
road and invites people to stop, rest, and forget about their journey. Indeed,
Barth talks about "the inevitable irony of its [the Church's] whole situation" (*R*, 402).[33] The greatest irony of the church is terrifying indeed: "It
was the Church, not the world, which crucified Christ" (*R*, 389). Nevertheless, by means of irony the church plays a necessary role: "The Church
seeketh after God, and when it meets Him, being unable to comprehend
Him, it rejects Him. But when this catastrophe is recognized, the reconcil-
ing of the world with God occurs" (*R*, 406). There is a double reversal here.
Not only does the church reject what it sets out to obtain, but by that very
rejection, what the church wanted is granted to it.

What then can Barth, who has no intention of leaving the church, say?
When confronted with this question, Barth himself turns to questions:

How are we to provide any further elucidation, explanation, and interpretation of the words of God to those who love Him — words which
only He can utter at the place where He wills that men should seek and
find Him? Is it not inevitable that anything we say must be said 'about'

or 'in addition to' or 'contrary to' what God has said? Must not our silence also, quite as much as our speech, obscure the truth concerning
the knowledge of love? (*R*, 326).

As I noted in chapter four, these are not rhetorical questions in the sense that
their answer is known before they are asked; they allow Barth to appear to
be saying something, while he actually establishes no positive line of
thought. It is tempting to suggest that Barth's theology in the end struggles
to say nothing at all. At the very least, everything is utterly ambiguous:
God's absolute irony means that theology itself must become ironic, must
say that which it does not mean. However, the instability of God's irony suggests that the response of theology, even in ironic form, will fail to imitate or
represent God's activity. The web of God's irony is too infinitely intricate
ever to be modeled by theology. Theology's ironic position, then, is a tension which cannot be resolved or resisted. Irony is a blurred genre, and if it
is too unstable it can easily become ambiguous and cynical. This is the risk
that Barth runs, and he readily admits it: the true Christian, he writes,
"adopts a point of view which is no point of view" (*R*, 58). Self-irony, then,
is the final implication of Barth's tropical strategy: theologians must realize
that all they can say—and this can be said, no doubt, in many different ways,
over and over again—is nothing at all.

AN UNSTABLE CORRECTIVE

The last forty or so pages of *Romans* are a remarkable retraction; they
constitute a conspicuous descent from the high places of Barth's discourse.
Here Barth's irony reaches a climax of irresolution. It is an odd conclusion
to this great text: in summarizing the Apostle Paul's theology, Barth realizes that there is nothing to summarize. Theology cannot conclude anything
because there is no place for it to end, no arguments or themes that it can
shelter or rescue from the crisis. This is, at any rate, what Barth has learned
from Paul: "Paul against 'Paulinism'! The Epistle to the Romans against the
point of view adopted in the Epistle" (*R*, 504). The reader cannot use Paul's
theology for any purpose, no matter how noble, because Paul does not really
mean what he appears to say. There are no handles here that can be grabbed.
Thus, Barth can write, "The man therefore who, armed with the knowledge
of the Epistle to the Romans, himself advances to the attack, has thereby
failed to perceive the attack which the Epistle to the Romans makes upon
him" (*R*, 505). Of course, the irony here is that Barth himself has used this
Epistle for precisely this purpose, to launch countless exaggerated attacks.
However, those attacks are now seen to be only part of the picture; if such

attacks were to be taken literally, then the true meaning of the crisis would be lost. "If the Krisis be not pressed home to the end, all would be but sounding brass and tinkling cymbal" (*R*, 505).

The end of the crisis is the end of theology, an end that theology itself cannot pronounce. This is Barth's conclusion. In fact, he argues that Paul's ability to turn his theology against itself is a sign of its authenticity. "And so, when at its ending the Epistle dissolves itself [*sich selbst aufhebt*], when it quite deliberately gives to its sympathetic, understanding, naturally Pauline readers the sharp command, 'Halt!', it does but corroborate itself. It is now that the reader is really tested" (*R*, 505). Indeed, any interpretation of Barth's text is confronted with an impenetrable ambiguity at this point. The Pauline Christian, Barth argues, defends a "position [which] is no position, and woe betide him, if he were to allow himself to be enticed onto ground where one point of view stands solidly and honestly in opposition to others" (*R*, 506). True theology cannot occupy any space at all. It must be an exercise in criticism, "destructive and Socratic; it dissolves the endeavors of others" (*R*, 507). Like Socrates, Barth can only ask questions, which, he hopes, will unmask the pretensions of those around him. These questions lead to no answers, prompting Barth to say, "Who is not aware of the grim humour in these words?" (*R*, 507).

At this point the reader is sure to protest that Pauline Christians must have some advantage over their more naive counterparts. Barth addresses this issue in an interpretation of Romans 14:1–4. Here Paul discusses the controversy between those whose faith is weak, allowing them to eat only certain foods, and those with a strong faith, which allows them to eat anything. This dispute has been traditionally understood as a conflict between ethical rigorism and freedom of conscience. Paul's advice, according to the usual reading, is that strong Christians should be willing to sacrifice their freedom in order not to offend weak Christians; nevertheless, strong faith does result in a certain amount of freedom from social customs and the demands of an excessively disciplined conscience. Barth does not think this passage is so simply explained. "Without doubt," he writes, "the noblest figures in history are marshalled behind the Roman eaters of vegetables" (*R*, 508). The liberal preference for freedom, then, ignores the advantages of ethical rigorism. Moreover, freedom as an end in itself is troubling: "If the paradox of the strong is that the strength of their character lies in an absence of pronounced characteristics, ought they to continue to cultivate this character-less character?" (*R*, 509). Or should they cease seeking their strength in their strength?

Barth concludes that the weak are justified in their accusations against the strong, while the strong have the advantage that they have a glimpse of

how futile the whole discussion really is. This glimpse, though, is not a basis
for judgment; the point is that humans cannot make any judgments at all
against one another. The real weakness is this readiness to judge, which is
the ironic temptation, Barth suggests, of the strong person who feels free to
judge the ethical rigorist. Perhaps the problem with both the weak and the
strong is that they do not realize that all judgments are relative and threaten
to turn against the judge. "All reformers are Pharisees. They have no sense
of humour. Deprive a Total Abstainer, a really religious Socialist, a Churchman, or a Pacifist, of the Pathos of moral indignation, and you have broken
his backbone" (R, 509). Here Barth abdicates all of his earlier judgments
against culture and the church. God's judgments have the capacity to simultaneously condemn and forgive. Our own actions cannot exhibit this double-
sidedness; we cannot both reject and elect. "The result is that we merely
suceed in erecting the wrath of God as an idol" (R, 516). This is a crucial
confession. Barth's attempts to announce the judgments of God have been
one-sided, exaggerated, lacking the cunning of irony. His attempt to be the
Pauline Christian freed from the illusions that blind his contemporaries is
misleading. The capacity of judgment, which the strong Christians exercise,
is itself a sign of pride and arrogance; it "must therefore find some other outlet. It must be turned against themselves, it must be proved" (R, 516).

If the Pauline or Barthian Christian cannot judge others, what action
is left to be taken? I will return to the issue of the ethical implications of
Barth's rhetoric in the next chapter. For now it is important to note that
Barth advises the Christian that by doing nothing, the most decisive event
will happen. The person of God should not intervene in the world: helping
the neighbor to attain peace, challenging the neighbor to change, showing
the neighbor a better way, will all merely contribute to a premature eclipse
of God's will. Instead, the person of God should let the neighbor travel along
her or his path to its end, where unrest will be revealed behind a defiant self-
will. The Christian should let God's irony take its course, trusting that the
defeats the neighbor will meet will reveal the neighbor's true situation.
Thus, Barth can say that the person with strong faith "does not stand out,
he withdraws; he is nowhere because he is everywhere" (R, 525). However,
Barth also says that this course of action is itself no standard or recipe for
Christian practice. In fact, there is, finally, no ethical help in either Paul or
Barth. The best that Paul provides us is God's insight into things: "Regarded as a 'point of view,' the point of view of the Epistle to the Romans is
God's point of view!" (R, 516). For this very reason, it cannot be appropriated by the Christian: "The best element in Paulinism is what is unmanage-
able and useless in it" (R, 525).

There is, then, no truth in either the Epistle or Barth's commentary. It
would be ludicrous to think otherwise; there is no secret knowledge, no mat-

ter how obscure or indirect, which can justify humanity before God. "In order to arrive at this mistaken notion," Barth observes, "there was surely no need to digress into a study of the Epistle to the Romans" (R, 519–20). This is the problem with Protestantism, Barth suggests. It thinks that Paul establishes a position which can rival Rome. Instead, Protestantism should be only a question mark, what Tillich would later call the Protestant Principle, ceaselessly critical but refusing to become a substantial position in its own right. Indeed, the Reformation cannot be recalled as the beginning of a new religion: "It would be a sign of real perception on our part were we to cease celebrating the Reformation and were we to learn seriously to regret it as a venture of Titanism" (R, 520). Barth's position, then, like the irony Kierkegaard criticizes in *The Concept of Irony,* threatens to evaporate or disappear. Barth acknowledges this: "Paulinism is itself dissolved, long before its opponents have found sufficient breath to utter their anxious warnings against it" (R, 527). Barth admits that this is difficult to understand. His discourse is, he confesses, "twice-broken" (R, 521). It is about a reality broken by God, and it is itself broken, a shattered mirror reflecting a shattered world.

To use another image, the crisis is not a bridge across which people can reach God; it is a gulf which demands a leap. Paul is no help because his thesis implies that he cannot be trusted. "Paul is nothing. Having withdrawn himself behind this not, he is perhaps, however, far more dangerous" (R, 532). The Epistle to the Romans does not appeal to any authority, intellect, experience, or religion. It appeals to "those who have seen through and are nauseated by the confusion of that supposed 'simplicity' of which our generation is so proud" (R, 527). But Barth can also say that this Epistle "puts into words what everybody has heard already" (R, 528). Ironically, Paul stirs up so much controversy because what he says is already known:

> The Epistle to the Romans offers no new, strange, personal truth, but rather the Truth which is old, familiar, and universal. It lays no claim to originality, nor does it pretend to be deeply spiritual. It cannot, however, be for this reason overlooked, for it possesses a real claim to serious consideration (R, 527).

That claim is a "knowing not-knowing" (R, 528), but even this it does not really know, prompting Barth to ask, "Must every answer be ruled out which is not itself a question?" (R, 528). Only with a question can Barth acknowledge his lack of answers.

In the end, "Paulinism condemns itself" (R, 529). It does not offer the most precipitous route to God, but no route at all, or a route that goes nowhere, caught in its own web of irony. Paul's theology is a pebble, which has "got in between the smoothly moving, interlocking wheels of the machinery of human progress" (R, 533). Irritating but inevitable, theology must practice self-denial if it is to affirm anything. Even that statement about theology is misleading: the more theology becomes aware of its ironic position, the more it is tempted to think that it has achieved something in the realm of the divine, and so the further confused it really is. Thus, Barth must warn his readers against himself: "Take care lest ye be deceived, especially by those who are nearest to you and most plausible! Beware of the annual market of religious goods, with its many, busy, glittering stalls!" (R, 536–7). A theology that draws attention to itself, as Barth's certainly does, is not to be trusted. Theology should appear to do nothing, act without direction, speak without words: "Filled with inexhaustible purpose and certain of final success, theology must appear on the scene without any purpose and acknowledging no success as such" (R, 530–1).

Unfortunately, in the face of such contradictions and ambiguities, the reader must persevere. How is such discourse to be interpreted? Perhaps the simplest way is to read Barth's irony as a corrective. Irony, after all, is frequently intended to stir the reader or listener into changing an attitude or belief. Barth himself sometimes leans toward this interpretation. In an essay first published in 1922, "The Need and Promise of Christian Preaching," he suggests that his theology is not a standpoint "but rather a mathematical point upon which one cannot stand—a viewpoint merely" (WG, 98). Here Barth uses a mathematical metaphor to demonstrate how uneasy the position of theology really is. A bit later he shifts his metaphors: "Take it rather as a kind of marginal note, a gloss which . . . loses its meaning the moment it becomes more than a note and takes up space as a new theology next to the others" (WG, 98). His ironic theology, then, is not a part of the main text of theology; it is a note jotted on the margins, an aside hidden in a footnote, a comment written between the lines of traditional theology. His theology is not meant to become a new text, a new edition of theology, replacing worn-out copies of this tired discipline. Barth writes on the margins, an unsystematic interference with or effacement of the main body of theology, occasionally rewriting theology but also erasing his own marks, not wanting anyone to look over his shoulder and think that he has written yet another book.

If Barth's irony is a corrective, then it is important to understand what kind of corrective. It is not the kind of correction which can be incorporated into a text, like the marks of a proofreader. Instead, it seeks to subvert—to transgress—the text of theology. Barth's irony is not superimposed upon theology; it arises from theology itself, in a space that demands to be filled but disruptively extends beyond any possible fulfillment. The result is an intentional instability, a movement of language that is always going beyond itself by taking itself back. Barth's dialectics thus needs special consideration. It might be helpful to compare it with Adorno's philosophy, a negative dialectics which sought to free that form from all affirmative traits. For Adorno, philosophy should be ruthlessly self-critical, to the point of asking whether philosophy should exist at all. The problem is that to think is to identify, yet all objects enter into thought incompletely, leaving a remainder which shows thought to be in contradiction with itself. Philosophy, then, should be the thought of nonidentity, a nonstandpoint; negative dialectics itself "remains the thing against which it is conceived."[34] Adorno suggests that one way thought can become disenchanted with the concept is by restoring rhetoric, or language, to itself. Only by acknowledging its indeterminacy can thought get at the essence it obscures, the concrete suffering that exposes the poverty of conceptuality but which makes thinking necessary. Barth and Adorno thus share a desire to turn dialectics against itself in order to reveal a reality that thought cannot grasp.

Perhaps an even better comparison could be made with Derrida.[35] He launches his philosophy in a critique of the claim that language is the medium through which presence (or meaning) is established, a claim that he traces in part to theology. His main move is to reverse the traditional relationship between writing and speaking and then to argue for a new understanding of language in general. Speaking gives the illusion of transparent meaning because the speakers are bodily present to each other. This presence leads philosophy to exaggerate the potential for meaning in discourse. For Derrida, writing is not an inferior form of speaking, something that must be done only when other people are absent. Writing, once liberated from the repression of philosophy, shows that there is never an identity between the signifier and the signified in discourse. There is a fracture or rupture in the structure of language, which undermines the attempt to achieve stability of meaning. Derrida's key term, *différance,* implies that language is never able to contain an otherness within a systematic unity. The unarticulated cognitive assumptions of texts, what is left unsaid, always can be shown to upset and reverse what the text purports to accomplish.

Rhetoric thus supplants grammar: language has no center, no foundation. The project of deconstruction, therefore, tries to show what philosophical texts try to hide: language gets in the way of pure meaning. But deconstructionism must itself be perpetually deconstructed so that it does not take meaning for granted. Otherwise, it will commit the crimes for which it has convicted others. Barth and Derrida thus share a similar theory of language. However, for Derrida, God, or the quest for unity, is the veil which philosophy uses to cover up the ambiguities of language; for Barth, God is the very reason why language can never achieve any permanent meaning. God is the difference that language tries to trace, but which leaves a trail that language can never follow. Nevertheless, Derrida and Barth share a similar predicament: both must incorporate the criticisms to which their opponents are blind into their own styles. Neither finally can explain the ambiguity that they see so clearly, because to inscribe it into a theory or system would be to betray it.

To speak the unspeakable: the divine reality is such that it can never be described in any other way. Barth often explains this with the image of trying to draw a bird in flight: "The religion which we are able to detect in ourselves and in others is that of human possibility, and, as such, it is a most precarious attempt to imitate the flight of a bird" (*R*, 184). The activity of the Word of God cannot be easily imitated or represented; most theologies try to describe it as if it were static and not dynamic. Such realistic portraits point to where God once was but now is not. Barth, in contrast, wants a theology which will do justice to God's dynamic activity: this is why the isolation of a few frames cannot do justice to the motion of Barth's prose. It is an attempt to fly without landing, a movement without rest. It is a bold flight, but because it cannot follow, in the end, the mysterious movement of God, it must make the arc of a boomerang. The result is a self-consuming artifact in which the victim of Barth's irony is not only himself but also his readers.[36] The reader cannot approach this text hoping to know more about God—or about Barth himself. His work is nearly unreadable, as de Man suggests all good rhetoric should be. His frustrating rhetoric is thus an allegory of the Christian predicament; his own authorship, the possibility of a stable system of meaning, is hidden and confused in his text just as God is never clearly present in the world or in history. This is no mere corrective maneuver; it is a reenactment or a recapitulation of the human situation. Reading Barth parallels the experience of trying to know God. It should be clear that now it can be said that Barth's rhetoric is his theology—to the extent that he has one.

CHAPTER 6

RETREAT AND RECONSTRUCTION:
RE-READING BARTH TODAY

RETREAT FROM RHETORIC

Of course, everything soon changed. Just as Barth rebelled against liberalism, he soon rebelled against his own rebellion. To many people, in fact,
the name Karl Barth represents the work he did after *Romans,* especially
the multivolume *Church Dogmatics,* and this is, perhaps, how it should be.
After all, he spent most of his life on the *Dogmatics* and the theology it represented, while he had increasing reservations about his earlier work. *Romans* came to stand for an aberration in Barth's thought, or a brief and intriguing option that did not work out, or a stepping stone toward the more
stable and positive dogmatic theology. Whatever the case, this movement
away from the theology, or better put, antitheology, of *Romans* is a complicated story. So many factors are involved that it would take another work
just to sort through them. Scholars still debate the continuities and discon-
tinuities between the two periods. To do justice to the result of this shift, to
analyze Barth's later work, can only be the task of many scholars, a process
that began concurrently with Barth's work and is continuing today. Ob-
viously, then, I cannot hope in this work to follow Barth much beyond the
limited territory of the *Romans* period. However, I do want to suggest that
rhetoric can contribute its own perspective to this discussion. I want to argue that Barth's later theology can be understood rhetorically as a kind of
realism, an attempt to evade his earlier configurations. I can only sketch this
rhetorical interpretation of Barth's shift here, but it is important to show
how Barth reevaluated his early rhetoric before I offer my own response.

Barth's shift away from expressionism in the 1920s should not be surprising. After all, as Hayden White has argued, irony is a difficult trope to
maintain. A theology suspended in the air of doubt and anxiety is going to
be tempted to land somewhere. It takes a certain kind of stamina to refuse

ceaselessly even a contingent affirmation. In any case, that is what happened to expressionism: its drive to innovate became exhausted, and a backlash ensued. Just as Barth was a fellow traveler of expressionism, he followed this new cultural route, and many commentators have noted this parallel, even though they never analyze it in any detail.[1] In this case, however, scholars are more justified in failing to connect Barth to his cultural context. The movement away from expressionism was diverse and fragmented, and Barth can be considered a part of it only in very general terms. Nevertheless, this cultural development is important for a rhetorical reading of Barth, and so it is worthy of comment. The important thing to note is that expressionism was criticized as early as 1920, and most scholars mark its demise, if not its death, at around 1924. The reasons for this downfall are many, not least of which is expressionism itself; its self-criticism and continual experimentation inevitably wore itself out. As a result people were ready not just for something new, but for a return to something old.

What replaced expressionism came to be called *Neue Sachlichkeit*, the new objectivity or new matter-of-factness. The art critic G. F. Hartlaub coined this label in an influential 1924 essay and organized, in 1925, an exhibition to demonstrate his point. Although originally limited to a particular movement in the fine arts, this phrase came to embody the new spirit of the time. It implies a neutral, sober, utilitarian attitude toward the arts. Clarity and balance were valued over distortion and disharmony, and a restrained and reasonable confidence replaced despair and self-doubt. Peter Gay discusses this movement under the rubric of "the revenge of the father," marking its beginning with the election of Hindenburg to the presidency of the Weimar Republic in 1925. John Willett suggests that it began with the stabilization of the German mark at the end of 1923, arguing that "inflation and expressionism had been apt companions."[2] Whatever its origins, most scholars agree that most aspects of German culture followed a similar development. In Willett's words, there was "a non-utopian, even rather prosaic concern with clarity, accuracy and economy of means, biased towards the collective rather than the personal, and informed by a realistic social analysis."[3] Art turned away from a preoccupation with the inner essence of things; the external world looked stable enough to be explored again.

The new objectivity was not necessarily a conservative reaction to expressionism because many of the objective artists were socialists or communists. Thus, it is not correct to describe the new objectivity as the end of German modernism and a foretaste of the reactionary art that was soon to dominate central Europe. It was a diverse group with plural aims; many artists, including, for a while, Beckmann himself, were members of the movement. In many ways it was a natural outgrowth of expressionism's desire for a new reality. Nevertheless, the change was dramatic: the social pressures that had driven expressionism subsided, and a new style emerged. In place of the hysteria and intoxication of expressionism grew a subdued modesty, which, at its worst, could be disposed to moods of resignation and cynicism and, at its best, could examine the harsh realities of the world with a cool analytical reason. Some have argued that this new style was in actuality a return to nineteenth century realism.[4] Thomas Mann's *Magic Mountain,* published in 1924, is certainly exhausting in its accumulation of detail. Peter Gay suggests that there were good reasons for this turn to realism: the new objectivity was "a search for reality, for a place to stand in the actual world . . . It called for realism in setting, accurate reportage, return to naturalistic speech, and, if there had to be idealism, sober idealism."[5] The new objectivity was one last attempt by the artistic world to prop up the republic by containing the self-destructive irrationality latent in much of expressionism. Unfortunately, by 1933 unemployment and political violence would begin a process that would overwhelm both art movements.

Barth's participation in the new objectivity, even though indirect, is not difficult to map. In 1921 he accepted a professorship in Göttingen, and this move from the pulpit to the classroom is crucial for understanding the development of his thought. Instead of being the outsider, a radical pastor in a small village, he had to assume the responsibilities of carrying on and communicating the tradition of academic theology. "The 'movement' stopped and the work began" (*B,* 126). Not only had Barth joined the academy, but he was now the leading representative of a new school of theology. "All at once we were in the front rank. We had to take on the responsibilities which we had not known about while we were simply in opposition . . . First of all the details had to be ascertained, clarified, and above all tested" (*B,* 127). At first Barth was unsure of himself, and he was later fond of telling stories about how hard he had to work to prepare for his lectures. He had to move slowly; just as earlier he had sought a theology that would do justice to the particular problem of preaching, now he sought the necessary foundation for teaching. Nearly all of the sections of the *Church Dogmatics* began as lectures, a format—the impartation of information—which replaced the pulpit behind which the prophet could judge and proclaim. Now Barth had an audience to which he was directly responsible; no longer could he just argue with books and distant figures. In *Romans* he could disturb his audience; in the classroom he had to build a consensus and give a convincing account of his views by developing the proper credentials.

This process was, understandably, very painful for Barth at the start. To counter his anxiety, he often played the role of the curious and astonished visitor to the academic scene, uncertain of what to make of all this earnest seeking after knowledge. His energy and intellect, however, guaranteed a rapid adjustment. He helped found a journal, *Zwischen den Zeiten,* reevaluated his prior uneasiness toward the reformation, continued various exegesis projects, and immersed himself in the study of the history of theology. It was soon clear that he was again going in a direction separate from his theological contemporaries. Already in 1923 he had dissociated himself from Tillich over the issues of paradox and Chistology, and in 1924 he criticized a book by Brunner on Schleiermacher. He also had suspicions about Bultmann and Gogarten. The front of dialectical theology was never, therefore, firmly united, and in 1924, when Barth delivered his first lectures on dogmatics, it was clear that he was fighting a new war almost all by himself (Thurneysen was, as always, a loyal supporter). To gain some guidance in this new territory Barth turned to an unlikely source, a volume of nearly forgotten dogmatics by the nineteenth century theologian Heinrich Heppe. Barth knew that it was rigid, dry, and unattractive, a compendium of Reformed theology, which read like a logarithm table. It was a discovery over which the other dialectical theologians could hardly become excited, or even mildly interested. Yet Barth found it inspiring; Heppe treated Christian truths in an objective and confident manner, thus setting Barth on a bold and definite course. "What happens is that after much racking of my brains and astonishment I have finally to acknowledge that orthodoxy is right on almost all points and to hear myself saying things in lectures which I would never have dreamt could be so either as a student or as a pastor at Safenwil" (*B,* 155).

Barth made several false starts in his quest for a dogmatic theology; he felt like a beginner, learning theology all over again. An initial formulation based dogmatics on the explication of the principles of Christian preaching. In 1927, now at Münster, Barth decided that dogmatics instead should focus not on preaching but on the proclaimed Word of God, and he published the first volume of a projected series under the title, *Die christliche Dogmatik im Entwurf (Christian Dogmatics in Outline).*[6] In order to purge this work of its existential elements, Barth later, in Bonn, abandoned this project and began his final major work, the *Church Dogmatics,* in which his Christological concentration became clear. Throughout this transformation Barth's earlier concern with crisis had itself been subjected to a crisis. No longer did theology need a starting point in the attempt to understand God. Talk about crisis, Barth came to believe, merely sidetracked theology. An analysis of the world situation as a presupposition to theology could only distort and delay theology's entry into its proper sphere, which became the task of describing the reality of the Word of God. Barth wanted to free theology from its preoccupation with philosophical issues; instead, theology should be bound solely to its own subject matter. In this sense, Barth could say that he was not writing a systematic theology, a pattern of thought constructed around one or several major principles and developing a set of categories or concepts hierarchically arranged. Instead, as his change in titles from Christian to church dogmatics implies, he was presenting and explaining church dogma:

> The church should always present revelation to men as 'doctrine' (what else? Surely not in lyric poems . . . or as random emotional outbursts?). And it should be presented with the claim that this doctrine is to be 'accepted as true' (how else? Surely not as a fairy tale?). Would to God that our doctrine were so worthy of belief that it could compel such acceptance of truth (*B*, 161–2).

Talk about dogma did not please many of Barth's contemporaries. Barth's work became a lonely enterprise, and he himself once complained that "my life's work seems to lack a certain power of attraction; indeed, one characteristic of it seems to be a certain explosive or at any rate centrifugal effect" (*B*, 249). Many people simply did not know what Barth was trying to do; he was charged with regressing to Protestant scholasticism and orthodoxy, promulgating an authoritarian position, advocating a closed system. Barth himself helped to stir this reaction with defiant comments like, "Fear of scholasticism is the mark of a false prophet."[7] However, for the most part Barth was right to take offense at these kinds of criticisms. His attempt to discuss the perennial themes of theology — to survey the whole range of issues that serve as the vocabulary and grammar of the theologian's discourse — simply cannot be understood as a narrowing of this discipline. In Barth's eyes, Protestant theology had become trivial and boring in comparison to the best of Roman Catholic thought. Protestant theology had become lost in existential thought (a relationship that Barth himself had helped initiate); to rescue it, Barth proposed a steady course through the traditional topics that belong to theology alone. Philosophy should not set the theological agenda, although it can be used, in an ecclectic manner, by the theologian. In all of these changes Barth's theology came to resemble the new objectivity of his surrounding culture. To be more specific, in rhetorical terms Barth came to write theology realistically. This complex rhetorical shift cannot be directly linked to the *Neue Sachlichkeit;* that movement did not have a monopoly on realism. Moreover, that movement was short-lived, while Barth's realism continued throughout all of his long and productive career. However, that movement can, as in the case of expressionism, point the rhetorician in the right direction for an analysis of Barth's new style.

What is realism? This term is just as complex and elusive as any of the tropes I have discussed. For my purposes, though, a rough definition can be sufficiently established in order rhetorically to place Barth's dogmatic theology. Historically speaking, realism as a literary genre developed in the nineteenth century, partly out of and in reaction to Romanticism.[8] Both in theory and practice realism depicts the novelist as a kind of scientist: observation and free inquiry are the means toward the goal of a deepening understanding of the world. Realism, then, is interested not only in the truth but in the whole truth. This is illustrated by Engels's famous comment about Balzac, that he tells us more about the nature of French society in his time than all the sociologists, historians, or political thinkers in the world. To achieve this effect realism tries to portray the world with a mimimal amount of distortion, and it develops characters without obvious or overt manipulation. One purpose of this descriptive strategy can be educative: the realistic novel informs and instructs. It shows the reader a plausible view of the world and how various characters choose to live in it. In sum, as C. P. Snow states, "In the great realistic novels, there is a presiding, unconcealed, interpreting intelligence. They are all of them concerned with the actual social setting in which their personages exist."[9] From this brief discussion, then, three traits of realism can be distinguished: a stable and trustworthy authorial voice is subservient to the external world in order to display the regular pattern of relationships that evolve as people adjust themselves to this world.

This does not mean that all realists share the same style. It does mean, though, that they usually share a similar attitude toward language and the role and purpose of the author. In realism language is representational or mimetic; it serves a preexisting reality. It is not, however, a slave to reality; language is still creative in the way in which it responds to reality, but it is primarily responsive, not creative. Language brings to appearance the essence of things, operating on the assumption that the structure of the world can be duplicated in the medium of language. It does not follow from this that realistic style is static; reality can be seen as a dynamic flux, which requires great feats of interpretation and subtle strategies of harmonization.[10] The author, therefore, must make many choices about the portrayal of reality and the development of the characters. Wayne Booth has argued that it is precisely this necessity that limits the goals of realism. The narrative voice of a novel can never be completely detached and indifferent to the novel's characters and plot development. Even in those novels which strive for pure objectivity, there are different ways of constructing a semblance of reality. Thus, there are various kinds of realism, depending on the narrative tone: narrators can be reliable or unreliable, overt or implied, involved or detached, and the list of options is almost endless. Booth's argument is that all authors are rhetorical, even if they write realistically; authors try to persuade the audience of their attitude toward the world that has been created. The author always has the reader in mind: "The author cannot choose whether to use rhetorical heightening. His only choice is of the kind of rhetoric he will use."[11]

Booth's argument must be kept in mind when I examine Barth's realism. Booth's claim is not that realism does not exist, but that the authorial voice—ever present—determines the style of the realism. This argument is important because theorists have traditionally defended realism as a way of avoiding the many perplexities of rhetoric. Realism, this argument goes, sacrifices language to reality; language becomes transparent, allowing the reader to see through it to the thing in itself. Realism pretends to be, therefore, a rejection of rhetoric, while in actuality it is merely another kind of rhetoric, one which orders itself according to some (rhetorically constructed) view of reality.[12] I will return to this discussion in a moment, but for now it is important to note that Barth's shift in styles can be seen as his own kind of retreat from rhetoric. He found it impossible to sustain his tropical configuration, and as I argued at the end of chapter four, he frequently warned his readers against taking his earlier configurations literally. In moving away from *Romans* he sought a more stable and manageable rhetorical terrain. In an autobiographical reflection, he explains this change: "Also at this time [1921–1935], gradually or more visibly, I came to learn, along with a great centralization of what was material, to move and express myself again in simple thoughts and words."[13] This relative simplicity is one of the keys to realism; the author rejects the need for tropical gestures of any kind. Language does not need to have a form of its own because it merely imitates the form which it finds in the external world.

Barth's taste for realism was not limited to theology. Busch tells us that in 1931 Barth's favorite author at that time was Balzac (*B*, 209). This was not a passing obsession. In a rare and revealing comment on literature, in 1944, Barth defends a strict realism:

> I expect him [the modern novelist] to show me man as he always is in the man of today, my contemporary—and vice versa, to show me my contemporary in man as he always is. I expect the novel to give evidence on every page that its author not only knows this man properly and sees right through him, from the depths of his heart to his outward manners and mode of speaking, but also treats him honestly, i.e. loves him as he is and as he is not, without regret or contempt. Furthermore, it should tell me what its author finds special in this man—that and no more. In

other words, it should have no plans for educating me, but should leave me to reflect (or not) on the basis of the portrait with which I am presented. Finally, its form should correspond to the portrait of the man whom it presents; its form should be necessary, strict and impressive to the extent that I do not forget the man I have been shown in his temporal and timeless aspects. I should be able to live with him, and indeed perhaps have to live with him again and again (*B*, 313).

Here are all the ingredients of realism. Barth advocates an unobtrusive author who simply reveals a character in exact and comprehensive detail. The style should be subordinated to the subject matter, and the themes should consist of those problems that universally besiege human nature. The novel should educate the reader only indirectly, allowing readers to make their own judgments about the characters and events, which are objectively portrayed. Written at a time when the modernist novel was becoming increasingly experimental, losing both characters and authors in nonrepresentational language, Barth's comments are a bold confession. They are not only about his (albeit dated) literary taste; they are also about his own work. The stable authorial voice, the reflection of a powerful reality, the adherence to perennial themes, all of these traits that Barth sought in realistic novels can be found in his own later work.

The objectivity of Barth's dogmatic theology has been analyzed by many scholars, although not in rhetorical terms. Donald Phillips, for example, has argued that the primary architectonic principle governing Barth's later thought is "a movement toward complete fidelity to the object of inquiry as determining the nature of scientific activity, rationality and discourse."[14] Thomas Torrance has also emphasized the scientific and objective nature of Barth's dogmatics.[15] Barth does at times advocate a general position of philosophical realism; "the goal of language," he writes, "must be determined by the unique object in question."[16] His most consistent position is that theology must be realistic because of what it is, not because of what philosophy is. Indeed, theology's realistic approach to God is not something that Barth expects philosophy to share; the object of theology is a field of inquiry available only to that discipline, a claim that tempers Barth's realism with a fairly heavy dose of idealism.[17] The theologian, then, is not realistic because philosophy dictates that particular epistemological program; the theologian is realistic because, as in rhetorical realism, there is an external reality that initiates and creates its own response. Moreover, that reality shapes the style of theology: the theologian cannot take a naive epistemological position on God because God is dynamic and free, and theology can never presume fully to describe that reality. This allows Barth's later work to be ironic, in its own way, about the possibilities of theology. In sum, the theologian is hardly a scientist, and the reality of God is not analogous to the natural world. In Barth's thought, God's actuality precedes any theological reflection; concrete divine acts call for a specific kind of response. This may or may not be true of other objects, but it is something theology cannot afford to avoid.

Hans Frei has come the closest to a rhetorical analysis of Barth's dogmatic theology, calling his method a kind of conceptual description. "He took the classical themes of communal Christian language molded by the Bible, tradition and constant usage in worship, practice, instruction and controversy, and he restated or redescribed them, rather than evolving arguments on their behalf."[18] Barth was aware that Christian language had been eclipsed by the discourses of science and secularism, but he had no desire to argue against this reversal. Instead, he wanted to rely on the power of representation to persuade his audience that Christian language can be spoken and used again. In Frei's words, he had to "recreate a universe of discourse."[19] He puts the reader in the middle of that universe by showing, not explaining or arguing, how such language can fruitfully function. Barth is depicting a world that has its own linguistic integrity. "In much the same way as the now old-fashioned 'newer' literary critics he set forth a textual world which he refused to understand by paraphrase, or by transposition or 'translation' into some other context . . ."[20] Technical theological and philosophical arguments serve to clarify, but do not hinder or replace, this redescriptive process. Although Frei does not explicitly say this, he portrays Barth as a kind of realistic novelist. Theology can do and often does other tasks, speculating about various divine and human possibilities; but Barth's God has done this and that, here and there, and demands a full and accurate description of these events and activities as they are mediated through the Bible and the church and salvation history.

I want to examine briefly two of Barth's works from his dogmatic period for evidence of this rhetorical realism. The first work is Barth's book on Anselm, first published in 1931, which was the turning point in his development of a realistic theology.[21] In the preface to the second edition of this book Barth complains that most commentators "completely failed to see that in this book on Anselm I am working with a vital key, if not the key, to an understanding of that whole process of thought that has impressed me more and more in my *Church Dogmatics* as the only one proper to theology" (*A*, 11). In 1939 he remarked that, "Among all my books I regard this as the one written with the greatest satisfaction."[22] This is a difficult book, not least because of its similarities with *Romans:* Barth is developing his own theological position by what appears to be a close reading of a single text, in this case the *Proslogion*. He realizes that he will be accused of inadequate exegesis, but, he asks, "Who can read with eyes other than his own?" (*A*, 9). With that caveat he sets out to situate the so-called ontological argument in its theological context. Much of this discussion consists of a highly technical interpretation of Anselm's use of certain key words, most specifically *probare* and *intelligere*, and scholars still debate the merits of Barth's line of reasoning.[23] It is a provocative text: Barth argues that for Anselm the search for understanding is spontaneously immanent in faith itself. Proof, as well as joy, follows as a necessary consequence of the miracle of faith. Theological reason cannot question its own basis. "It is the presupposition of all theological inquiry that faith as such remains undisturbed by the vagaries of the theological 'yes' and 'no'" (*A*, 18). The success or failure of theology does not and cannot affect the truth of revelation.

The existence of faith, therefore, does not require knowledge; rather, the nature of faith demands description. Reason can advance our understanding of faith, but it cannot initiate or prove that faith. Faith is a given; reason need neither storm its gates nor sacrifice itself. In other words, *fides* both makes and meets the demand on *intelligere*. But the quest of reason cannot be direct; theology cannot exactly describe its object. Here Barth qualifies his realism: "Strictly speaking, it is only God himself who has a conception of God. All that we have are conceptions of objects, none of which is identical with God. Even the most worthy descriptions are only relatively worthy of him" (*A*, 29). Thus Barth can still sound like his former self and speak of God shattering the concepts of human thought, but a different voice can be heard here. Theological statements can be made with some degree of certainty (subject, of course, to future qualification and modification, as with all scientific statements) because God can be known in God's self-revelation. Barth can say, therefore, that theology can make progress, but it is also vulnerable. The criterion for its progress is scripture, which is interpreted in the form of a body of practices and beliefs held by the church. "And this *Credo* makes the science of theology possible and gives it a basis. It is thus and only thus that the characteristic absence of crisis in Anselm's theology can be understood" (*A*, 26). Barth has come a long way from *Romans;* here the church serves the positive function of mediating the scriptural basis of theology.

Anselm thus was not making an argument at all in the *Proslogion*. In fact, Barth suggests that the key to that text is its opening and closing prayers. Correct theology can come only from correct faith. Thus, "prior to any desire or ability to find theological answers is the question of dedication on the part of the theologian himself" (*A*, 34). This is not just a matter of the theologian expressing a certain amount of piety. Instead, theology is only possible because of the prevenient grace of God. God shows God's self to the theologian, granting the theologian access to the divine. God establishes the knowledge of God's self, which the theologian must recognize; or as Barth says in more technical language, the ontic precedes the noetic. The revelation of God's necessity provides for theology's own certainty; theology must be mastered by its object if it is to know anything. Thus, there is no anxiety in theology, as long as it humbly and obediently responds to what is already existent. That is theology's only responsibility; it cannot apologetically defend Christian truths in an attempt to convert the nonbeliever. Conversion is possible only with the mysterious movement of God's grace. Since theology speaks from faith, it cannot speak to nonfaith, except indirectly, by properly describing faith. Thus, the theologian can invite the nonbeliever into the world of faith, but only on the basis of theology itself. This is what Barth means when he says, "The unbeliever's quest is not simply taken up in any casual fashion and incorporated into the theological task but all the way through it is in fact treated as identical with the quest of the believer himself" (A, 67). The theologian addresses the world in an assumed solidarity, which is based on the hope that God's revelation will one day be complete and undeniable.

Theologians thus have nothing else to offer than theology. They have nothing to prove in the sense of that term as it is used today, but they have plenty to show. This means in part that theology does not need to make compromises with the world; nor does it need to rely on philosophical arguments. Theology enters the world not in a truce but as a conqueror. Theology offers the world the name of God, which is, after all, how Anselm begins his proof. That name manifests a "command not to imagine a greater than he" (A, 107). If that name is properly understood, then God will be known. Theology cannot persuade the world of the value of that name, but it can give a partial description of that name. The rest is up to God. Theology is thus "distinguished by a provocative lack of all doubt, including all 'philosophical doubt,' of all anxiety, including all apologetic anxiety and in this connection by a no less provocative intellectual coolness" (A, 151). The 'fool' does not reject such clear thinking because of pride or ignorance; the fool is the victim of the wrath of God. The fool exists because God has (not yet) revealed God's self completely. This must be because no mere human could withstand Anselm's proof, which is, in the end, God's proof of God's self. God has spoken, and in that activity theology is created. Theology's deepest form, then, is a kind of grateful response: it describes the divine out of gratitude for its own existence, pointing like Grünewald's John the Baptist —but this time without the exaggerated forefinger—toward a greater reality.

The second text I want to examine is part one of the first volume of the *Church Dogmatics,* originally published in 1932.[24] Here Barth launches his constructive dogmatics, and so I want to examine this work in some detail.

He realizes that his project will appear to many to be archaic in its overall design; few theologians were bold enough to survey and interconnect the entire range of Christian beliefs. However, with gentle irony he suggests that it is not his fault that this is the task of theology:

> Shall I excuse myself by pointing out that the connexion between the Reformation and the early Church, trinitarian and christological dogma, and the very concepts of dogma and the biblical Canon, are not in the last resort malicious inventions of my own? (*CD,* xiii–xiv).

Barth argues that he is not trying to begin another movement or found a new school; he is merely writing about and for the church. He is even aware that the church itself has no desire to listen to doctrine; people will think, in fact, that he is offering them stones and not bread. Yet, he is willing to face these problems because he wants to return theology to its proper setting. On one level, the church is always doing theology to the extent that it confesses God. There is, however, another level of theology that is needed: when the church pauses to take its own measure, the result is a scientific theology. Theology as a science measures the church's language against the basis of the church's existence. "Theology follows the language of the Church, so far as, in its question as to the correctness of the Church's procedure therein, it measures it, not by a standard foreign to her, but by her very own source and object" (*CD,* 2).

The issue of truth in theology, then, is a matter of correspondence. While the language of the church has been criticized from many different quarters, theology accepts the task of criticizing it from its very own essence. The other sciences can help in this project only indirectly. Does this mean that theology is one science among many, each given its own special task? Barth at times talks in this way. His most consistent position is that theology is a science only when that term, science, is used analogically. Barth admits that the task of theology appears to be very similar to other sciences, but it does not receive its task from a general concept of science. This would subject theology to the common self-understanding of the sciences, and Barth wants to argue that theology receives its task only from its own quite particular object. Theology cannot accept the standards and procedures of the other sciences even if those methods closely resemble the way of theology. However, there is an ambiguity here because Barth does suggest a general definition of science in these remarks: a science is limited to a study of a specific object within a specific sphere of activity. It is ordered according to the law of an object's being, and it tests its language against this object. In the case of theology, then, its constitution can only be conceived according to the reality of God. This reality, however, is unique, so that theology cannot become just one among the many sciences.

Theology, then, does not need to situate itself in relationship to other sciences. This is what most theologians mean when they talk about the need for a prolegomena to theology. Since everything has changed so much over the course of church history — the way of knowledge is more complex and tenuous today than in the past — theology must reflect on knowledge in general before it can speak about what it actually knows. Barth rejects this approach, arguing that "there is no theological foundation for the assumed difference between our own time and earlier times" (*CD*, 28). Christianity has always been opposed by the world, truth and falsehood have always been at odds. The tragedy of modern godlessness is nothing out of the ordinary, Barth explains; the situation of the world has always been the same, just as revelation is always the same. The only struggle that faith needs to be concerned about is its struggle with itself; faith should not take unbelief seriously. "The Church should fear God and not fear the world. But only if and as it fears God need it cease to fear the world" (*CD*, 73). The only unbelief that is important to theology is the unbelief that lies within faith, when faith does not adequately correspond with its own object. Repairing that connection is the best way for theology to witness to the world.

What is the reality that makes theology so distinctive? Theology begins with the fact that the church speaks about God. That speech is made possible by another fact: God creates the church. God creates the church with the command that it proclaim God's word. Proclamation, then, is the object of theology. "Theology as such is not proclamation, but science, instruction and investigation" (*CD*, 51). Proclamation is the preaching of the Word of God. It is not moral instruction or the expression of personal piety. It is not even a *representation* of God's word; that task belongs to theology. Instead, preaching is a *presentation* of God's word, so that God's word is heard through it. "Proclamation is human speech in and by which God Himself speaks like a king through the mouth of his herald . . . " (*CD*, 52). Whether God speaks through preaching is God's free choice: "When and where it pleases God, it is God's own World" (*CD*, 72). The freedom of God's voice implies that it is not limited to the proclamation of the church. "God may speak to us through Russian Communism, a flute concerto, a blossoming shrub, or a dead dog" (*CD*, 55). However, Barth suggests that unless we are prophets, we are not commissioned to pass on what we have heard as independent proclamation; the theologian, then, is limited to the proclamation of the church. Only subsequently, *a posteriori*, can the theologian consider revelation outside the church, and even that consideration must keep its focus on the center of the church, that is, Jesus Christ.

What makes theology so important is the recognition that church proclamation is not unassailable. At its best, it is loyal only to God's word; however, it can confuse that loyalty with other interests and concerns. The precarious situation of proclamation makes dogmatic theology a necessity. The
fact that the Word of God cannot be confirmed independently from proclamation makes theology an inexact science. "The Church can neither question its proclamation nor correct it absolutely. It can only exert itself to see
how far it is questioned and how far it ought to be corrected" (*CD*, 75–6).
Dogmatics, then, is a guide, a corrective exercise. Stylistically, it does not
stand on its own: "Dogmatics does not seek to give a positive, stimulating
and edifying presentation" (*CD*, 82). It is not a higher truth than proclamation, an esoteric science; it does not have access to some source of knowledge that is unknown by the church. It is critical of but not superior to proclamation; it is not an end in itself but a means toward revision and
modification. Its basis does not reside in personal conviction.

> For in so far as these convictions are capable of rational presentation,
> the persons concerned should be referred again to the way of scientific
> exposition, and in so far as they are wholly or predominantly irrational
> they should be referred to the possibility of musical, poetic or artistic
> expression (*CD*, 89).

Dogmatics, then, is neither science nor art; it is a religious discourse, made
possible by the Word of God. In sum, "Dogmatics must always be undertaken as an act of penitence and obedience" (*CD*, 22).

How does theology know the Word of God, so that it can correct
church proclamation? The Word of God is the speech of God, Barth says,
and as speech it requires hearing and obedience. "Speech, including God's
speech, is the form in which reason communicates with reason and person
with person" (*CD*, 135). But notice that, "God did not need to speak to us.
What He says by Himself and to Himself from eternity to eternity would
really be said just as well and even better without our being there ... "
(*CD*, 140). God does allow us to overhear his speech; and what we hear is
real and true, nothing that we could ever say to ourselves. What we hear is
who God is. Nonetheless, we hear this word from God indirectly. God's
Word always takes a form — what Barth calls its secularity — and theology
must listen to both the form and the content of God's speech. More specifically, God's Word takes three forms, written, preached, and revealed. Of
these, the written form is the most important for theology because proclamation is ventured on the basis of the recollection of the Word of God. This
recollection, though, is not timeless, like Plato's doctrine of *anamnesis*. It is

the recalling of scripture, the concrete object of the Bible, which has a free power over the church. God acts through the Bible, which is not in itself God's revelation but is the witness to that revelation.

The result of this approach is that theology must be a purely responsive discipline with the task of representing—describing, ordering, clarifying—a speech that has already been spoken and accepted as true and final. Barth explains this position by saying that the theologian does not know the Word of God, but instead acknowledges that Word. Barth defines knowledge "as the confirmation of human acquaintance with an object whereby its truth becomes a determination of the existence of the man who has the knowledge" (CD, 198). Knowledge is an experience in which the object changes the subject. Acknowledgement, then, is receptive, respectful, a decision to obey. This is the experience of faith. Barth argues that this experience cannot be described in general terms because it belongs only to a specific person, that is, to the Christian. Moreover, it belongs to the Christian only in the form of a gift. "The Word of God becomes knowable by making itself known" (CD, 246). The object of theology, finally, is a dynamic reality, which demands and creates its own reception. It can never be completely contained in any human form. It not only decides when and where it will be known, but it also decides how it will be known. Theology is thus caught in an hermeneutical circle, which it can make productive by the *analogia fidei*, teaching only what it has already learned from God. To describe the Word of God, then, humanity need not be taken into account. There is no predisposition in humanity to know this Word, and there is no necessity in the Word that it be known. In its freedom, then, the Word is, in the end, mystery.

This mystery of the Word of God is an important feature in Barth's discussion. So far, I have only commented on the positive, confident and objective side of Barth's dogmatics, but there is another side. Although there is no longer a metaphor of crisis operative here, and the church is no longer hyperbolically denounced, there is still some irony left in Barth's position. Because dogmatics pursues an ultimately mysterious reality, it can only be a humble project, a *theologia crucis* and never a *theologia gloriae*. The conformity it seeks can never be clear and unambiguous. This gives Barth room to echo, on occasion, his old voice in *Romans*. "Our concept of God and His Word can only be an indication of the limits of our conceiving," he can write (CD, 164). Dogma, which correlates proclamation and revelation, can never be complete and final. In fact, dogmatics is not a question of knowledge at all, but one of obedience. Thus, there is an ironic distance between the goal and the practice of theology: "What God said and what God will say is always quite different from what we can and must say to ourselves and others about its content" (*CD,* 141). This irony is, however, very limited and controlled; it is not destructive, as it was in *Romans,* but, to return to Booth's categories, stable. It humbles theology, but it does not derail it from its course. Theology, Barth is saying, like all sciences, has its limits.

When Barth does turn irony onto himself, in this later work, it is more endearing and gentle than disturbing and aggressive, as in this example:

> The angels laugh at old Karl. They laugh at him because he tries to grasp the truth about God in a book of Dogmatics. They laugh at the fact that volume follows volume and each is thicker than the previous one. As they laugh, they say to one another, "Look! Here he comes now with his little pushcart full of volumes of the *Dogmatics!*" —and they laugh about the men who write so much about Karl Barth instead of writing about the things he is trying to write about. Truly, the angels laugh.[25]

Here Barth pokes fun at both himself and his readers, but no great damage is done. Barth often spoke of his later work in this way. Once he wondered if he was building Solomon's temple or the tower of Babel: "I am quite sure that the angels sometimes chuckle at my enterprise, but I would like to think that the chuckle is well-meaning" (*B,* 374). He continued to warn his readers against making his thought into a system or a school. "If there are 'Barthians,' I myself am not among them" (*B,* 375). In these cases irony functions to counter the positive confidence of his theology; it is a small sign of modesty, the recognition of a certain finitude. It is also an expression of solidarity that all theology resides on the same plane of human ignorance and pretension. Yes, we can agree, the angels laugh, we do look foolish, but theology must go on.

In this diluted form irony undoubtedly continues into Barth's later work; however, the other tropes are gone.[26] Theology does not need to prefigure its field in order to express itself because it has already been configured by an external and overwhelming presence. Frei has argued that the style that results from this dogmatic theology is mimetic or representational.[27] Theological language here is realistic according to the three criteria I outlined: it responds to an external reality, under the control of a stable authorial voice, with the goal of explicating perennial themes. In *Romans* the external reality is absent and, when present, tensively disruptive and inaccessible. In the *Dogmatics* the reality of God is understood in progressively stable and positive terms. "Saying no is hardly a supreme art," Barth now claims, "nor is the overthrow of all kinds of false idols an ultimate task."[28] This means that theological language can relax as it adopts the form of a greater reality. Frei argues that this representative role of theology

changes from the first volume, which I have analyzed, to the rest of the project. Instead of portraying theology as a matter of a static correspondence,
theology becomes involved in a dynamic coherence. Barth's vision of theology "became increasingly and self-consciously temporal rather than cog-
nitivist."[29] Theology cannot depict the divine reality in one comprehensive
sweep, constituted by the act of God's speech; instead, theology must gradually unfold the truths of the biblical world, following God's own self-
unfolding. This leads Frei to suggest that the *Dogmatics* increasingly takes
a narrative form; it depicts, with conceptual help, the plot-like development
of God's creation and redemption of the world.

In the course of Barth's evolving position, excessive incitements and
uncanny obfuscations fade more and more into the background, as Barth becomes increasingly absorbed in and sure of his material. Whereas Barth's
voice in *Romans* was fragmented into many different contradictory voices,
in the *Dogmatics* the case is totally different. Note, for example, the subparagraphs in the *Dogmatics,* printed in small type, which indicate the biblical and theological presuppositions of Barth's argument, its connections
to historical theology, and its polemical relations. Barth says that this allows
for a smooth reading of his text because the nonspecialist can skip over
these passages, which often include quotations from the Bible and the
church fathers in the original languages (*CD,* xii). But the subparagraphs do
not merely give this text a cohesiveness to the nontheologian; they also show
that Barth is in control of his text, marshalling the evidence for his arguments and ordering its composition. These subparagraphs, which frame and
thus defuse their polemical material, are, then, the marks of an intrusive author who displays a consistent and trustworthy face. They are full of the kind
of detail one would expect in a realistic novel, detail that makes the structure
of the work feel solid and weighty. In some of the asides, for example, Barth
puts his past work into perspective, showing that his whole authorship, beginning with *Romans,* constitutes a continuous development, with plot-like
changes and reversals, no doubt, but a development nonetheless that now
reaches its consummation with the veracity of dogmatics. In these paragraphs Barth is not just a voice behind his theology, but Barth becomes one
of his own characters, a personality to be liked or disliked, but one whose
intentions and goals are clear.

The full rhetorical force of Barth's later work is harnessed by Frei in
his own constructive project, *The Eclipse of Biblical Narrative.*[30] Frei tells
the story of how a certain way of reading the Bible was transplanted by other
ways. He argues that traditionally the church construed the Bible as a realistic narrative which structured the individual's faith.[31] Reading the Bible in
this precritical way was a matter of participating in a grand story, which for

the Christian is "the one and only real world."[32] The Bible did not serve as evidence for historical events, nor did it express truths that could be verified from a general reflection on human nature. The Bible is a unique world which invites the reader to become one of the characters in its cosmic drama. It is a lens through which the Christian sees all of reality. The role of the theologian is to show — like a good literary critic — how powerful and coherent this narrative really is. Frei's theological agenda is a good response to those who have argued that Barth's theology stands alone, majestically or otherwise, never contributing to new theological developments.[33] It has been discussed from many different perspectives, and it has created a new school of theology, called postliberalism.[34] There are many ways to argue with this theological movement. I merely want to note that, in continuation with Barth, it commits theology to a realistic style. The realism of the Bible, according to Frei, is a "feature that can be highlighted by the appropriate analytical procedure and by no other, even if it may be difficult to describe the procedure — in contrast to the element itself."[35] It is difficult to describe the method of theology because it really does not have a method other than the seemingly simple and yet difficult task of describing a rich and complex world, which already fully and finally exists.

On rhetorical grounds it is very difficult to argue against Frei's or Barth's realism. This is not because style is a matter of private, indisputable taste, but rather because style is connected to so many issues that the decision about what style is best for a particular discipline is complex and multifaceted. One way to respond to Frei and Barth would be to place their rhetoric in a cultural context: a survey of modern literature might show that realism, as a style, is, according to most observers, if not dead then at least mortally wounded.[36] In my discussion of irony I already noted that only popular literature is nonironical, and Alan Wilde recently has argued that the styles of modernism and postmodernism can be distinguished according to an increasing reliance on unstable or what he calls suspensive irony.[37] Indeed, the history of language in this century has been a gradual rejection of realism in all of its forms. Whether in literature or philosophy (or even science) the representational power of language is doubted and dismissed.[38] Whatever else postmodernism might be, at the very least it is an act of displacement against representationalism. Representation means to *re-present*: what is represented has been presented before. No object can be located in its pure state, and so language is always a representation, to some degree, of itself. Representation re-presents another presentation. This is what postmodern writers mean by intertextuality: the other of language is wrapped up in words, so that language must make a choice as to how to portray that otherness. Language is not constrained by some external reality, which is given to it from outside the structure of representation; language is free and, therefore, also responsible to choose its own style. The what of language will not dictate how language must speak. Realism, then, is just another style, and it must be self-conscious that it does not have any privileged access to reality over against any other style.

Realism tries to hide this freedom from language. It is not for that reason a wrong or failed style, but once the freedom of language is recognized, realism will seem to be a limited or unimaginative choice, as the history of modern literature attests. But what is the alternative? The freedom of language does not mean that language must turn inward in a narcissistic display of impotence; nor does it have to lash out at the world in a destructive spasm of anarchy. In fact, here I would want to return to my analysis of language in chapter two. The choice of language will take different concrete forms, which are themselves represented by the various tropes. Barth's early rhetoric, for example, although unstable and undecidable at certain key points, can nevertheless be mapped according to a fairly specific tropical strategy. To this rhetoric, then, my discussion of Barth's retreat must return. The question then becomes: how is this rhetoric, which is openly figurative, to be judged? In the midst of so many decisions, what tropical gestures are to be accepted and rejected? In the end, there can be no definitive criteria for the freedom of language; that is the nature of freedom. However, certain pragmatic considerations can count for or against various tropical strategies. Some tropes are more effective at achieving certain ends than other tropes.[39] With that observation I want to return to Barth's early rhetoric and examine it from a pragmatically ethical viewpoint. I will not only ask after the social and political consequences of Barth's rhetoric; I will also inquire, finally, into its usefulness today, in a completely changed situation.

ANOTHER OTHER

The relationship of Barth's theology to ethics has always been controversial. In all phases of Barth's career he has been accused of disregarding the importance of ethical reflection. Indeed, Barth refused to make of ethics a separate discipline from theology; ethics, he thought, should flow naturally from dogmatics. The commandment of God is the basis of ethics, which must take the form of obedience, not deliberation. It is not productive to reflect on general ethical principles because, for the Christian, ethical action must be the response to the specific Word of God, which is free and unpredictable. The 'good' and the 'right' have no meaning apart from God's will for each situation. To many critics this formulation of ethics is not helpful in concrete cases. As one ethicist remarks,

> The critics' complaint seems to be that Barth's ethics lacks specificity.
> He speaks broadly of good and evil, but he refuses to identify the good
> and the evil with something so particular as a defense policy or a welfare
> reform bill. He refuses to speak of evil in terms of petty promise break-
> ing or marital infidelity.[40]

How can we know what God really wants without speaking in terms of general Christian principles? By making ethics a byproduct of dogmatics, Barth
risks the abandonment of a systematic ethical position, which could guide
both the individual and the church through ambiguous and complex issues
and situations.

Recently, a different interpretation of Barth's ethics has argued that
Barth's theology is itself ethical throughout. This point of view connects
and subordinates Barth's theology to his socialist beliefs.[41] This argument
does have a certain biographical plausibility. In chapter three I noted
Barth's early commitment to socialism. Anyone who is familiar with
Barth's life is forced to admire the way in which he almost instinctively
understood the danger of the German political situation and from the very
beginning protested against Nazi Germany.[42] The rhetoric of his dogmatic
period, which advocates a singular focus of the church on the divine, can
only be understood and appreciated, in the last analysis, in this context of
the rise of facism. Barth confronts the unlimited power of facism with the
jealous power of God, playing off one exclusive rhetoric against another; this
explains, in part, his rejection of any divided loyalties in theology, and his
condemnation of natural theology, which could serve as the basis for nation-
alism and militarism. In war time sharp lines must be drawn. After the war,
ever ready to keep the Word of God from being used by political or cultural
forces, Barth, again courageously, resisted the Cold War rhetoric and criticized the rearmament of West Germany. Barth was quite clear that the Word
of God opposes fascism, while he was suspicious that Western anticom-
munism was merely an excuse for a continuation of military build-up and a
cover for the unwillingness of the West to deal with its own domestic social
problems.[43]

Barth's experience with fascism also helps to put his earlier rhetoric in
an interesting light: the disgraceful activity of the church (the so-called German Christians) during this period—and Barth acted in a very constructive
manner, helping to form the Confessing Church—makes the rhetoric of *Romans* look, at times, like understatement and not exaggeration. It is that
early rhetoric that I want to briefly examine for its political and social rami-
fications. Eberhard Jüngel has challenged those who find in Barth's early
work the basis for a socialistic interpretation of his theology. For Jüngel, this

interpretation, which seeks to link Barth with his political beliefs and practices, is preposterous, both abstract and reductive. He realizes that Barth
was a practicing socialist, and he finds evidence for the importance of socialism predominant in the first edition of *Romans,* but he thinks that by the
second edition the concept of revelation has been depoliticized. There can
be no synthesis of revelation and history; both socialism and liberalism
stand under the crisis of the judgment of God. In fact, Jüngel argues that
Barth's ultimate concern was always theology. There is no nontheological
basis for talk about God. "Politics was a predicate—the 'political side'—of
his theology, but his theology was never a predicate of politics."[44] The Christian's best political activity is the confession of faith; Barth was "a socialist,
not as a pastor, but as a human being and a citizen."[45] The revolution, which
he advocates in *Romans,* is a purely theological matter with no direct political consequences.[46]

The problem of the ethical implications of the second edition of *Romans* is something I have not yet discussed; with this problem a different
kind of otherness is posited from the otherness that, I have argued, shapes
and informs the body of Barth's text. I want to situate my comments in the
middle of the debate between the socialistic interpretation of Barth and Jüngel's reaction. Surely Jüngel overstates his case; I tried to show in chapter
three that socialism was, admittedly in an increasingly ambiguous fashion,
one of the factors that contributed to Barth's break with liberalism; there is,
then, a special relationship between *Romans* and socialism that is difficult
to deny. It is true that in the second edition socialism no longer serves as a
sign of the coming of the Kingdom of God; the crisis has become too complete to allow for any exemption. However, socialist values are still privileged in this text. What, then, does Barth say about how people should treat
each other, about the responsibilities and demands which are usually discussed under the rubric of ethics? More specifically, I want to ask Barth a
final question: What is the relationship of his rhetoric of an absolute otherness, an absent God who makes his prose reckless and wild, and a finite otherness, the very present neighbor who demands our attention and action?

Barth's ethical arguments, like all of his arguments, are plural in form
and cannot be easily summarized. I have already noted in chapter four that
his hyperbolic critique of the church sputters into nearly vacuous tautolo-
gies and scepticisms. Neither the church nor the critique of the church can
alter the situation of the world. Moreover, in the chapter on irony I noted that
Barth qualifies and retracts all of his constructive comments, so that anything he might say about ethics cannot be taken literally. At this point one is
tempted to understand Barth through Mann's comment that irony is the only
alternative to radicalism. However, there are passages in *Romans* that either

contain or imply fairly specific ethical positions, passages that have not received sufficient attention in the secondary literature.[47] For example, one of the implications of the general and massive crisis is that all individuals are put on an equal footing. "The observable superiority which one man has over another is only his person, his mask, his form, the part he takes in the play. To their fellow men it is only this mask which distinguishes one man from another. They can see no more than this" (R, 63). By turning reality against appearance, the crisis obliterates every essential distinction that separates and divides people. True, Barth does not say that people should take off their masks; only God can see through the outward appearances of humanity. But the crisis does subtract from the seriousness and importance of these masks, the roles that society forces people to play. At its deepest level, humanity is united in an absolute equality.

There is, then, an ultimate sameness which draws humanity together under the terrifying otherness of God. This does not mean that Barth wants — or is able — to depict a new humanity awakened to this knowledge. He does talk about the "new man" in *Romans*, but this discussion does not parallel Nietzsche's talk of an *Übermensch*. The crisis does demand a reevaluation of all values, but humanity is unable to act on this demand. Typically, Barth describes the "new man" as an incomprehensible void. The new subject is not new at all: "Speaking dialectically: this identification must always be shattered by the recognition that man is not God" (R, 149). What holds humanity together in a comprehensive sameness is nothing that humanity can claim to know or understand — it is, in fact, nothing: humanity shares something purely negative, the absence of God. "Thus the new subject emerges in the negation of the old, known, human subject; and by the invisible and personal action of God human personality is fashioned" (R, 150). God creates the new subject; but that creative act is hidden to us, unknown, beyond all human experience.

In fact, Barth can even argue that we do not really know the old subject, let alone the new: "Sin is, moreover, meaningless and incomprehensible except as the negation of the righteousness which is in Christ" (R, 171). Both the old and the new subject, then, are hidden in the mystery of God: "The different characteristics of the old and the new proceed from the same invisible origin. They are old or new according to their relation to God" (R, 179). Barth describes this battle between the old and the new subject as war. "There is no third alternative between death and life. In the war which is waged between them, there are no deserters, no mediators, and no neutrals" (R, 211). However, it is difficult not to think of individuals as, at best, observers or, at worst, victims, in this war, especially when Barth's emphasis on predestination is recalled. In fact, there is not much that people can do; taking sides will not help. "There is no 'good cause' which is, in actual fact, God's," Barth writes (*R*, 301), a statement that supports Jüngel's apolitical interpretation of *Romans*.

However, in the commentary on chapters twelve through fifteen of the Epistle, Barth returns to the issue of ethics in what seems, at times, to be a constructive manner. He admits that he has made an insurmountable problem out of ethics because "the object about which we are concerned has no objectivity, that is to say, it is not a concrete world existing above or behind our world" (*R*, 424). He confesses that he has no simple advice or consolation to offer anybody: "To be sincere, our thought must share in the tension of human life, in its criss-cross lines, and in its kaleidescopic movements" (*R*, 425). He can even say that, "The problem of ethics reminds us that our act of thinking cannot be justified" (*R*, 426). Yet he does want to discuss the practical implications of his thought. Barth's dilemma raises the suspicions I discussed in chapter one: can an openly rhetorical mode of thought leave any room for ethical principles? Barth's answer to this question, which was consistent throughout his career, is that practical theology is not a second thing existing by the side of a theory of religion; the ethical question has been involved in his rhetoric from the beginning. "We have not been searching out hidden things for the mere joy of so doing" (*R*, 427). So what, then, can the church and the individual Christian do? The moral exhortation of the church, Barth writes,

> can be naught else but a criticism of all human behaviour, a criticism which moves through every one of the 360 degrees of the circle of our ambiguous life. This means that very great reserve is necessary when judgements concerning human capacity of will and action, whether they be positive or negative, have to be made—not for fear lest the criticism should be too sweeping, but lest it should not be sweeping enough (*R*, 428).

This criticism from the church cannot be identified with the critique of socialism; its origin must come from theology, or rather, from the crisis that God initiates. It must be a complete critique, just as the crisis is comprehensive, and thus socialism too must come under the church's disapproval.

Ethics, under the crisis, must try to disclose the incredible force of God's judging grace. In the end, though, ethics must, like everything else, dissolve itself: "The decisive word about ethics must disclose their full ambiguity, ambiguity covering every aspect of human behaviour" (*R*, 428). Barth is aware that this is a difficult or impossible project: "The task of ethics, thus defined and directed, becomes both serious and impressive, for it lies wholly beyond this world" (R, 429). The ethical life is identified with grace, which exists only eschatologically; in the present, then, there is no ethical life as such. Our ethical acts can only be signs or parables of the coming Kingdom of God; in themselves they possess no significance or substance. "Thus it is that all human duties and virtues and good deeds are set upon the edge of a knife. They hang on a single thread" (R, 433). Just as the theological thinking is indirect, obscure and finally self-destructive, ethical acts are mingled with egoism and eroticism and never accomplish what they intend. When we do experience something good in this world it only reminds us of how far we are removed from the world to come: "When a human work or production sings to us a theme of supreme beauty—Mozart!—then, precisely then, it strikes chords of deep distress" (R, 434).

Is there, then, no practical significance or political presuppositions to the critique that the church must carry out in the name of the crisis? There is something that can be done: "Since the truth lies in the ambiguity of human existence, we must exhort them to affirm that ambiguity" (R, 436). This act of rethinking, Barth argues, can only lead to repentance, which becomes the primary ethical act. "For the vast ambiguity of our life is at once its deepest truth. And moreover, when we think this thought, our thinking is renewed, for such thinking is repentance" (R, 437). Barth is clear that this act of rethinking and repentance must be done on an individual, not social level. It is a constructive act, though, one that recognizes the utter sameness of the human condition. The otherness of the neighbor can be acknowledged by a mutual recognition of the otherness of God as a common problem. The other can be accepted because the Other also confronts her or him. "It must be fellowship which is encountered in the community: but this means an encountering of the Other in the full existentiality of his utter Otherness. In the neighbor it must be the ONE who is disclosed" (R, 443). Christian fellowship is a mutual recognition of a shared relationship to a common and catastrophic otherness. Community, then, is not built on some liberal notion of tolerance: "Tolerance is, no doubt, a virtue without which none of us can live, but we must nevertheless, at least understand that it is, strictly speaking, destructive of fellowship, for it is a gesture by which the divine disturbance is rejected. The One in whom we are veritably united is Himself the great intolerance" (R, 445). Community makes present but does not neutralize an absence which is otherwise both intolerable and easily ignored.

In sum, the neighbor is accepted because in that otherness a greater otherness can be acknowledged; the neighbor is a cipher for a greater reality, the most concrete of all Barth's figures, prefiguring that which otherwise cannot be imagined. With an allusion to Grünenwald, Barth can say that the neighbor "who stands at the side of each one of us is the uplifted finger which by its 'otherness' reminds us of the Wholly Other" (R, 444). The rad-

ical equality that flows from this position is analogous to the equality socialism demands. True, it is a theological equality: "The maxim, 'To every
one his own,' can never lead to ethical action. 'To every one the One.' is the
true maxim" (R, 445). But there is a certain solidarity Barth is advocating,
a solidarity that extends beyond the confines of the church to include all human beings. "There is, for this reason, much in the cause of socialism which
evokes Christian approval" (R, 463). And he can say, "All ethical action is
of the nature of a protest" (R, 468). Barth is not necessarily expressing a
sympathy for state socialism, what is now called communism; instead, he is
drawing an analogy between Christianity and the utopian kind of socialism
that hopes for a community of equality that will not let any one position
dominate all others. No viewpoint here is absolute; there is a real plurality
of opinions and positions—a critique of the totalizing tendency of thought
—all sheltered beneath the storm of the crisis. "By putting an end to all absolute ethics, Christianity finally puts an end to all the triumph and sorrow
that accompanies the occupation of any human eminence ... We are deprived by the Truth of the energy with which we immerse ourselves in A
truth" (R, 466).

Barth says that in some ways his theology has tried to bring the world
war. "War is the concrete expression of what men are, of their impossibility,
and of our determination to be rid of them" (R, 470). His deeper desire is to
bring peace. By forcing people to recognize their common situation, all apparent differences have been obliterated, not because of who people are, but
because of who God is. This is not an advocacy of pacifism, but it is something close to that position. "Thou and the enemy smitten by God are one.
Between thee and him there is complete solidarity. His evil is thy evil; his
suffering thy suffering; his justification thy justification" (R, 475). More specifically, Barth says that his position is neither legitimism nor revolution. In
fact, on his theological scales revolution and reaction are not equally
balanced.

> We are anxious about the forces of revolution and not about the forces
> of conservativism, because it is most improbable that anyone will be
> won over to the cause of reaction—as a result of reading the Epistle to
> the Romans! On the other hand, it is not unlikely that its reading may
> foster a contempt for the present order and an attitude of negation
> towards it (R, 478).

Moreover: "The revolutionary Titan is far more godless, far more dangerous, than his reactionary counterpart — because he is so much nearer the
truth" (R, 478). The problem with political revolution is that when the good

and the true is established, it becomes the status quo, and thus further per-
petuates evil. Revolutionaries forget the ambiguity of their position. Unfortunately, "Even the most radical revolution can do no more than set what
exists against what exists" (R, 482).

Barth does not reject revolution; he wants a more permanent and universal revolution, one that will create a lasting, an eternal change. For this,
love, the ultimate protest, is needed—not human love, eros, but God's love,
agape. In this love can be found the God in the other. "If I hear in the neighbor only the voice of the other and not also the voice of the One—that is to
say, if I do not detect in him both question and answer—then, quite certainly
the voice of the One is nowhere to be heard" (R, 495). Barth can even say
that the neighbor answers the question: Who am I? By understanding the
love of God for the other, individuals can find God's love for themselves.
"Love is the relation between men and their fellow men which is grounded
—and therefore broken!—in the knowledge of God" (R, 495). In love the
One is disclosed in the other, reducing the many to a real (even if not yet realized) community; that is the ultimate revolution. It shares many characteristics with socialism, but it must be brought about by God, not by any human movement. Of course, this entire discussion is followed by the
retraction of the last chapter of Romans, which I analyzed in my chapter
five, so it cannot be taken literally. But it does offer some of the most constructive statements that can be found in Romans. It is important because it
develops a distinctive theory of otherness. In the singular Otherness of God
the multitude of others is fused together; we can know the other as a fellow
victim of a greater Other. This is Barth's anthropology: the only common
element in human nature is something that people do not know, cannot experience or feel, but nonetheless share, a force—a negative monism—
which ruthlessly breaks down all differences and oppositions, changing
everything and nothing.

TOWARD A RECONSTRUCTION

Barth's discussion of finite otherness in Romans is usually overlooked; scholars choose to focus instead on Barth's conception of God's infinite otherness. This is an understandable decision: the one otherness does
overshadow and engulf the other. Nevertheless, Barth's discussion is significant because the problem—the figure—of otherness has come to define the
present situation.[48] Today, in fact, the existence of really 'other' others constitutes a new crisis for theology: we live in an age of pluralism and suspicion in which no knowledge is certain and yet many truth claims abound in
a sea of conflicting currents. Pluralism—the conflict of ideologies, episte-

mologies, and theologies — makes us essentially unsure of ourselves, and yet we must listen to the many voices that are demanding to be heard. Pluralism as both fact and problem forces us to respond to radical otherness, not only the No-God of Barth's early theology but also the Not-I's of the many conflicting realities in which we find ourselves. As a fact of our common existence pluralism is both a challenge and a promise: the challenge lies in efforts to define and address a situation that is fragmented, constantly changing, seemingly chaotic and out of control; the promise resides in the hope that new voices can come to be heard above the clamor of competing claims and defeating confusions. The problem is that pluralism can be both a romantic notion (all other cultures, especially so-called primitive cultures, are better than our own) and a utopian ideal (we hope to learn to live in a world at peace and harmony with itself). In any case, as Langdon Gilkey has argued, we can no longer afford to deny the apparent rough parity among the religions, a parity that calls into question all the assumptions which have guided theology in the past.[49]

The initial problem in any reflection on pluralism, a term whose currency is already in danger of becoming inflated, dispersed and thus devalued, is to deal with both the *fact* of plurality (both within and outside the church) and the attempt to understand that fact as a description of our *common* reality. There is something uncanny in evaluating the current individual, social and cultural situation as one of plurality. The question that immediately arises is this: How can we deal with pluralism when that very word threatens to defer all of our solutions? In other words, the fact of plurality seems to undermine any commonality that our situation might engender. Pluralism itself escapes again and again from the clutches of conceptuality. By its very nature it means different things to different people; it is discovered, in fact, not by any analysis of shared assumptions and values but by the trace of difference which it leaves, as a remainder, in all such analyses. Any discussion of pluralism, then, cannot follow the contours of the clarity of theoretical elaboration. If pluralism is not to become a meaningless catchword that only connotes an attitude of "anything goes," if it is to be kept from slipping into a sloppy relativism or, even worse, an oppressive monism, then we must deal with the question of how pluralism can be best articulated as a vision of reality that both holds together a variety of positions and issues and allows for real conflict within communication. We must deal with the hope that pluralism can become not a permanent state of miscommunication and despair, not a way of shrinking from the task of developing new visions for culture and religion, but a way in which a new holism can be found that is inclusive without being exclusive and therefore destructive.

Some way of thinking and acting is needed that will do justice both to one's own tradition and to the existence of many traditions that challenge and contradict each other. The issues at stake are enormous. In the midst of such contradictions many people resort to private fantasies, unwilling to venture into the public realm: as the authors of *Habits of the Heart* have shown, many Americans live without ever finding their own voices because they cannot join voices with any whole greater than themselves.[50] Everything is tolerated because nothing really matters.[51] The result, according to Peter Berger, is that many individuals are not connected to any particular tradition or cultural framework; "homeless minds" feel at best nostalgia or homesickness for ways of life that once answered their deepest questions.[52] On the other hand, some individuals—and institutions—react to pluralism by becoming increasingly exclusive, reaffirming their own position by rejecting all others, thus turning the fundamentals of their tradition into yet another "ism." Others deplore the attempt to exclude religious traditions from the political realm, responding to the problem of the "naked public square" by reviving discussions of civil religion, often in an exclusive fashion.[53] Very practical perplexities, then, make pluralism a most serious issue: how can conflicting traditions not only coexist but come to learn from and grow with each other? How can absolute claims be held in the midst of contingent and relative qualifications?

Because this problem cannot be resolved conceptually, a rhetorical approach must be sufficient. Pluralism is, after all, a question of communication, not an issue of theoretical certainty. Perhaps more than anyone David Tracy has recognized this and has undertaken the project of developing an imaginative theological response to the problem of otherness.[54] He follows Tillich in defending a method of correlation between theology and other disciplines; however, his correlation is not based on an ontology that would demand an ordering and ranking of the insights that the correlation would produce. Instead, correlation becomes conversation in Tracy, rhetorical and not ontological, unpredictable and yet urgent, freed from a systematic philosophical position that would arrange the categories within which the correlation would fit. In fact, his proposal depends on the tropical strategy of analogy: both the similarity and the difference of the other must be recognized at the same time. From that recognition, true dialogue — mutually critical interaction—can take place.[55]

More recently, however, Tracy has confronted the plurality and ambiguity that threaten even the most articulate attempts at conversation and dialogue.[56] In the midst of such radical plurality, the question remains whether analogy is enough. As many authors have argued, analogy is related to metaphor; both seek an identity through an opposition. It could be argued that metaphors and analogies, in today's situation, promise more than they can give. In the midst of so many differences, similarities cannot be so easily identified. If this is true, then a return to the broad outline of Barth's rhetoric might expand the theological imagination in an important way. Hyperbole and irony give more than they can promise. In fact, hyperbole and irony break the promise that is only ambiguously present in all communication. Hyperbole gives the ontological shock of metaphor in a more provisional, almost comedic form, while irony warns us that all of our new quests for (metaphorical) knowledge can turn out to be mystifying journeys of self-deception along the way.

This does not mean that Barth's rhetoric should be simply reiterated today. Barth was right to suggest that the difference of the other prefigures an even more fundamental difference, but he was wrong to move too quickly toward a reflection on the utter unity of that deeper otherness; no single discourse on that singular otherness can prevail in the midst of radical plurality. The many others must be refigured not as instances of a monolithic otherness but as marks of differences and reversals. Barth's focus on a fundamental otherness too quickly reduces diversity to sameness. Moreover, all tropes have their dangers. While metaphor risks a too comprehensive ambition, the parallel risk of hyperbole is that some exaggerations can seem shrill and irresponsible while unstable irony can become mere ambiguity or worse, simply cynicism. Yet Barth's focus on these two tropes, if read through a new metaphor of crisis, the different otherness, can help theology to prepare for radical plurality. By limiting its own claims with an ironic sensibility, theology can let the world be the world and yet theology can still speak to the world, albeit in a broken voice. Irony alone is not enough, however, and Barth was correct to be dissatisfied with the overwhelmingly negative thrust of his early work. A positive moment in communication, a yes to balance the no, was needed to avoid the many circuitous perplexities of the kind that have plagued the work of deconstructionism. Let me, then, recall Marvick's analysis of the sublime, where he argued that hyperbole and irony must work together to both manifest and displace the quest for the sublime other. In Barth hyperbole is finally put to the service of irony; hyperbole exploits the crisis within which only irony is allowed to move and work. Perhaps a more traditional coupling of these two tropes could help theology today.

It just might be that a hyperbolic imagination of the extremes of God's graces in the plurality of othernesses and an ironic suspicion and suspension of the necessity and ability of theology to capture and tame all of God's manifestations could be an appropriate envisionment of theological rhetoric today. Such figures of speech could help us to refigure theological communication in an age of excessive pluralism and suspicion, when there is too much otherness ever to be fully known, and yet know we must try. Perhaps this strategy can meet Barth's demand that the Word of God be granted an absolute freedom.[57] My point is that a theology freed from ontology must take rhetoric seriously; theology is now forced to choose a language, a style, rather than a philosophy.[58] Hyperbolically we can seek God's love in every other; ironically we can be prepared to live with the failure of that search. That God is love, then, does not mean that God and love are somehow metaphorically fused together in the theological consciousness; instead, God is love is an exaggeration, an extravagant willingness on our part to find God wherever we discover love, and to see in the practice of love the work of God —and to find both God and love more present than appearances would allow. Pluralism seems to demand such excess. After all, to transform the juxtaposition of two others into a fruitful communication, risks must be taken that transcend the usual cordialities of the exchange of information and the cultivation of channels of persuasion, which the term conversation too often denotes.

Yet the attempt to encompass the other with loving understanding and the likelihood that conversation can be freed from all interruptions leads to the need for irony. The theologian must be suspicious of all attempts to establish common ground: conversation itself should not be reified into an absolute category and thus treated as a simple answer to a complex problem. Irony must qualify hyperbole because we know that all too often our conversations with others lead us astray in strategies of exclusion or capitulation and with the force of violence, which we are always too slow to recognize. Nevertheless, the only alternative to conversation, besides violence, is silence, and that is only for those who have already spoken.

In the end, we cannot say ''God is love'' with a straight face and a steady voice; we must be willing to say it ironically, because we have heard it said too often, and we know that it is too frequently betrayed and abused.[59] In this way—from the metaphor of the crisis of the other through the hyperbole of love and to an ironic reservation and qualification about that love— Barth's early rhetoric, broken by the Other of others and not the Other in itself, can be made if not to speak again then at least to echo, like a lion's roar, along the fringes of theology.

NOTES

CHAPTER 1: READING KARL BARTH

1. Aristotle, *Rhetoric*, in *Introduction to Aristotle,* ed. Richard McKeon and trans. W. Rhys Roberts (Chicago: University of Chicago Press, 1973), 731 (1355b).
2. Robert Hariman, "Status, Marginality, and Rhetorical Theory," *Quarterly Journal of Speech* 72 (1986): 38–54.
3. For a good review of the possibilities here, see John S. Nelson, Allan Megill, and Donald N. McCloskey, eds., *The Rhetoric of the Human Sciences* (Madison, Wisconsin: University of Wisconsin Press, 1986). For a good overview of the history of rhetoric, see George A. Kennedy, *Classical Rhetoric and its Christian and Secular Tradition from Ancient to Modern Times* (London: Croom Helm, 1980).
4. See *Plurality and Ambiguity* (San Francisco: Harper & Row, 1987), 28. This is ironic because in *Blessed Rage for Order* (New York: Seabury, 1975) Tracy was accused of foundationalism due to his attention to metaphysics and transcendental arguments. Note, however, that such arguments are still present in his more recent work, where they are used *rhetorically;* transcendental arguments do not prove anything, but they do help the conversation along when they are needed. They are breaks in the conversation, which should not be pursued for their own end.
5. Sallie McFague, *Speaking in Parables, a Study in Metaphor and Theology* (Philadelphia: Fortress Press, 1975), 40.
6. I should note here that, as McFague's argument implies, rhetoric in biblical studies is a fast growing field, even if rhetoric in theology has been a bit slower to develop. For two representative texts, see Amos N. Wilder, *The Language of the Gospel: Early Christian Rhetoric* (New York: Harper & Row, 1964) and Robert Funk, *Language, Hermeneutic, and the Word of God: The Problem of Language in the New Testament and Contemporary Theology* (New York: Harper & Row, 1966). In a more recent work, Stephen Prickett argues that traditionally rhetoric and literary theory were united with biblical studies, so that the recent interest in biblical poetics constitutes a return to the roots of literary criticism. See *Words and The Word, Language, Poetics and Biblical Interpretation* (Cambridge: Cambridge University Press, 1986). It is interesting that McFague argues that a renewed appreciation of biblical language as rhetorical can teach theology to be creative in its own use of language; it was precisely this move — toward biblical language—that ignited Karl Barth's own theological rhetoric.

7. "Much of this [discussion of figurative and rhetorical language in religion] seems so self-evident that we wonder why we miss it so often; why we insist on trying to step out of our skins when we think . . . The metaphorical tradition . . . is in large part the legacy of Christianity, yet the main tradition in Christian theology has often retreated from faith in its own foundation" (McFague, *Speaking in Parables*, 62). McFague, like many others, blames this understanding of rhetoric on the Cartesian search for conceptual foundations.

8. Michael C. Leff, "Modern Sophistic and the Unity of Rhetoric," in Nelson, Megill and McCloskey, eds., *The Rhetoric of the Human Sciences*, 20.

9. Friedrich Schleiermacher, *Brief Outline on the Study of Theology*, trans. Terrence N. Tice (Atlanta: John Knox Press, 1966), 98–99. For a good discussion of Schleiermacher's attitude toward practical theology, and an example of the increasing importance of practical theology in theological circles today, see John E. Burkhart, "Schleiermacher's Vision for Theology," in *Practical Theology*, ed. Don Browning (San Francisco: Harper & Row, 1983). As the articles in this book show, though, practical theology is more often connected to sociology and critical theory than to rhetoric. Don Browning, for example, in his contribution, gives rhetoric the limited role of being an adjunct to preaching (see "Pastoral Theology in a Pluralistic Age," 189). Leander Keck's contribution to this volume, although helpful in explicitly raising the issue of rhetoric, also limits rhetoric to the problem of preaching (see "Toward a Theology of Rhetoric/Preaching"). He at least has the foresight to criticize practical theologians like Hermann Diem who argue that "a textual sermon can dispense with rhetorical means of carrying the thought because it is borne by the text" (quoted on p. 127). None of these thinkers see the theoretical importance of rhetoric which I will pursue in this book. I should also note here that Barth's very rhetorical *Epistle to the Romans* was dismissively accused by Jülicher of being merely practical theology! (See Adolf Jülicher, "A Modern Interpretation of Paul," in *The Beginnings of Dialectical Theology*, ed. James M. Robinson [Richmond: John Knox Press, 1968], 72–81.)

10. Clifford Geertz, *Works and Lives, the Anthropologist as Author* (Stanford: Stanford University Press, 1988).

11. Ibid., 2.

12. Paul de Man, *Allegories of Reading* (New Haven: Yale University Press, 1979), 10.

13. Ibid.

14. In *Blindness and Insight, Essays in the Rhetoric of Contemporary Criticism*, rev. ed. (Minneapolis: University of Minnesota Press, 1983), de Man argues that critical texts are also literary; they too are subject to the disruptive force of rhetoric. In fact, he suggests that, because literary criticism tries to read in a systematic way texts which are essentially rhetorical — tries to put rhetoric into literal terms — such criticism can make its points only by disregarding the rhetoric of the texts it questions. In other words, insight comes about only by blindness: "Critics' moments of greatest blindness with regard to their own critical assumptions are also the moments at which they achieve their greatest insight" (109). Critics are doomed, therefore, to say things quite different from what they mean; the result is that the process of interpretation itself is thoroughly rhetori-

cal and neverending. In later work de Man has called this the insecurity of contemporary literary theory. See *The Resistance to Theory* (Minneapolis: University of Minnesota Press, 1986), 12. The upshot of this position is that there can never be a true rhetorical reading of a literary text because such a reading must try to reduce or undermine rhetoric in order to make sense of it. For an introduction to the entire scope of de Man's thought, see Christopher Norris, *Paul De Man, Deconstruction and the Critique of Aesthetic Ideology* (New York: Routledge, 1988). I will deal with another version of this position, in the works of Jacques Derrida, throughout this thesis. I hope that it will become clear that while my reading of Karl Barth is tremendously influenced by deconstructionism, I do not want to follow the deconstructionists into their skeptical labyrinths, primarily because I do not agree, as I will point out in chapter two, that rhetoric and reason are bitter and irreconcilable opponents.

15. Maurice Wiles, *Remaking of Christian Doctrine* (London: SCM Press, 1974), 24–25.

16. T. F. Torrance, *Karl Barth: An Introduction to His Early Theology, 1910–1931* (London: SCM Press, 1962), 41. Stephen Sykes echoes this argument in *The Identity of Christianity* (Philadelphia: Fortress Press, 1982), 174.

17. "Ist etwa ein einziges meiner Worte *das* Wort, das ich suche, das ich aus meiner grossen Not und Hoffnung heraus eigentlich sagen mochte? Kann ich denn anders reden als so, dass ein Wort das andre wieder aufheben muss?" Karl Barth, *Der Römerbrief, 1922* (Zurich: Theologischer Verlag, 1940), 243 [my translation].

18. Karl Barth, *Epistle to the Romans,* trans. Edwyn C. Hoskyns (Oxford University Press, 1968), 225. In all, there were six editions of *Der Römerbrief* published between 1919 and 1928. Hereafter *Romans* will be used to refer to the English translation, which is of the sixth edition (unrevised from the second), and quotations in the text will be marked in parentheses with the symbol, *R.*

19. The bomb analogy is often made and is originally attributed to Karl Adam. See, for example, T.H.L. Parker, *Karl Barth* (Grand Rapids, Mich.: Eerdmans, 1970), 56.

20. In an introduction to the second part of a collection of letters between him and Thurneysen, Barth admits that their language then "was rich, not to say over-rich, in images of all kinds, among which quite noticeable the military and particularly those drawn from the field of artillery played a decisive role. One may shake his head in disapproval, but one can do nothing about it! The first world war was at that time still very much alive in our imaginations, and in fairness also it must be recognized that our decidedly embattled situation during those years drew such forms of expression inevitably from our pens" (*Revolutionary Theology in the Making: Barth-Thurneysen Correspondence, 1914 – 1925,* trans. James D. Smart [Richmond, Va: John Knox Press, 1964], 71). (Hereafter this book will be cited in the text as *RTM.*) In the preface to the English edition of *Romans* Barth exaggerates this military context of the book: "When I first wrote it . . . it required only a little imagination for me to hear the sound of the guns booming away in the north" (*R,* v). Biographically speaking, this stylistic preference should be no surprise; Barth's earliest childhood interests were in military history, and he was obsessed with the American Civil War.

21. See, for example, John Updike, *Roger's Version*, 42. Updike's interest in Barth is evident from his earliest publications; note "Faith in Search of Understanding," review of Barth's book on Anselm, in *Assorted Prose* (New York: Knopf, 1965). 212–219. For a more recent discussion, see Updike's "To the Tram Halt Together," in *Hugging the Shore* (New York: Random House, 1983), 825–836.

22. Langdon Gilkey, "An Appreciation of Karl Barth," *How Karl Barth Changed My Mind*, ed. Donald K. McKim (Grand Rapids, Mich.: Wm. B. Eerdmans, 1986), 152.

23. Hans Frei, "An Afterword: Eberhard Busch's Biography of Karl Barth," in *Karl Barth in Re-View, Posthumous Works Reviewed and Assessed*, ed. H.-Martin Rumscheidt (Pittsburg: Pickwick Press, 1981), 98 and 100.

24. Ibid., 97–98.

25. John Bowden, *Karl Barth, Theologian* (London: SCM Press, 1983), 13. Herbert Hartwell also uses a musical analogy (without much elaboration) to describe Barth's style, calling *The Epistle to the Romans* "a very hymn in praise of the Godness of God." *The Theology of Karl Barth: An Introduction* (London: Duckworth, 1964), 9.

26. Ibid., 14.

27. With this comment I am in agreement with Eberhard Jüngel, who, in *Karl Barth, A Theological Legacy*, trans. Garrett E. Paul (Philadelphia: Westminster Press, 1986), writes, "Barth scholarship — and here I include everything that passes for Barth scholarship — is particularly concerned to reduce the extraordinary wealth of his theology to a few meager structural principles, so that his theology may be totally circumscribed and then commended or refuted" (14). Jüngel says that Barth is "seductive": "Without a doubt, Barth's theology had style, great style" (12). Jüngel's reading of Barth, though, is not concerned with his style but with Barth's intentions; he investigates what Barth really means by examining the biographical and contextual resources. I will be more concerned with Barth's style than with biographical or historical questions of intention, although I will try not to ignore Barth's intentions, when applicable.

28. See Eberhard Jüngel, *The Doctrine of the Trinity: God's Being in Becoming*, trans. H. Harris (Grand Rapids, Mich.: Wm. B. Eerdmans, 1976); Phillip J. Rosato, *The Spirit as Lord: The Pneumatology of Karl Barth* (Edinburgh: T. & T. Clark, 1985); Hans Küng, *Justification: The Doctrine of Karl Barth and a Catholic Reflection*, rev. ed., trans. Thomas Collins, Edmund E. Tolk and David Granskou (Philadelphia: Westminster, 1964); Stephen Sykes, "Barth and the Power of the Word," *The Identity of Christianity*, chapter 8 (Philadelphia: Fortress Press, 1982); Steven G. Smith, *The Argument to the Other: Reason Beyond Reason in the Thought of Karl Barth and Emmanuel Levinas* (Chico, Calif.: Scholars Press, 1983); Friedrich Wilhelm Marquardt, "Socialism in the Theology of Karl Barth," in *Karl Barth and Radical Politics*, ed. and trans. George Hunsinger (Philadelphia: Westminster, 1976); George Berkouwer, *The Triumph of Grace in the Theology of Karl Barth* (London: S.P.C.K., 1956); Colm O'Grady, *The Church in the Theology of Karl Barth* (London: Geoffrey Chapman, 1968); and Mark I. Wallace, "The World of the Text: Theological Hermeneutics in the Thought of Karl Barth and Paul Ricoeur," (Ph.D. diss., University of Chicago, 1986).

29. George Hunsinger, "How to Read Karl Barth: The Shape of His Theology," (Ph.D. diss., Yale University, 1988). His five motifs are actualism, particularism, objectivism, personalism, and realism. In fairness to Hunsinger, I should note that he says that these themes are "adjectival in force, not substantive" (31). They are qualifications of Barth's subject matter, he argues, never the subject matter itself.

30. Hans Urs von Balthasar, *The Theology of Karl Barth,* trans. John Drury (Garden City, New York: Doubleday, 1972).

31. Torrance, *Karl Barth: An Introduction to his Early Theology, 1910–1931.*

32. For an excellent study of Barth's Marburg period see Simon Fisher, *Revelatory Positivism? Barth's Earliest Theology and the Marburg School* (New York: Oxford University Press, 1988).

33. Von Balthasar, *The Theology of Karl Barth,* p. 67.

34. Wilhelm Pauck, *Karl Barth: Prophet of a New Christianity?* (New York: Harper, 1931), 19. Probably the first person to call Barth an expressionist was Adolf Harnack. He used the term to mean that Barth was unscientific. See Martin Rumscheidt, "The Correspondence Between Harnack and Barth," (Ph.D. diss., McGill University, 1967), 28, 91 and 93. For a recent use of this analogy, note Jüngel's comment: "These early writings spoke not only with the expressionist language of their time but also with a vigorous recklessness that emphasized the new ... " *Karl Barth, A Theological Legacy,* 12.

35. Von Balthasar, *The Theology of Karl Barth,* 23–4.

36. In this chapter I will not discuss the more general problem of comparing literature and the fine arts. For a comprehensive and provocative treatment of the *ut pictura poesis* tradition, with focuses on the modern period, see Wendy Steiner, *The Colors of Rhetoric, Problems in the Relation Between Modern Literature and Painting* (Chicago: University of Chicago Press, 1982).

37. John Dillenberger, *A Theology of Artistic Sensibility* (New York: Crossroad, 1986), 217. Dillenberger quotes Barth as saying that images and symbols "have no place at all in a building designed for Protestant worship" (From Karl Barth, "The Architectural Problem of Protestant Places of Worship," in *Architecture in Worship: The Christian Place of Worship,* ed. Andre Bieler [Edinburgh and London: Oliver and Boyd, 1965], 93). In fact, Barth's entire theology, which pits the dialectic of the heard Word against the illusory identity of appearance and reality, can be considered as essentially antiaesthetic and iconoclastic (with the exception of his limited but original discussion of beauty as an attribute of God in *Church Dogmatics,* ed. G. W. Bromiley and T. F. Torrance [Edinburgh: T. & T. Clark, 1939–1969], II/1: 650ff). Barth was, by the way, aware of his iconoclastic tendencies, and in the following passage he tries to soften them by transfering them from humans to God: "That is why we must not omit to add by way of warning that we have not to become Philistines or Christian iconoclasts in face of human greatness as it meets us so strikingly in this very sphere of religion. Of course it is inevitable and not without meaning that in times of strong Christian feeling heathen temples should be levelled to the earth, idols and pictures of saints destroyed, stained glass smashed, organs removed: *to the great distress of aesthetes everywhere.* But *irony* usually had it that Christian churches were built on the very sites of these temples and with materials taken from their

pillars and furnishings. And after a time the storm of iconoclasm was succeeded by a fresh form of artistic *decoration*. This goes to show that while the devaluation and negation of what is human may occasionally have a practical and symbolical significance in detail, it can never have any basic or general significance. And it must not, either. We cannot, as it were, translate the divine judgment that religion is unbelief into human terms, into the form of definite devaluations and negations" (*Church Dogmatics*, I/2: 300, my emphases). In practice, then, iconoclasm is significant, but since it is ironically always followed by more art (read: decoration), it should be left up to God, the great Iconoclast. For Barth's support of the Second Commandment as a ban against all Christian art see *Dogmatics in Outline* (New York: Harper & Row, 1959), 41.

38. See "The Christian's Place in Society." *The Word of God and the Word of Man* (New York: Harper, 1957), 292. Hereafter cited in the texts as *WG*.

39. See Eberhard Busch, *Karl Barth: His Life from Letters and Autobiographical Texts*, trans. John Bowden (Philadelphia: Fortress, 1976), 125. Hereafter cited in the text as *B*.

40. For a discussion of Grünewald's influence on expressionism, see Frank Whitford, *Expressionism* (London: Hamlyn, 1970), 30–31.

41. Barth definitely intends to make of his own approach a general hermeneutical rule: "I cannot, for my part, think it possible for an interpreter honestly to reproduce the meaning of any author unless he dares to accept the condition of utter loyalty" (*Romans*, 18).

42. What is perhaps still the most comprehensive treatment of expressionism is Bernard S. Myers, *The German Expressionists, A Generation in Revolt* (New York: Frederick A. Praeger, 1956). A more general account can be found in John Willett, *Expressionism* (New York: McGraw-Hill, 1970). The publication of the most recent major exhibition of this movement in the Unites States is *Expressionism, A German Intuition, 1905–1920* (New York: Solomon R. Guggenheim Foundation, 1980). For more technical recent work, see Gerhard P. Knapp, *Die Literatur des deutschen Expressionismus* (München: C. H. Beck, 1979), and the collection of essays in *Expressionismus and Kulturkrise* (Heidelberg: Carl Winter Universitätsverlag, 1983). For a comprehensive treatment of all varieties of German art during this period see Harald Olbrich, editor, *Geschichte der deutschen Kunst, 1890–1918* (Leipzig: VEB E. A. Geemann, 1988).

43. Ulrich Weisstein, "Expressionism," in *Princeton Encylcopedia of Poetry and Poetics*, ed. Alex Preminger (Princeton, N.J.: Princeton University Press, 1965), 267.

44. See, for example, Richard Samuel and R. Hinton Thomas, *Expressionism in German Life, Literature and the Theater, 1910–1924* (Cambridge: W. Heffer and Sons, 1939), 12.

45. John Dillenberger, in the introduction to Paul Tillich, *On Art and Architecture*, ed. Dillenberger and Jane Dillenberger, trans. Robert P. Scharlemann (New York: Crossroad, 1987), xvi.

46. Tillich, *On Art and Architecture*, 177.

47. For an excellent study of the literary style of expressionism, see Walter H. Sokel, *The Writer in Extremis, Expressionism in Twentieth-Century German Literature* (Stanford: Stanford University Press, 1959). Sokel argues that a basic contra-

diction of expressionism resided between its missionary zeal about revolution and its elitist and technical stylistic innovations. Thus, Sokel can argue that expressionism was connected to Nazism because the latter also promised a revolutionary program but in a more accessible and traditional form. For a good book on style in expressionist drama, see J. M. Ritchie, *German Expressionist Drama* (Boston: Twayne Publishers, 1976). This work emphasizes abstraction — as opposed to the detailed work of projecting the illusion of reality — as the key to expressionism. One could also examine expressionism in music (for example, the work of Arnold Schoenberg).

48. Lucille Virginia Palmer, "The Language of German Expressionism," (Ph.D. diss., University of Illinois at Urbana, 1938), 4.

49. Samuel and Thomas, *Expressionism in German Life, Literature, and the Theater, 1910–1924,* 151. They argue that in this tendency lies the danger of expressionism: "Language becomes merely a toy. The same danger arose in the Baroque age, with the language of which Expressionist style has often been compared and which ended in meaningless bombast" (167).

50. I have found two exceptions to this general observation. Armin Arnold mentions Barth as an expressionist in his *Prosa des Expressionismus, Herkunft, Analyse, Inventar* (Stuttgart: W. Kohlhammer, 1972), 17. And a comprehensive book by Wolfgang Rothe discusses Barth not as an expressionist but as the theologian who most closely represents the expressionist view of religion. See *Der Expressionismus, Theologische, soziologische und anthropologische Aspekte einer Literatur* (Frankfurt am Main: Vittorio Klostermann, 1977), 43–7.

51. Frei, "An Afterword," 97.

52. I do not mean to imply that these two works are representative of expressionism as a whole. Both lack the utopian and revolutionary zeal of much expressionism to make that claim. However, they serve my purpose by showing in a specific way some of the parallels between Barth and expressionism.

53. Quoted in Wolf-Dieter Dube, *The Expressionists,* trans. Mary Whittal (London: Thames and Hudson, 1972), 161. For a good overall portrait of Beckmann, see the book by his longtime friend and supporter, Stephen Lackner, *Max Beckmann* (New York: Crown Publishers, 1983). I should note that Beckmann repudiated the expressionist label as early as 1922, although his early work is always associated with the movement. As Peter Gay has argued, "Whatever Beckmann liked to call himself, no one stated more eloquently than he the program, or rather the longing of the Expressionist years." *Weimar Culture, the Outsider as Insider* (New York: Harper & Row, 1968), 109. This remark is not completely accurate because Beckmann was rather apolitical, thus not capturing the political idealism which served as the background to much of the movement.

54. Quoted in Gay, *Weimar Culture,* 109.

55. The painting is now located in the Kunstsammlung Nordrhein-Westfalen, Düsseldorf, West Germany.

56. Dube, *The Expressionists,* 166–67.

57. Matthias Eberle, *Max Beckmann, Die Nacht, Passion ohne Erlösung* (Frankfurt am Main: Fischer Taschenbuch, 1984), 43–45.

58. Gay, *Weimar Culture,* 102–105.

59. Gay's reading of the film is influenced by the rather overstated thesis by Siegfried Kracauer connecting expressionism to fascism. See Kracauer, *From Caligari to Hitler: A Psychological History of the German Film* (Princeton, N.J.: Princeton University Press, 1947). Kracauer uses the history of film to expose the deep psychological dispositions of the German people. He argues that *Caligari* is the archetype of all German films from this period: it is macabre, sinister, morbid, ultimately a riddle. In this film Kracauer finds the mechanisms which allowed Hitler to gain power. Briefly put, his argument is that the film puts into opposition the two fundamental forces of tyranny and chaos. The fair scenes, during which the murders occur, represent the chaos of the Weimar period. Caligari, both as a ruthless experimenter with Cesare and as the benign asylum director, represents tyranny. Kracauer suggests that the Germans liked this film because it both portrays chaos in fascinating terms but also shows that only tyranny can overcome such chaos. Only a strong authority figure can successfully exert control over the asylum which is contemporary Germany. Many commentators have tried to link expressionism with Nazism; most argue that extreme experimentalism and artistic anarchism helped to cause a backlash which resulted in the demand for more authority and control, in both the arts and the wider culture. This debate is complicated; what should be remembered is that Hitler condemned expressionism as degenerate art and cultural bolshevism, a condemnation which climaxed in the notorious Degenerate Art Exhibition of 1937. That should be sufficient evidence that the relationship between expressionism and fascism is indirect at best. However, there is a shift away from expressionism and toward traditionalism and authority in Germany in the 1920s, but this shift does not necessarily foreshadow fascism and it cannot be completely attributed to the expressionists. For my purposes this shift is interesting because Barth basically participates in this cultural current; he has his own reaction against expressionism, which I will analyze in rhetorical terms in chapter six.

60. It would take the expertise of a Pauline scholar to fully address Barth's various interpretations of Romans in any detail. Fortunately, for my purposes, Barth rarely analyzes the Pauline text in order to better understand Paul but rather uses it as a starting point for his own reflections. In fact, Paul is just one of the many voices which Barth weaves together in his theological mosaic. However, there is a definite need for a comprehensive study of Barth's actual reading of Paul. Perhaps a good model for this study would be Harold Bloom's *The Anxiety of Influence, A Theory of Poetry* (New York: Oxford University Press, 1973). Here Bloom deals with the predicament of all strong poets, that is, the dependency of their need to create on their relationship to their (fatherly) precursors, resulting in the necessity of misreading past poems. His analysis easily could be applied to the creation of new theologies. Several of his key methodological terms are especially apt for Barth's reading of Paul: clinamen, where the poet swerves away from the precursor's poem, implying that "the precursor poem went accurately up to a certain point, but then should have swerved, precisely in the direction that the new poem moves"; tessera, where the new poet completes the old poem by reading back into it antithetical terms, "as though the precursor had failed to go far enough"; and daemonization, where the "later poet opens himself to what he believes to be a power in the parent-poem that does not

belong to the parent proper, but to a range of being just beyond that precursor. He does this, in his poem, by so stationing its relation to the parent-poem as to generalize away the uniqueness of the earlier work'' (all quotes, 14–15). This last defensive strategy strikes me as most applicable to Barth: what Barth pretends to find in Paul is really above and beyond Paul and best stated by Barth himself.

61. Paul Ricoeur, *Time and Narrative,* vol. 3, trans. Kathleen Blamey and David Pellauer (Chicago: University of Chicago Press, 1988), 162.

CHAPTER 2: TOWARD A TROPOLOGY

1. This argument is presented in Tzvetan Todorov, "The Splendor and Misery of Rhetoric," *Theories of the Symbol,* trans. Catherine Porter (Ithaca, New York: Cornell University Press, 1982). The quotation is from page 66.

2. John Nelson, "Seven Rhetorics of Inquiry, A Provocation," in Megill, Nelson and McCloskey, eds., *The Rhetoric of the Human Sciences,* 418.

3. Max Black was the first to use this label in "Metaphors," *Models and Metaphors* (Ithaca: Cornell University Press, 1962), 25–47.

4. For an excellent historical placement of Descartes, see Jeffrey Stout, *The Flight fom Authority, Religion, Morality and the Quest for Autonomy* (Notre Dame: University of Notre Dame Press, 1981), Part 1. He is especially helpful in situating Descartes in terms of the historical development of ideas about probability and assent.

5. Richard Bernstein, *Beyond Objectivism and Relativism, Science, Hermeneutics, and Praxis* (Philadelphia: University of Pennsylvania Press, 1983). It is Bernstein's desire to go beyond the false dilemma proposed by Descartes: "It [Cartesianism] is the quest for some fixed point, some stable rock upon which we can secure our lives against the vicissitudes that constantly threaten us. The specter that hovers in the background of this journey is not just radical epistemological skepticism but the dread of madness and chaos where nothing is fixed, where we can neither touch bottom nor support ourselves on the surface" (18). He rejects this dilemma by a reinterpretation of the category of praxis; one could just as well revise the theory of language on which it rests.

6. Voltaire, *Philosophical Dictionary,* in *Works: A Contemporary Version,* revised and modernized new translation by W. F. Fleming (London: The St. Hubert's Guild, no date), 64.

7. John Locke, *Essay Concerning Human Understanding,* Vol. 2 (Oxford: The Clarendon Press, 1894), 146–7.

8. Giambattista Vico, *The New Science of Giambattista Vico,* trans. Thomas Goddard Bergin and Max Harold Fisch (Ithaca: Cornell University Press, 1948).

9. Friedrich Nietzsche, "On Truth and Lying in an Extra-Moral Sense," in *Friedrich Nietzsche on Rhetoric and Language,* ed. and trans. with an introduction by Sander L. Gilman, Carole Blair, and David J. Parent (New York: Oxford University Press, 1989), 250. The introduction of this book, which contains the first publication of Nietzsche's complete lectures on rhetoric, conveys the importance of rhetoric for Nietzsche's philosophy.

10. Jacques Derrida, *Margins of Philosophy,* trans. Alan Bass (Chicago: University of Chicago Press, 1982), 207–271.

11. Janet Soskice, *Metaphor and Religious Language* (Oxford: Clarendon Press, 1985), 41.

12. Black, "Metaphor," *Models and Metaphors,* 25. All further quotations from Black will be cited in the text with the symbol *M.*

13. For a spirited defense of the comparative view which argues that it need not be connected to the substitution view, see Robert J. Fogelin, *Figuratively Speaking* (New Haven: Yale University Press, 1988).

14. I. A. Richards, *The Philosophy of Rhetoric* (Oxford: Oxford University Press, 1936), 93.

15. For a comprehensive anthology of this shift from the perspective of "analytical" philosophy, see Richard Rorty, editor, *The Linguistic Turn, Recent Essays in Philosophical Method* (Chicago: University of Chicago Press, 1967).

16. See Richard Rorty, *Philosophy and the Mirror of Nature* (Princeton: Princeton University Press, 1979), especially 11–12 and 371.

17. "Man acts as though he were the shaper and master of language, while in fact language remains the master of man." Martin Heidegger, "Building Dwelling Thinking," *Poetry, Language, Thought,* trans. Albert Hofstadter (New York: Harper & Row, 1971), 146.

18. Compare their very similar criticisms of Heidegger in Richard Rorty, *Consequences of Pragmatism* (Minneapolis: University of Minnesota Press, 1982), 37–39 and Paul Ricoeur, *The Rule of Metaphor* (Toronto: University of Toronto Press, 1977), 309–311.

19. Paul Ricoeur, *Freedom and Nature: The Voluntary and the Involuntary,* trans. Erazim V. Kohak (Evanston: Northwestern University Press, 1966).

20. Paul Ricoeur, *Fallible Man,* rev. and trans. Charles A. Kelbley (New York: Fordham University Press, 1986).

21. Paul Ricoeur, *Hermeneutics and the Human Sciences* ed. and trans. John B. Thompson (Cambridge: Cambridge University Press, 1981), 33. Ricoeur explains this gap in *Fallible Man* (see 133–146) by arguing that phenomenology can only ascertain the structure of human limitation or finitude, whereas evil is not a consequence of the person's being in the world; finitude is a precondition for evil, but evil already exists outside the structure of limitation which makes it, evil, possible. To make the leap from the possibility to the actuality of evil, Ricoeur decides he must write a philosophical anthropology which has its source in a hermeneutic of the symbols of evil. "Fragility is not merely the 'locus,' the point of insertion of evil, nor even the 'origin' starting from which man falls; it is the 'capacity' for evil. To say that man is fallible is to say that the limitation peculiar to a being who does not coincide with himself is the primordial weakness from which evil arises. And yet evil *arises* from this weakness only because it is *posited.* This last paradox will be at the center of the symbolics of evil" (*Fallible Man,* 146).

22. See Don Ihde, *Hermeneutic Phenomenology, The Philosophy of Paul Ricoeur* (Evanston: Northwestern University Press, 1971).

23. The quote to which I am refering reads: "It is the text, with its universal power of world disclosure, which gives a self to the ego." *Interpretation Theory: Discourse and the Surplus of Meaning* (Fort Worth: Texas Christian University Press, 1976), 95. At this point in the development of Ricoeur's hermeneutics his concern with language has been narrowed to a theory of the text.

24. Paul Ricoeur, *The Symbolism of Evil*, trans. Emerson Buchanan (Boston: Beacon Press, 1967).

25. Paul Ricoeur, "Toward a Hermeneutic of the Idea of Revelation," *Essays on Biblical Interpretation*, ed. Lewis S. Mudge (Philadelphia: Fortress Press, 1980), 101.

26. Ricoeur, *The Symbolism of Evil*, 349.

27. Ibid., 352.

28. See Hans-Georg Gadamer, *Truth and Method* (New York: Crossroad, 1975), 241ff and pp. 267ff.

29. See "Hermeneutics and the Critique of Ideology," in Ricoeur, *Hermeneutics and the Human Sciences*.

30. Paul Ricoeur, "The Hermeneutics of Symbols and Philosophical Reflection," *The Conflict of Interpretations* (Evanston: Northwestern University Press, 1974), 289.

31. Ibid., 290 (italics are Ricoeur's).

32. Paul Ricoeur, *Freud and Philosophy: An Essay on Interpretation*, trans. Denis Savage (New Haven: Yale University Press, 1970), 12.

33. Ibid., 16.

34. Monroe Beardsley, *Aesthetics* (New York: Harcourt, Brace and World, 1958), 134. Ricoeur expands this statement by suggesting that the form of the metaphor "is like an abridged version within a single sentence of the complex interplay of significations that characterize the literary work as a whole" (*Interpretation Theory*, 46). All further reference to *Interpretation Theory* will be cited in the text as *IT*.

35. Richards, Black and Beardsley have already been cited. For Philip Wheelwright see *Metaphor and Reality* (Bloomington: Indiana University Press, 1962) and *The Burning Fountain, a Study in the Language of Symbolism* (Bloomington: Indiana University Press, 1968); for Colin Murray Turbayne see *The Myth of Metaphor*, rev. ed. (Columbia: University of South Carolina, 1970). Turbayne comes close to equating metaphor with model because of his desire to distinguish between using metaphors and being used by metaphors. In particular, he argues against the use of the metaphor which depicts the world as a great machine. I will further discuss the relation between metaphor and model in chapter three.

36. Ricoeur is especially influenced by Wheelwright's discussion of the tensive movement of metaphor. See *Metaphor and Reality,* chapters three and four.

37. For Gilbert Ryle's development of the notion of a category mistake, see *The Concept of Mind* (New York: Penguin Books, 1966), 17–24.

38. See Soskice, *Metaphor and Religious Language,* 86–90.

39. All further references to this book will be included in the text with the abbreviation *RM*.

40. Compare this position with Theodor Adorno's succinct definition of rhetoric according to the traditional perspective: "In philosophy, rhetoric represents that which cannot be thought except in language." *Negative Dialectics*, trans. E. B. Ashton (New York: Continuum, 1983), 55. Adorno's argument is that that which lies outside of language cannot be thought.

41. Paul Ricoeur, "The Metaphorical Process as Cognition, Imagination, and Feeling," *On Metaphor*, ed. Sheldon Sacks (Chicago: University of Chicago Press, 1979), 146.

42. Paul Ricoeur, in Richard Kearney, *Dialogues with Contemporary Continental Thinkers* (Manchester: Manchester University Press, 1984), 17.

43. Paul Ricoeur, *Time and Narrative*, vol. 1, trans. Kathleen McLaughlin and David Pellauer (Chicago, University of Chicago, 1984). Ricoeur explains the relationship between this work and the book on metaphor in the preface to this volume.

44. Paul Ricoeur in Kearney, *Dialogues with Contemporary Continental Thinkers*, 23.

45. Dominick LaCapra, *Rethinking Intellectual History: Texts, Contexts, Language* (Ithaca: Cornell University Press, 1983), 120.

46. Ibid.

47. Hayden White, *Tropics of Discourse, Essays in Cultural Criticism* (Baltimore: The Johns Hopkins University Press, 1978), 99. Hereafter refered to in the text as *TD*.

48. Hayden White, *Metahistory, the Historical Imagination in Nineteenth-Century Europe* (Baltimore: The Johns Hopkins University Press, 1973), xi. Hereafter refered to in the text as *MH*.

49. For example, in an enlightening interview, Derrida has argued that, "It is totally false to suggest that deconstruction is a suspension of reference. Deconstruction is always deeply concerned with the 'other' of language . . . I totally refuse the label of nihilism which has been ascribed to me and my American colleagues. Deconstruction is not an enclosure in nothingness, but an openness towards the other" (Kearney, *Dialogues with Contemporary Continental Thinkers*, 123–124).

50. LaCapra, *Rethinking Intellectual History*, 76.

51. Ibid., 79.

52. Ricoeur, *Time and Narrative*, vol. 1, 179.

53. Ricoeur, *Time and Narrative*, 3:142–3.

54. Ibid., 154.

55. For a similar use of White and Ricoeur in a completely different context, See C. J. T. Talar, *Metaphor and Modernist: The Polarization of Alfred Loisy and His Neo-Thomist Critics* (Boston: University Press of America, 1987).

CHAPTER 3: METAPHOR OF CRISIS/CRISIS OF METAPHOR

1. This article can also be found in Black, *Models and Metaphors* and will be cited in the text as *MA*.

2. See Charles Sanders Peirce, *Selected Writings*, ed. Philip P. Wiener (New York: Dover, 1966), 368 and 391.

3. Ian G. Barbour, *Myths, Models and Paradigms, the Nature of Scientific and Religious Language* (London: SCM Press, 1974), 42–43.

4. Frederick Ferre, "Metaphors, Models and Religion," *Soundings* 51 (1968): 327–45.

5. Soskice, *Metaphor and Religious Language*, 102.

6. See Ian Ramsey, *Models and Mystery* (Oxford: Oxford University Press, 1964) and *Models for Divine Activity* (London: SCM Press, 1973).

7. This criticism is put forth in Mary Gerhart's review of Soskice's book in *Journal of American Academy of Religion* 56 (1988): 184–5.

8. McFague, *Speaking in Parables*, 87.

9. Sallie McFague, *Metaphorical Theology, Models of God in Religious Language* (Philadelphia: Fortress Press, 1982) and *Models of God, Theology for an Ecological, Nuclear Age* (Philadelphia: Fortress Press, 1987). The latter book is especially influenced by Gordon Kaufman's *Theology for a Nuclear Age* (Philadelphia: The Westminster Press, 1985) in two respects: first, she agrees with Kaufman that the issue of the prospect of nuclear war and the ecological problem should govern contemporary theological concerns, and second, she basically agrees with his methodology in portraying the imagination as constructive of talk about God but not responsive in such talk. Both books result in a rather cavalier handling of the theological concepts of tradition and authority. Note that while Kaufman talks about theology as an imaginative discipline, he links theology to a conceptual construction of the doctrine of God from the material of reflection on human experience. Kaufman is thus more concerned with epistemology than rhetoric. He treats the imagination as a tool of the understanding, just as many authors treat metaphor as a kind of model. See Gordon D. Kaufman, *An Essay on Theological Method*, rev. ed. (Missoula, Montana: Scholars Press, 1979), especially ch. 3.

10. McFague, *Metaphorical Theology*, 23.

11. George Lakoff and Mark Johnson, *Metaphors We Live By* (Chicago: University of Chicago Press, 1980).

12. Mary Gerhart and Allan Russell, *Metaphoric Process, The Creation of Scientific and Religious Understanding* (Fort Worth: Texas Christian University Press, 1984), 120. These authors are influenced by Paul Ricoeur's discussion of the ontological vehemence of the metaphor in his *Rule of Metaphor*.

13. Stephen C. Pepper, *World Hypotheses* (University of California Press, 1942), 91.

14. David Tracy, "Metaphor and Religion: The Test Case of Christian Texts," in *On Metaphor*, ed. Sheldon Sacks (Chicago: University of Chicago Press, 1979). He writes: "In a particular religion root metaphors form a cluster or network in which certain sustained metaphors both organize subsidiary metaphors and dif-

fuse new ones. These networks describe the enigma and promise of the human situation and prescribe certain remedies for that situation" (89). I will return to the tropical analysis of "God is love" in chapter six.

15. White, "The Burden of History," *Tropics of Discourse*, 35. It is interesting to note that Jülicher, in his review of *Romans*, makes a similar observation: "Without doubt we have not to reckon with a period in the history of culture that is not historically oriented . . . " (*The Beginnings of Dialectical Theology*, 81). He thought that Barth was a fair theologian, but a poor historian: "Much, perhaps even very much, may someday be learned from this book for the understanding of our age, but scarcely anything new for the understanding of the 'historical' Paul" (81).

16. Allan Megill, *Prophets of Extremity* (Berkeley: University of California Press, 1985).

17. Langdon Gilkey, *Reaping the Whirlwind, a Christian Interpretation of History* (New York: Seabury Press, 1981), 218. In a letter to Thurneysen written on January 1, 1916, Barth talks about "how frightfully indifferent I have become about the purely historical questions" (*Revolutionary Theology in the Making*, 36). Gilkey's comment shows how Barth could afford such indifference by stripping history bare of any religious content.

18. For just one example, see Stephen Neill, *The Interpretation of the New Testament, 1861–1961* (London: Oxford University Press, 1964), 206. Interestingly, Neill speaks of exaggeration as one of Barth's characteristics (205) and criticizes him for "certain extravagances of language" (208). David Klemm, who also discusses Barth in terms of the metaphor of crisis, also traces that crisis to World War I. See "Toward a Rhetoric of Postmodern Theology: Through Barth and Heidegger," *Journal of the American Academy of Religion* 55 (1987): 445. Although the war did have a dramatic impact on Barth, there is little doubt that, as my discussion of his pre-war theology will show, he had a tendency to exaggerate its significance on his own development.

19. Karl Barth, *God, Grace and Gospel*, trans. James Strathearn McNab (Edinburgh: Oliver & Boyd, 1959), 57.

20. Soon after the war began, for example, Barth could say this about the conflict: "It is not the war that disturbs peace. The war is not even the cause of our unrest. It has merely brought to light the fact that our lives are all based on unrest. And where there is unrest there can be no peace" (Busch, *Karl Barth*, 85). Hereafter Busch's book will be cited in the text as *B*.

21. Karl Barth, *Theology and Church, Shorter Writings 1920–1928*, trans. Louise Pettibone Smith (London: SCM Press, 1962), 238. This will be cited in the text as *TC*.

22. Karl Barth, "On Systematic Theology," *Scottish Journal of Theology* 14 (1961): 225–228.

23. Karl Barth, "Moderne Theologie und Reichsgottesarbeit," *Zeitschrift für Theologie und Kirche* 19 (1909): 317–475.

24. Quoted in James D. Smart, *The Divided Mind of Modern Theology: Karl Barth and Rudolf Bultmann, 1908–1933* (Philadelphia: Westminster, 1967), 47.

25. Karl Barth, "Der christliche Glaube und die Geschichte," *Schweizerische Theologische Zeitschrift* 29 (1912): 1–18, 49–72.

26. Smith, *The Argument to the Other,* 15.

27. Karl Barth, "Der Glaube an den personlichen Gott," *Zeitschrift für Theologie und Kirche* 24 (1914): 21–32, 65–95.

28. Smith, *The Argument to the Other,* 17.

29. Ibid., 19.

30. "Our difficulty in addressing the Social Democrats became clear to me: either one strengthens them in their party loyalty by providing a religious foundation and all manner of Christian aims for their political ethos — or one tries to lead them out beyond themselves and thereby, as I had the impression yesterday, one lays upon them a burden which is too heavy for many of them to bear. In spite of everything, the latter is the right thing to do if one is going to give such lectures at all" (*Revolutionary Theology in the Making,* 27).

31. Quoted in Pauck, *Karl Barth, Prophet of a New Christianity?,* 58.

32. For a good analysis of Barth's sermons from this period, see Jochen Fähler, *Der Ausbruch des 1. Weltkreiges in Karl Barths Predigten 1913–1915* (Bern, Frankfurt am Main, Las Vegas: Peter Lang, 1979). Barth and Thurneysen published two volumes of sermons during these years; see *Suchet Gott, so werdet ihr leben!* (Bern: G. A. Baschlin, 1917) and *Come Holy Spirit,* trans. G. W. Richards (New York: Round Table, 1933). Barth's sermons are very important for any analysis of his theological thought. In the sermons, for example, it is easy to see Barth's penchant for using cutting and even irritating hyperbole for its shock value. See Barth's very honest, "Der Pfarrer, der es den Leuten recht macht," *Die christliche Welt* 30 (1916): 262–7. Also note that although the "Wholly Other" did not become a slogan until 1919, under the influence of Otto, already in his prewar sermons he is beginning to use this language; for example, see *Predigten 1913,* ed. G. Sauter and N. Barth (Zurich: TVZ, 1976), 168, 249 and 305. In his letters, Barth often credits Thurneysen, not Otto, for making him see the centrality of this phrase.

33. Karl Barth, *A Karl Barth Reader,* ed. Rolf Joachim Erler and Reiner Marquard (Grand Rapids, Mich.: Eerdmans, 1986), 33.

34. Ibid., 34.

35. See Karl Barth, *The Word of God and the Word of Man,* trans. Douglas Horton (New York: Harper & Brothers, 1957), 28–50. Hereafter all references to this collection of essays will be abbreviated in the text with *WG*.

36. Karl Barth, *Der Römerbrief* (Bern: G. A. Baschlin, 1919; reprinted 1963 by Evangelischer Verlag, Zurich). This book was actually printed by December 1918, but it has 1919 as its date of publication. It is also interesting to note that although this edition was destined to fade into oblivion, it was this first edition that got Barth his first academic position, a professorship at Göttingen.

37. See von Balthasar, *The Theology of Karl Barth,* 48–52. In fact, Barth says in this first edition of *Romans* that Moses, Plato, Kant and Fichte all stand in one line, serving as prophets to God's righteousness.

38. David Paul Henry, *The Early Development of the Hermeneutics of Karl Barth as Evidenced by His Appropriation of Romans 5: 12–21* (Macon, Georgia: Mercer University Press, 1985).

39. Smart, *The Divided Mind of Modern Theology,* 82.

40. Barth often mused about the impact of *Romans* as if it were as much a shock to him as to anyone else. "On a certain day in 1916, Thurneysen and I very naively agreed to go back to academic theology to clarify the situation. If we had known what was to happen we would not have found the *parrhesia* [confident authority] to do this . . . Even in 1918 I had no inkling of the repercussions which would follow . . . " (*Karl Barth/Rudolf Bultmann Letters, 1922–1966*, ed. Bernd Jaspert, trans. Geoffrey W. Bromiley [Grand Rapids, Mich.: Eerdmans, 1981], 154–5). It is my contention that Barth's insight—the metaphor of crisis—was, like all good metaphors, a genuine surprise to him as well as to others, and it enabled him to organize his thoughts into a new theological paradigm the contours of which not only he understood fully.

41. This is a limited list; I could have included Barth's father, Fritz, his brother, the existentialist philosopher, Heinrich, and Plato and Kant, but I wanted to limit the list to those names directly responsible for Barth's deepening notion of crisis. Thurneysen and Nietzsche would belong in this list, but Thurneysen's influence is broad and permeates all aspects of Barth's early development, so that it is hard to pinpoint, while I think that Nietzsche's influence is mediated to Barth through Overbeck. Moreover, I discuss Nietzsche in connection with Barth's use of hyperbole. For more detailed discussions of this period in Barth's development, see Henri Boullard, *Karl Barth*, 3 vols., vol 1: *Genese et evolution de la theologie dialectique* (Paris: Aubier, 1957).

42. For an article by Barth about Blumhardt, see "Past and Future: Friedrich Naumann and Christoph Blumhardt," in *The Beginnings of Dialectical Theology*, 35–45. Barth's admiration for Christoph Blumhardt and his father was controversial not only because of their socialism; both of them, especially the father, dabbled in faith healing and exorcism, which Barth for a time seemed to admire.

43. One of Nietzsche's primary influences on Overbeck—as well as Barth—concerns his philosophy of history. Nietzsche argued that a full explanation of historical events could not be found in history itself; the great deeds of the past are embedded in myth. The historian must overcome any pretension to objectivity and learn to use the historico-mythical past in terms of those unhistorical elements which can also be found in the present. See Nietzsche's "On the Uses and Disadvantages of History for Life," in *Untimely Meditations*, trans. R. J. Hollingdale (Cambridge: Cambridge University Press, 1983).

44. Barth was also very influenced by Overbeck's many reflections on the importance of death and the way in which people try to avoid thinking about death. In fact, in *Romans* Barth often identifies the crisis as death itself.

45. For comments on Feuerbach in *Romans*, see the 1921 preface to the second edition and also page 236.

46. See Eduard Thurneysen, *Dostoevsky* (Richmond: John Knox Press, 1966).

47. For explicit references to Dostoevsky or the Grand Inquisitor in *Romans*, see 67–8, 122, 141, 232, 300, 391, 501–2, 504–5.

48. For Barth's own reflections on his tenuous relationship to Kierkegaard, see Karl Barth, "A Thank You and a Bow: Kierkegaard's Reveille," *Canadian Journal of Theology* 11 (1965): 164–73. For further reading, see Alastair McKinnon, "Barth's Relation to Kierkegaard: Some Further Light," *Canadian Journal of Theology* 13 (1967): 31–41.

49. See Berkouwer, *The Triumph of Grace*, 24.

50. Ibid., 29. Berkouwer's concern is to show how grace triumphs in all of Barth's works, so he downplays the negative aspects of the second edition of *Romans;* in fact, he tends to read the second edition in the light of the first.

51. In a fascinating rhetorical study of Pascal, Sara E. Melzer argues that figurative language for Pascal is a direct result of humanity's fall into sin. See *Discourses of the Fall, A Study of Pascal's Pensees* (Berkeley: University of California Press, 1986). The historical fall away from God results in an epistemological fall from truth into language. This position gives Pascal's language an undecidable and paradoxical edge: the prisonhouse of language prohibits any direct knowledge of God as the origin which precedes the fall. Yet the desire for truth persists, and in the end this desire can be satisfied only by a wager of the heart which transcends the boundary of language. For Barth too the fall necessitates figurative language; however, he does not advocate a pietistic solution to this predicament. On the contrary, he tries to turn language against itself in order to open up a space, within language, for faith.

52. Jacques Derrida, *Of Grammatology*, trans. Gayatri Chakraorty Spivak (Baltimore: The Johns Hopkins University Press, 1976), 283.

53. "In der Auserstehung berührt die neue Welt des heiligen Geistes die alte Welt des Fleisches. Uber sie berührt sie wie die Tangente einen Kreis, ohne sie zu berühren, und gerade indem sie sie nicht berührt, berührt sie sie als ihre Begrenzung, als neue Welt." *Der Römerbrief, 1922,* 6.

54. Hans Frei is one of the few commentators I have read who has noted Barth's distinctive use of metaphor. "It [second edition of *Romans*] is not exactly nonobjective [art], but the recurring metaphors certainly aren't mimetic. For the most part they are vaguely mathematical. There are points, tiny, disappearing. There are lines, life and death lines bisecting each other; there is talk about empty space between temporally filled spaces, and so forth and so on." From *Karl Barth and the Future of Theology,* ed. David L. Dickerman (New Haven: Yale Divinity School Association, 1969), 5. T. H. L. Parker has also commented perceptively on Barth's use of metaphor. "It is noteworthy that few of the images are organic, not many human (e.g. the watchman, the soldier, the rebel) but most either technological, inanimate, or taken from the realm of pure thought, i.e. mathematical" (*Karl Barth,* 44).

55. "Ein Tröpfchen Ewigkeit hat mehr Gewicht als das ganze Meer der der Zeit unterworfenen Dinge" (*Der Römerbrief, 1922,* 51).

56. "Gibt es höhepunkte in der Geschichte, die mehr sind als grösste Wellen im Strom der Vergänglichkeit, stärkste Schatten unter andern Schatten?" (*Der Römerbrief, 1922,* 52).

57. Barth argues, in fact, that an objective view of history is not only irrelevant to faith, but it can contradict faith. "Judged by the record of what He [Jesus Christ] did and omitted to do, His sinlessness can be as easily denied as ours can, more easily, in fact, that can the sinlessness of those good and pure and pious people who move about in our midst . . . Is there any historical occurrence so defenceless against brilliant and stupid notions, against interpretations and misinterpretation, against use and misuse; is there any historical happening so inconspicuous and ambiguous and open to misunderstanding — as the appearance in history of God's own Son? There is no single incident in His life known to us in such a way as to be free from ambiguity and free from the possibility of giving

offence. A hundred incidents are manifestly offensive: 'Here we feel otherwise than Jesus felt' — a truth so desperately obvious that one would have thought hardly worthwhile mentioning" (*Romans*, 280). A little later he adds that the life of Jesus is "a playground where men can exercise their ingenuity in propounding all manner of noble and absurd ideas and notions, but a playground so covered with stones that each man stumbles after his own fashion" (*Romans*, 281). Objective history can and indeed does contradict Christian belief because history itself is contradicted by the eternity of the divine message.

58. For a brilliant reading of the perplexities involved in Barth's understanding of God, see Robert P. Scharlemann, "The No to Nothing and the Nothing to Know: Barth and Tillich and the Possibility of Theological Science," *Journal of the American Academy of Religion* 55 (1987): 57–72.

59. "Der wahre Gott ist aber der aller Gegenständlichkeit, der Richter, das nicht-sein der Welt (mit Einschluss jenes 'Gott' menschlicher Logik)" (*Der Römerbrief, 1922*, 57).

60. As I have discussed above, many scholars have argued that metaphor and analogy are closely related, suggesting that metaphor provides the groundwork for analogy. Thus, Barth's difficulties with metaphor in *Romans* could be construed as a foreshadowing of his later and more explicit rejection of analogy in Godtalk. In other words, before Barth theologically rejected the use of analogy, he figuratively stumbled over the use of metaphor. Note his most famous statement about analogy: "I regard the *analogia entis* as the invention of Antichrist, and think that because of it one cannot become Catholic" (*Church Dogmatics*, I/1: x).

CHAPTER 4: MAGIC OF THE EXTREME

1. Jonathan Barnes, *The Complete Works of Aristotle*, the Revised Oxford Translation, vol. 2 (Princeton: Princeton University Press, 1984), 2255 (1413a29–30).

2. Robert Evans, "Hyperbole," *Princeton Encyclopedia of Poetry and Poetics*, ed. Alex Preminger (Princeton, New Jersey: Princeton University Press, 1965), 359.

3. Chaim Perelman and L. Olbrechts-Tyteca, *The New Rhetoric, A Treatise on Argumentation*, trans. John Wilkinson and Purcell Weaver (Notre Dame: University of Notre Dame Press, 1969). All further references to this book will be included in the text and marked *NR*.

4. Louis Wirth Marvick, *Mallarme and the Sublime* (Albany, N.Y.: SUNY Press, 1986). References to this book will be given in the text and marked *MS*.

5. See Barth, *Revolutionary Theology in the Making*, 47. For a later criticism of Otto, see *Church Dogmatics*, I/1: 135. For Otto, see *The Idea of the Holy*, trans. by John W. Harvey (London: Oxford University Press, 1958), especially chapter four.

6. Fogelin, *Figuratively Speaking*, 13.

7. See Walter Kaufmann, *Nietzsche, Philosopher, Psychologist, Antichrist* (New York: The World Publishing Company, 1956). Kaufmann treats Nietzsche as a naturalist, someone who wanted to protect human instincts against the en-

croachment of excessive rationalization. He downplays aspects of Nietzsche which he finds inconsistent and incomprehensible, like the doctrine of the eternal return. Moreover, in stressing the philosophical doctrines in Nietzsche's work, he makes the opposite mistake of those who read Nietzsche for style alone: "I had been reacting against the view that Nietzsche was primarily a great stylist, and the burden of my book had been to show that he was a great thinker" (iii). For Heidegger, see his *Nietzsche*, 4 vols., trans. by David Farrell Krell and Frank A. Capuzzi (San Francisco: Harper & Row, 1979–1982). Although Heidegger was one of the first to recognize the importance of Nietzsche as a philosopher (these lectures were originally given in the 1930s), his interpretation of Nietzsche has been questioned recently because he argues that Nietzsche is primarily a systematic metaphysician who reduplicates in reverse form the Platonic heritage of philosophy. For Heidegger, then, Nietzsche did not overcome metaphysics, but he did put an end to metaphysics by inverting its traditional values, thus clearing the way for new thinking (Heidegger's, of course). Those interpretations which focus on Nietzsche's style see a much more fragmented, inconsistent, self-critical and troubled philosopher than either Kaufmann or Heidegger allow. Megill's book, by the way, does a good job of showing how much Nietzsche and Heidegger have in common—the promotion of the aesthetic to the highest level of philosophy—something the latter would not admit.

8. For two of the best collections of essays that addresses this new reading of Nietzsche, see Daniel O'Hara, *Why Nietzsche Now?* (Bloomington: Indiana University Press, 1985) and Michael Allen Gillespie and Tracy B. Strong, eds., *Nietzsche's New Seas, Explorations in Philosophy, Aesthetics, and Politics* (Chicago: University of Chicago Press, 1988).

9. Megill, *Prophets of Extremity, Nietzsche, Heidegger, Foucault, Derrida*, 343. Megill actually applies his observation to all of the prophets he studies.

10. Ibid.

11. Alexander Nehamas, *Nietzsche, Life as Literature* (Cambridge: Harvard University Press, 1985), 23.

12. Robert Solomon, introduction, *Nietzsche, A Collection of Critical Essays* (Notre Dame, IN: University of Notre Dame Press, 1980), 1.

13. Arthur C. Danto, *Nietzsche as Philosopher* (New York: Macmillan Company, 1965), 13–14.

14. Ibid., 13.

15. For a good study of the Dionysian throughout all of Nietzsche's works, see Adrian Del Caro, *Dionysian Aesthetics, The Role of Destruction in Creation as Reflected in the Life and Works of Friedrich Nietzsche* (Frankfurt am Main: Peter Lang, 1981).

16. Christopher Middleton, ed. and trans., *Selected Letters of Friedrich Nietzsche* (Chicago: University of Chicago Press, 1969), 339.

17. Nehamas, *Nietzsche, Life as Literature*, 23.

18. Middleton, *Selected Letters of Friedrich Nietzsche*, 122.

19. Ibid., 317.

20. Friedrich Nietzsche, *The Will to Power*, trans. Walter Kaufmann and R. J. Hollingdale (New York: Random House, 1967), 396. The emphasis is Nietzsche's.

It is interesting that this note, whih is number 749, is crossed out in the original manuscript.

21. The many and often obsure biological comments in *Ecce Homo* are often ignored by interpreters; it is interesting that Morgot Norris, in a brilliant reading of this text, traces its hyperbole to Nietzsche's use of nature as a model for human activity. See *Beasts of the Modern Imagination, Darwin, Nietzsche, Kafka, Ernst and Lawrence* (Baltimore and London: The Johns Hopkins University Press, 1985). Norris claims that Nietzsche's references to diet, climate and the environment are attempts to deny the influence of culture and consciousness on human development; in their place Nietzsche substitutes the importance of instinct and natural endowment, in a word, physiology. Thus, Nietzsche's exaggerations are an aspect of the animal aggressiveness which his philosophy must valorize; they are "high animal spirits" and "discharges" (74) constituting a "rhetoric of bounty . . . a harvest celebration, a thanksgiving prayer" (83). It is true that in this book Nietzsche portrays his work as the result of a natural and even spontaneous development; he does not write because of some inner lack or emptiness, or the need to share with others. His books are the overflowing product of a true health which has overcome many obstacles; he has no reason, therefore, to be tempted by *ressentiment,* which plagues nearly all of his enemies. However, Norris's interpretation, while it places Nietzsche's hyperbole in an interesting context, goes too far in reducing his position to that of a rather crude form of philosophical naturalism. Moreover, Norris risks making Nietzsche's style an inconsequential symptom of his philosophical content; I want to argue that his hyperbole is philosophically significant in its own right.

22. Megill, *Prophets of Extremity,* 33.

23. Barth is not unique in his reliance on Nietzsche; nearly all the expressionists paid tribute to him. For an excellent survey of the many uses of Nietzsche during this period, see R. Hinton Thomas, *Nietzsche in German Politics and Society, 1890–1918* (La Salle, Illinois: Open Court, 1983). This book argues that contrary to popular belief, Nietzsche during this period was used by progressive and dissident groups, not by militaristic and imperialistic forces. Unfortunately, Thomas does not discuss the expressionist—or religious—use of Nietzsche.

24. Friedrich Nietzsche, *Human, All Too Human, A Book for Free Spirits,* trans. Marion Faber, with Stephen Lehmann (Lincoln: University of Nebraska Press, 1984), 215.

25. Ibid., 244.

26. Friedrich Nietzsche, *Ecce Homo,* trans. by R. J. Hollingdale (New York: Penguin Books, 1979). This work will be cited in the text as *EH.*

27. I am grateful for conversations with Langdon Gilkey for this insight into Barth's use of rhetorical questions.

28. It is interesting that Augustinus P. Dierick, in *German Expressionist Prose* (Toronto: University of Toronto Press, 1987), argues that one consistent theme in expressionism is the critique of institutional religion. "Expressionist hostility to organized religion is inspired by the belief that religion is yet another attempt by established powers to reinforce an already intolerable hold on society." (240). He connects this hostility to the pervasive feeling of an absent God. There is "a painful awareness of an enormous distance separating man and God. Intense

longing and the realization that God is *deus absconditus* therefore create much of the religious pathos of Expressionism, and also inform the search for alternatives so characteristic of the period" (241). The result is an ambiguous rejection of and renewed quest for religion. Dierik argues that this mixture of feelings often led the expressionists to synthesize religion and socialism. In fact, "In the synthesis of socialism and religion Expressionism seems to have reached its logical apex" (258). That these comments can be so aptly applied to Barth is further evidence of his connection to expressionism, even though he is never mentioned in this book. But note that Barth did not rest with the synthesis of religion and socialism. His notion of crisis encompasses both of these camps, an issue to which I will return when I examine the ethics of *Romans* in chapter six.

29. "Die Lage der Kirche kann darum nicht sharf genug gesehen werden, wie sie ist" (*Der Römerbrief 1922*, 379). Although Barth does not use the German word for exaggeration in this statement, the translator's interpretation is accurate. A more literal translation would read: The church's position therefore cannot be seen as sharply as it is.

30. Note that Barth thinks that the duality of predestination is only apparent; in the end there is only one predestination, and that is to salvation. Thus he can speak of "the eternal victory of election over rejection" (*Romans*, 347).

31. The tone of resignation in this passage is not unique; it can be found throughout Barth's text. Note this example: "The world remains the world and men remain men even whilst the Gospel is being received. The whole burden of sin and the whole curse of death still press heavily upon us. We must be under no illusion: The reality of our present existence continues as it is!" (*Romans*, 38).

32. Rene Girard, *To Double Business Bound* (Baltimore: The Johns Hopkins University Press, 1978), 22.

33. Karl Barth and Emil Brunner, *Natural Theology,* trans. by Peter Fraenkel (London: Geoffrey Bles, The Centenary Press, 1946). Hereafter cited in the text as *NT.*

34. I should note that Barth during this period increasingly came to connect natural theology—and theological liberalism in general—with the dangerous tendency of the church to make alliances with worldly powers. In the light of the rise of fascism, then, Barth's critique of natural theology was especially politically potent. This is one underlying reason why he reacts so strongly against Brunner. Unfortunately, the connection between Barth's theology and politics during this time is extremely complex and has never been adequately analyzed. Some theologians, for example, thought he was taking advantage of the political situation to advance his own theology. Certainly some forms of theology were more liable to reactionary cooption, but the link between natural theology and fascism has never been adequately drawn, to my mind, and Barth therefore overstates his thesis. In any case, Barth's theology was well suited to oppose fascism because he fought one absolute power with another; the focus of the church on only one power was built into the very fabric of his thought. Today, in a different political situation, the political value of this position must be re-thought. I try to do this in chapter six.

35. "And who knows whether one could not find passages in the *Epistle to the Romans* in which I have said something of the sort myself" (*Natural Theology,*

115). He is talking about the use of a negative natural theology to prove God's existence, a use which certainly does pervade—albeit ambiguously—*Romans.*

36. For a classic statement of the shift in Barth's doctrine of God, see the title essay in Karl Barth, *The Humanity of God* (Atlanta: John Knox Press, 1960). Here Barth surveys his past excesses with humour and grace. "All this, however well it may have been meant and however much it may have mattered, was nevertheless said somewhat severely and brutally, and moreover—at least according to the other side—in part heretically. How we cleared things away! And we did almost nothing but clear away! Everything which even remotely smacked of mysticism and morality, of pietism and romanticism, or even of idealism, was suspected and sharply interdicted or bracketed with reservations which sounded actually prohibitive! What should really have been only a sad and friendly smile was a derisive laugh! Did not the whole thing frequently seem more like the report of an enormous execution than the message of the Resurrection, which was its real aim?" (43). "We viewed this 'wholly other' in isolation, abstracted and absolutized, and set it over against man, this miserable wretch—not to say boxed his ears with it—in such a fashion that it continually showed greater similarity to the deity of the God of the philosophers than to the deity of the God of Abraham, Isaac, and Jacob" (45).

37. *Church Dogmatics*, II/1:634.

38. "The result was that we could not speak about the posttemporality of God in such a way as to make it clear that we actually meant to speak of God and not of a general idea of limit and crisis. That we had only an uncertain grip of the matter became apparent, strangely enough, in those passages of the exposition in which I had to speak positively about the divine future and hope as such" (*Church Dogmatics*, II/1: 635).

39. *Church Dogmatics*, IV/1: 755.

40. *Church Dogmatics*, II/1: 635.

CHAPTER 5: WEB OF IRONY

1. For one example, note how John Bowden, who is very attentive to Barth's style, calls *Romans* "the bombshell, the earthquake, the volcano, the thunderbolt that Barth unleashed on the world," and "theological dynamite" (*Karl Barth, Theologian*, 24 and 33). Bowden does comment on Barth's use of irony, but he links it to his tendency toward polemics and his general wit. "Barth's wit is a mixed blessing. At worst it can be a vicious weapon of destruction, so that one American theologian called him a 'verbal sadist.' Even so, provided that one agrees with Barth, his irony and ridicule to the point of maliciousness can be extraordinarily entertaining" (11). I hope to show that Barth's theological position drives him to a more fundamental form of irony with the result that he is harder on himself—and his readers—than his opponents.

2. Kenneth Burke, *Grammar of Motives* (Berkeley: University of California Press, 1962), 517.

3. D. C. Muecke, *The Compass of Irony* (London: Methuen, 1969), 3. Hereafter cited as *CI.*

4. Wayne Booth, *A Rhetoric of Irony* (Chicago: University of Chicago Press, 1974), ix. Hereafter cited as *RI*.

5. For Hegel irony is also the form taken by the cunning of reason. Although people think that they are free, and act as they please, the results of their actions really fit into God's total plan for history. For a concise statement of Hegel's philosophy of history, see *Reason in History*, trans. Robert S. Hartman (Indianapolis: Bobbs-Merrill, 1953).

6. Cleanth Brooks, *The Well Wrought Urn* (New York: Harcourt Brace Jovanovich, 1947), especially 209–10. Note Muecke's response to Brooks: "By taking this view he has done his best to finesse the word 'irony' out of useful existence" (*CI*, 13).

7. Umberto Eco, *Reflections on the Name of the Rose*, trans. William Weaver (London: Secker and Warburg, 1985), 67–8. This connection between postmodernism and irony is also made by Charles Jencks in *What is Post-Modernism?* (New York: Academy editions/St. Martin's Press, 1987), 14–27. I will return to the question of postmodernism in chapter six.

8. Richard Rorty, *Contingency, Irony, and Solidarity* (Cambridge: Cambridge University Press, 1989). See Part II.

9. This is from *Meditations of a Non-Political Man*, as quoted in Muecke's *The Compass of Irony*, 235.

10. John Searle, *Expression and Meaning* (Cambridge: Cambridge University Press, 1979), 113.

11. Augustine, *On Christian Doctrine*, trans. by D. W. Robertson, Jr. (Indianapolis: Bobbs-Merrill, 1983), 10–11.

12. Compare my comment to Paul de Man's potent and compact conclusion to his *Allegories of Reading:* "Irony is no longer a trope but the undoing of the deconstructive allegory of all tropological cognitions, the systematic undoing, in other words, of understanding. As such, far from closing off the tropological system, irony enforces the repetition of its aberration" (301). Irony is that part of the tropical system that makes it unsystematic. I am arguing that metaphor and hyperbole can also undo the understanding, and that in Barth irony serves as both a climax to this situation and a kind of unsystematic resolution.

13. Louis Mackey, *Kierkegaard: A Kind of Poet* (Philadelphia: University of Pennsylvania Press, 1971), 259. For a collection of essays that shows the development of Mackey's position from 1960 to 1982, see his *Points of View: Readings of Kierkegaard* (Tallahassee: Florida State University Press, 1986).

14. Søren Kierkegaard, *The Point of View for my Work as an Author: A Report to History*, trans. and intro. Walter Lowrie (New York: Harper & Brothers, 1962). Hereafter cited as *PV*.

15. Walter Lowrie, *Kierkegaard*, vol. 2 (New York: Harper & Brothers, 1962), 490.

16. Ibid., 492.

17. This is noted by Howard A. Johnson in a supplement to Kierkegaard's *Attack upon "Christendom,"* trans. Walter Lowrie (Princeton: Princeton University Press, 1968), xxvi.

18. It is a remark on the low standing of hyperbole among the tropes that even those who recognize that Kierkegaard's attack was in the form of exaggeration still think it is direct and thus debate its relationship to his earlier, indirect discourse.

19. Quoted in Lowrie, *Kierkegaard*, 2: 553.

20. Ibid., 493.

21. Søren Kierkegaard, *The Concept of Irony, With Constant Reference to Socrates*, trans. Lee M. Capel (Bloomington: Indiana University Press, 1965). Hereafter cited as *KCI*.

22. See Lee M. Capel's excellent introduction to this work for an analysis of its place in Kierkegaardian scholarship. For an excellent example of an ironic reading of this book, see the first essay in Mackey's *Point of View*, "Starting from Scratch: Kierkegaard Unfair to Hegel."

23. For an excellent portrayal of the negative implications which Kierkegaard attributes to irony, as well as a good summary of Kierkegaard's criticisms of Schlegel, see the short story by Donald Barthelme, "Kierkegaard Unfair to Schlegel," in *Sixty Stories* (New York: E. P. Dutton, 1982). This "story" is a *tour de force* of irony; on one level it argues against Kierkegaard's claim that irony is self-defeating and vain, but on another level, by its very dreariness and boredom, it accepts Kierkegaard's argument. The climax of the story is the reversal in which one of the voices (character would be saying too much) recognizes that Kierkegaard was not being unfair to Schlegel, but rather Kierkegaard was being only too fair in disapproving of the irony which the voice represents. But even this recognition is so couched in irony — it takes place in an interview, which reads like a satire of a psychiatric therapy session—that it is difficult to take it seriously. This story shows how closely irony and humour are related, both relying on odd and unexpected juxtapositions of events and meanings.

24. Søren Kierkegaard, *Either/Or*, Part 1, ed. and trans. Howard V. Hong and Edna H. Hong (Princeton: Princeton University Press, 1987).

25. Søren Kierkegaard, *Concluding Unscientific Postscript*, trans. David F. Swenson and Walter Lowrie (Princeton: Princeton University Press, 1941), 245.

26. Ibid., 402. I should note that this story does not illuminate Kierkegaard's full position on religion. It really deals with what Kierkegaard calls religiousness "A," which is a general kind of relationship to the infinite, not religiousness "B," which is Christianity, and involves the paradoxical but concrete moments of forgiveness and redemption.

27. Ibid., 442.

28. Frei, "An Afterword," 100.

29. Karl Barth, *Die christliche Dogmatik im Entwurf* (Munich: Christian Kaiser Verlag, 1927), ix.

30. From an autobiographical sketch included in *Karl Barth/Rudolf Bultmann Letters, 1922/1966*, trans. Geoffrey W. Bromiley, (Grand Rapids: William B. Eerdmans, 1981), 152.

31. Later Barth will say that all theology is made possible by the language always already spoken by God. The relationship of opposition and contradiction between these two discourses, then, is replaced by a relationship of representation and imitation.

32. The original reads: " . . . allein im Lichte göttlichen Ernstes und göttlichen Humors . . . " (*Der Römerbrief 1922*, 114). Although in this passage Barth does not use the German word for irony, the word *der Humor* can actually serve as the

German equivalent of the English irony, as the translation suggests. *Wahrig Deutsches Wörterbuch* defines this word as the ability to observe even the downside or disadvantages (*die Schattenseiten*) of life with cheerful composure and intellectual superiority.

33. "Dazu ist die Kirche angerannt—dazu ihr misslingen, ihre Unglaubwürdigkeit, der unfreiwillige Humor, mit dem sie umgeben ist . . . " (*Der Römerbrief 1922*, 387).

34. Adorno, *Negative Dialectics*, 147.

35. My reading is based on two early representative texts by Jacques Derrida, *Speech and Phenomena* (Evanston: Northwestern University Press, 1973), and *Of Grammatology*. My summary and all too brief account does not pretend to do justice to any of his most recent work. For a brilliant comparison of Barth and Derrida, see Walter Lowe, "Barth as Critic of Dualism: Re-Reading the *Römerbrief*," *Scottish Journal of Theology* 41: 377–395.

36. For a full analysis of this term, see Stanley Fish, *Self-Consuming Artifacts* (Berkeley: University of California Press, 1972). Fish defines this kind of text, which he calls dialectical, not rhetorical, as one which consumes both the reader and itself, "for by conveying those who experience it to a point where they are beyond the aid that discursive or rational forms can offer, it becomes the vehicle of its own abandonment" (3).

CHAPTER 6: RETREAT AND RECONSTRUCTION: RE-READING BARTH TODAY

1. For an example, note the remark of Hans Frei: "Certainly in the famous second edition of his *The Epistle to the Romans*, Barth's deliberately abrupt and staccato style, his distended, exaggerated metaphors and the provocative, allusive force of his rhetoric are all strikingly reminiscent of Expressionism, although he soon abandoned that mode and (once more astonishingly similar to an identical turn in contemporary German letters), moved on to the style of a *neue Sachlichkeit*" ("An Afterword," 102). Although Frei does not pursue the specifics of these cultural comparisons, he is, more than any other scholar, sensitive to Barth's stylistics. For another mention of *Neue Sachlichkeit* see Pauck, *Karl Barth, Prophet of a New Christianity?*, 20.

2. Willett, *Expressionism*, 189. Also see his *Art and Politics in the Weimar Republic, The New Sobriety, 1917–1933* (New York: Pantheon Books, 1978).

3. Ibid., 190.

4. George Lukács was one of the most important critics of expressionism's rejection of realism. He accused it of harboring an exaggerated subjectivism, connected it to the rise of fascism, and during its peak called for a return to the historical novel. See his *Essays on Realism*, ed. Rodney Livingstone and trans. David Fernback (Cambridge, MA: MIT Press, 1980), 91–113.

5. Gay, *Wiemar Culture*, 122.

6. Karl Barth, *Die christliche Dogmatik im Entwurf. Erster Band: Die Lehre vom Worte Gottes. Prolegomena zur christlichen Dogmatik* (Munich: Chr. Kaiser Verlag, 1927). This untranslated volume should be distinguished from the later *Dogmatik im Grundriss* (Christian Kaiser Verlag, 1947), English translation by G. T. Thomson, *Dogmatics in Outline* (New York: Harper & Row, 1959).

7. *Church Dogmatics*, I/1: 279.

8. For a historical treatment of realism, see Monroe C. Beardsley, *Aesthetics from Classical Greece to the Present* (University, Alabama: The University of Alabama Press, 1966).

9. C. P. Snow, *The Realists* (New York: Charles Scribner's Sons, 1978), xi.

10. William W. Stowe makes this argument about realism: at its best, it offers a moving picture of the world, not a snapshot. See his *Balzac, James, and the Realistic Novel* (Princeton: Princeton University Press, 1983).

11. Wayne C. Booth, *The Rhetoric of Fiction* (Chicago: The University of Chicago Press, 1961), 116.

12. Tzvetan Todorov gets at the problematic nature of realism by locating this paradox: "Artistic imitation is, as it happens, a paradoxical notion: it disappears at the very moment that it achieves perfection" (*Theories of the Symbol*, 112). Realism is a style which does not want to be a style.

13. *Karl Barth and Rudolf Bultmann Letters, 1922/1966*, 158.

14. Donald Phillips, *Karl Barth's Philosophy of Communication* (New York: Georg Olms Verlag, 1981), x.

15. See Torrance, *Karl Barth, An Introduction to His Early Theology, 1910–1931*, especially 151 to 158. Also see Graham White, "Karl Barth's Realism," *Neue Zeitschrift für systematisch Theologie und Religionsphilosophie* 26 (1984): 54–70, and George Hunsinger, "Beyond Literalism and Expressivism: Karl Barth's Hermeneutical Realism," *Modern Theology* 3 (1987): 209–223.

16. *Church Dogmatics*, I/2: 125.

17. For Barth's own understanding of the combination of realism and idealism in his theology, see his recently translated 1929 essay, "Fate and Idea in Theology," in *The Way of Theology in Karl Barth*, ed. H. Martin Rumscheidt, trans. George Hunsinger (Allison Park, Penn.: Pickwick Publications, 1986). Here Barth argues that theology can be described in two different ways: as an ordered investigation of the divine (idealism) and as a human and ambiguous discipline (realism). More specifically, Barth equates realism in theology with the tendency to seek God in fate (*Schicksal*). Realistic theology takes the empirical route of identifying God with fate—the rules, orders and principles of existence—either in its inward or outward forms. Idealistic theology surpasses naive realism to strive after the unseen, the divine dimension itself. The problem with idealism is that it forgets that God reaches down to us first, and thus it strays into mysticism; it believes that reality is a transparency through which the mind can reach ultimate truth. Similarly, realism is too quickly captured by subjectivism—the thought that God acts according to principles known and established by human being—and thus reduces the divine to the human sphere. Barth concludes this essay by trying to dialectically relate both realism and idealism. He wants to treat God as a particular actuality (realism) without neglecting God's mystery and freedom (idealism).

18. Frei, "An Afterword," 110.

19. Ibid., 111.

20. Ibid., 115.

21. Karl Barth, *Anselm: Fides Quaerens Intellectum,* trans. Ian W. Robertson (London: SCM Press, 1960). Hereafter cited as *A.*

22. Karl Barth, *How I Changed My Mind* (Richmond: John Knox Press, 1966), 43.

23. For a review of the recent literature on Anselm that includes critical comments about Barth's interpretation, see Arthur C. McGill, "Recent Discussions of Anselm's Argument," in John H. Hick and Arthur C. McGill, eds., *The Many-faced Argument* (New York: The MacMillan Company, 1967).

24. Karl Barth, *Church Dogmatics,* I/1, *The Doctrine of the Word of God,* trans. by G. W. Bromiley, (Edinburgh: T & T Clark, 1975). This volume will be cited in the text as *CD.* All other references to other volumes of the *Dogmatics* will be cited in footnotes.

25. Quoted by Robert McAfee Brown in his introduction to Georges Casalis, *Portrait of Karl Barth* (Garden City, New York: Anchor Books, 1964), xiii.

26. One could argue that hyperbole remains in Barth's later work as the exaggeration of the difference between theology and other disciplines, a difference which does not allow for any overlap or correlation. Theology is identical to all other disciplines only to the extent that all disciplines have their own subject matter and do not have any reason to address each other directly. Ironically, this exaggerated difference, according to Barth, is a more effective apologetic than liberal theological attempts at conciliation and mutual understanding. Liberal apologetics seek understanding by exaggerating the possibilities for identity and ironically lose their own identity. Barth displaces this irony by reversing its hyperbolic ground: by sacrificing any intention to identify with the world — by retreating from a difference which itself cannot be defined—theology makes the best claim to be heard and taken seriously.

27. See Hans Frei in Dickerman, ed., *Karl Barth and the Future of Theology* 5–8. In describing Barth's dogmatics Frei says that he is "somehow drawn to some things Erich Auerbach has said about Dante" (6). According to Auerbach, Dante's world is neither allegorical nor descriptive, but rather is both itself and points beyond itself. Auerbach, and Frei following him, calls this figurative, because something can stand for itself and another reality. For Frei, Barth's vision of the Bible is figurative because it points to the central wonder of the incarnation; Christ, then, serves as the figurative center of Barth's entire theology. Although Frei uses the term figurative to analyze Barth's theology, he is using this term in a distinctive way which differs from my use of it. For Frei, Barth describes the biblical world, and in that description something else is posited. He calls that activity, in this essay, both figurative and mimetic; I prefer to reserve the term figurative for discourse which is openly rhetorical, following tropical contours, while I agree with Frei that Barth's later work can be called mimetic, in the sense that its language allows itself to be shaped by a previously existing reality. For another excellent analysis of Barth's theology in rhetorical terms, see George Lindbeck, "Barth and Textuality," *Theology Today* 43 (1986): 361– 376. Lindbeck argues that Barth developed an intratextual theology in which the Bible, as a privileged text, functions as the comprehensive framework for the

Christian's understanding of reality. This is to be opposed to intertextuality, in which all texts, operating on the same level, interpret each other. He admits that intratextuality takes a certain kind of reading skill which many in the church have lost or forgotten.

28. *Church Dogmatics*, III/4: xii.

29. Frei, "An Afterword," 112.

30. Hans Frei, *The Eclipse of Biblical Narrative, A Study in Eighteenth and Nineteenth Century Hermeneutics* (New Haven: Yale University Press, 1974).

31. Frei argues that the primary characteristic of realistic narrative is that "characters or individual persons, in their internal depth or subjectivity as well as in their capacity as doers and sufferers, of actions or events, are firmly and significantly set in the context of the external environment, natural but more particularly social" (*The Eclipse of Biblical Narrative*, 13). Thus the character in the narrative cannot be separated from the structure of the story itself. The plot cumulatively renders the character, so that the narrative cannot be paraphrased without a permanent loss of meaning.

32. Ibid., 3.

33. This is a common observation. For example, John Bowden comments that "it is difficult to point to any fruitful positive developments along the line which Barth himself initiated" (*Karl Barth, Theologian*, 93).

34. For an excellent critique of Frei, see Lynn M. Poland, *Literary Criticism and Biblical Hermeneutics*. Poland compares Frei's vision of theology with the literary criticism practiced by the New Critics. Although the categories of formalism and realism only partially overlap, I have learned much from this critique. For a different development of Postliberalism, see George A. Lindbeck, *The Nature of Doctrine, Religion and Theology in a Postliberal Age* (Philadelphia: Westminster Press, 1984). Although Lindbeck's point of departure is not realistic narrative, he portrays the theological enterprise in similar terms as Frei: theology is a descriptive discipline. For Lindbeck, though, the theologian is more like an anthropologist than a literary critic, describing the language games which Christians play. Lindbeck also differs from Frei in that he connects Postliberalism to a fairly specific philosophical program (best articulated by Wittgenstein) while Frei tries to continue Barth's strategy of adopting philosophical positions only ecclectically and unsystematically (*ad hoc*) when useful. William C. Placher continues Lindbeck's line of development, offering the most consistent philosophical defense of Postliberalism, but at the cost of surrendering the Barthian position on the independence of theology. See his *Unapologetic Theology*, (Philadelphia: Westminster, 1989). In the terms that I am using, it could be suggested that Lindbeck and Placher defend a version of realistic theology based on philosophical and scientific considerations, while Frei's realism is more rhetorical and literary. This division in Postliberalism can be traced back to Barth's own ambiguities on the status of theology as a science.

35. Frei, *Eclipse of the Biblical Narrative*, 10.

36. This does not mean that contemporary authors do not use narrative as a device in their novels. Rather, they do not simply tell stories but shape those stories in very specific ways, commenting on them and subverting them as they tell them. Narrative alone does not suffice. Note this comment from Nathan A. Scott, Jr.:

"Substantial evidence of the diminished status of story in recent literature can easily be gathered from the various capitals of European literary life, but our American situation does itself make a fully representative case. Here, of course, Saul Bellow and William Styron and John Updike and Bernard Malamud—who are perhaps our ranking novelists—clearly intend still to practice that old magic whereby the storyteller mesmerizes us by his tale. But these writers, for all their eminence, are not amongst those to whom one turns for typical expressions of our postmodern period-style. It is rather such figures as John Hawkes, Donald Barthelme, Thomas Pynchon, John Barth, William Gass, Robert Coover, and Randolph Wurlitzer who, in Matthew Arnold's phrase, carry 'the tone of the centre'—and these and numerous others of a similar bent are writers who are notable for the very considerable ambivalence of feeling that they represent in regard to the traditional arts of narration" ("The Rediscovery of Story in Recent Theology and the Refusal of Story in Recent Literature," in *Art/Literature/Religion: Life on the Borders,* ed. Robert Detweiler [Chico, California: Scholars Press, 1983], 142). Scott's entire essay constitutes a warning against a naive reliance on narrative in theology.

37. See Alan Wilde, *Horizons of Assent, Modernism, Postmodernism, and the Ironic Imagination* (Philadelphia: University of Pennsylvania Press, 1987). Wilde's book is interesting for my purposes because he comments on many of the texts which I have used in chapter five. Although he criticizes many authors for not developing an adequate conception of the radically unstable movement of irony, he himself coins the term "anironic" to denote the vision that complements and balances (contains?) irony (see 30), and he interprets Donald Barthelme, the most absurd of the postmoderns, as somehow affirming (assenting to) some vision of humanism. I prefer to think of irony as a much more dangerous trope which is dependent on other tropes—and even narrative itself—for the visions which it subverts and destroys. For another excellent analysis of Postmodern literature, see Brian McHale, *Postmodern Fiction* (New York: Methuen, 1987).

38. For an analysis of this move away from representationalism in both literature and philosophy, see Allen Thiher, *Words in Reflection, Modern Language Theory and Postmodern Fiction* (Chicago: University of Chicago Press, 1984). In our pluralistic culture, this movement has not been uniform. In fact, Postliberalism can be understood as the theological correlate of the neorealistic segment of American literature best represented by Saul Bellow among others.

39. Perhaps realism is even the most effective style in certain disciplines, such as the natural sciences, or for certain kinds of theology. Theologies which seek to tell the story of oppressed peoples, stories which have not yet been told, probably can use realistic narrative without seeming to be naive and outdated. However, for those who live in cultures where the biblical story has been told too many times, it must be appropriated and communicated in explicitly figurative terms. Note that postmodernism does not mean the rejection of narrative altogether; that attitude is more appropriate for modernism, which stretched narrative out of any recognizable shape. Postmodernism means the recognition that narrative is both inescapable and naive; thus, postmodern writers employ all sorts of figures to turn narrative against itself in order to display its fictive status. For an example, note John Barth's satirical rewriting of the genres of epic and historical

novels in *The Sot-Weed Factor* and *Giles Goat-Boy*. When Barth talks about the literature of exhaustion, he does not mean that literature has nothing more to say. He means that literature must replenish itself by using old structures in new ways, always conscious of its rhetorical (re)construction. See John Barth, *The Friday Book* (New York: G. P. Putnam's Sons, 1984), 62–76 and 193–206. Theology is in a similar situation with the Bible; postliberalism thinks that the ways of talking about the Bible have been exhausted, and so the biblical story can be only repeated. A postmodern theologian thinks that such ways have hardly begun. Thus, Hayden White's complaints and suggestions about history apply equally to theology: "But the aim of the writer of a novel must be the same as that of the writer of history" and "History is no less a form of fiction than the novel is a form of historical representation" (*Tropics of Discourse*, 122). There is no reason why theology cannot be as creatively written as the best contemporary literature.

40. Robin W. Lovin, *Christian Faith and Public Choices*, (Philadelphia: Fortress Press, 1984) 24. Lovin argues that Barth provides no ground for public discussion and decision-making about ethical issues. "An ethic of the Word of God thus avoids all claims to know or to state the principle by which a moral act can be identified" (22). "For Barth's critics who think in these terms, the lack of specificity in his ethics results, paradoxically, from his failure to generalize" (24). "The problem with Barth's eschatological redemption is that it gives us no specific ethical guidance for choices in the present" (41). "For all its theological integrity, Barth's position is impossible for a public ethics" (42). For a different reading of the nature of the 'public' in Barth's theology see William C. Placher, "Revisionist and Postliberal Theologies and the Public Character of Theology," *The Thomist* 49 (1985): 392–416. Placher argues that Barth's theology is public because he addresses a quite specific public group, namely, the church. Note that Barth does explicitly discuss specific ethical issues in *Church Dogmatics*, III/4.

41. See Friedrich-Wilhelm Marquardt, *Theologie und Sozialismus. Das Beispiel Karl Barths* (Munich and Mainz: Kaiser/Grunewald, 1972) and George Hunsinger, ed., *Karl Barth and Radical Politics* (Philadelphia: Westminster Press, 1976). Marquardt protests against the abstract treatment of Barth's theology (a protest with which I agree) and wants to link his theology with his social praxis (much as I try to link his theology to rhetoric). He argues that Barth's theology not only arose from but aims at social action. His book was submitted as a dissertation at the Kirchliche Hochschule in Berlin, where it was rejected. It was then accepted at Berlin's Free University. Amidst this controversy, Prof. Helmut Gollwitzer resigned from the Hochschule and joined the University, where Marquardt also attained a position. It should be emphasized that Marquardt finds the substance of Barth's socialism in his doctrine of God and his Christology. He traces this socialistic theology to Barth's work on Romans. "Barth turned to theology in order to seek the organic connection between the Bible and the newspaper, the new world and the collapsing bourgeois order" (*Karl Barth and Radical Politics*, 54). "In Safenwil the proletariat was the material of Scriptural exegesis" (60).

42. Even a cursory reading of Busch should be enough to demonstrate Barth's political wisdom. It is odd, perhaps even paradoxical, that the theologian who re-

jected any correlation between theology and culture was so perceptive about culture and politics. Recall Barth's famous and often quoted statement, "One broods alternatively over the newspaper and the New Testament." Hans Frei has suggested that Barth's deepest imagination is "profoundly sceptical and secular, in a value-neutral, neither perjorative nor laudatory sense of those terms" (Dickerman, ed., *Karl Barth and the Future of Theology*, 8). Barth was able to confront the secular on its own terms because he was not trying to persuade it of an inner or essential connection to religion. An exception to the admiration of Barth's politics can be found in John Howard Yoder's pacifist critique of Barth, *Karl Barth and the Problem of War* (Nashville: Abingdon Press, 1970). Yoder argues that Barth's ethics leans toward Christian pacifism but in the end becomes indistinguishable from the casuistry of the Roman Catholic Just War tradition. He wonders why Barth did not advocate peaceful resistance to Germany as a middle ground between passivity and compliance or armed resistance.

43. Barth's political views are complex and my summary is not meant to be exhaustive. Many critics disagreed with Barth's refusal to overtly criticize the Soviet Union after the War, suggesting that Barth contradicted himself by opposing Nazi Germany but refusing to oppose communism with equal vehemence. As in his theology, Barth politically always swam against the stream. Unfortunately, I cannot further examine the relationship between Barth's rhetoric and his politics in his dogmatic period, but I hope these comments are suggestive and point in the right direction. I should note that Marquardt attributes Barth's criticisms of the Cold War to his sympathy for socialism. See Hunsinger, ed., *Karl Barth and Radical Politics*, 49.

44. Eberhard Jüngel, *Karl Barth, A Theological Legacy* trans. Garrett E. Paul (Philadelphia: Westminster Press, 1986), 41.

45. Ibid., 92.

46. Jüngel continues this argument in the last two chapters of the English translation of his book, which are dedicated to demonstrating that in the *Church Dogmatics* Barth argues that (1) sin never can be understood independently or apart from the Gospel; sin must be examined after the discussion of Christology and redemption. Therefore, there never should be an ethical reflection on the human condition which is not preceded by dogmatics; and (2) humanity receives its integrity and dignity, and people can achieve full personhood, only because of the incarnation; Christology therefore serves as the foundation for anthropology. Only in Jesus Christ can we find the true essence of humanity.

47. Barth's discussion of finite otherness in *Romans* is original and significant; it is often overlooked by scholars. Steve Smith, for example, in his *The Argument to the Other*, meticulously analyzes the concept of an infinite other in *Romans* without mentioning this "other" discourse.

48. For a comprehensive analysis of the problem of otherness which focuses on philosophers who were Barth's contemporaries, see Michael Theunissen, *The Other, Studies in the Social Ontology of Husserl, Heidegger, Sartre, and Buber*, trans. Christopher Macann (Cambridge: MIT Press, 1984). Giles Gunn has treated the problem of otherness from the perspective of the imagination and culture criticism. See his *The Interpretation of Otherness, Literature, Religion*

and the American Imagination (New York: Oxford University Press, 1979). In Gunn's most recent work, he continues to talk about otherness as the crisis of our culture, but he increasingly advocates a philosophical (American pragmatism) rather than an imaginative or rhetorical response. See *The Culture of Criticism, the Criticism of Culture* (New York: Oxford University Press, 1987).

49. Much of my discussion of pluralism has been guided by lectures and conversations with Langdon Gilkey. For an example of his response to this problem, see *Society and the Sacred* (New York: Crossroad, 1981).

50. Robert N. Bellah, et al., *Habits of the Heart, Individualism and Commitment in American Life* (Berkeley: University of California Press, 1985).

51. See Herbert Marcuse, "Repressive Tolerance," in *A Critique of Pure Tolerance* (Boston: Beacon Press, 1969), 81 – 123.

52. See Peter Berger, Brigitte Berger and Hansfried Kellner, *The Homeless Mind, Modernization and Consciousness* (New York: Vintage Books, 1974).

53. See Richard John Neuhaus, *The Naked Public Square, Religion and Democracy in America* (Grand Rapids: Eerdmans, 1984). Not all attempts to reestablish civil religion take a conservative form; for a survey of this issue, see Robert Bellah and Phillip Hammond, *Varieties of Civil Religion* (San Francisco: Harper & Row, 1980). Also see the call for a public philosophy in William M. Sullivan, *Reconstructing Public Philosophy* (Berkeley: University of California Press, 1986).

54. Another "theologian" who has confronted not the problem of otherness but the issue of difference in a rhetorical fashion is Mark C. Taylor; see his *Altarity* (Chicago: University of Chicago Press, 1987). This complex and imaginative book cannot be summarized here, but I can note that he does propose a rhetoric of difference which depends on strategies of juxtaposition, contrast and resonance. Taylor's approach is, broadly speaking, deconstructive.

55. See Tracy, *The Analogical Imagination,* especially chapters 8 – 10. Note that Tracy's theory of correlation is not an arbitrary imposition but an attempt to understand and encourage Christian conversations as they actually take place. Indeed, Tracy's tropical reflections are connected to his understanding of the particular configurations of Roman Catholic piety. See David Tracy, "The Catholic Theological Imagination," *Catholic Theological Society of America Proceedings* 32 (1977):234–44.

56. See David Tracy, *Plurality and Ambiguity, Hermeneutics, Religion, Hope* (San Francisco: Harper & Row, 1987).

57. Carl Raschke has suggested, in his own way, that this demand of Barth's must be met today. See his *Theological Thinking, An In-quiry* (Atlanta: Scholars Press, 1988), ix, 12 and 15.

58. Barth often stressed the freedom of theology; in one of his last works, *Evangelical Theology* (New York: Anchor Books, 1964), this was a ruling theme. "In the school of witnesses theology can in no way become monolithic, monomanic, monotonous, and infallibly boring. In no way can it bind or limit itself to one special subject or another" (28). "Every possible means must be used" to pursue the Word (30). Barth even admits that, "The real question is the problem of the language which must be employed by those who undertake to proclaim this Word" (162). However, he argues that theological speech must meet the two

conditions of declaration and address; it must be both a solemn and common-place speech which "is taught its content by exegesis and dogmatics" (162). In the end, Barth reduces the question of language to the ancillary discipline of practical theology. "Practical theology is studied in order to seek and to find, to learn and to practice, this speech that is essential to the proclamation of the community in preaching and teaching, in worship and evangelization" (162). Thus, just when Barth recognizes the importance of language he relegates it to the sphere of practice, which is dominated by dogmatics; he really thinks that theology has no choice in the realm of rhetoric. Even in this book Barth describes theology as a science which must be true to the logic of its own being. "In short, theology is not a creative act but only a praise of the Creator and of creation — praise that to the greatest possible extent truly responds to the creative act of God" (13). And "In relation to God's Word itself, theology has nothing to inter-pret" (14). Theology reflects the Bible, which is itself a "mirror and echo" of the Word of God (25). For Barth, realism seems to be the natural style of theol-ogy; theology is a free science, then, only with regard to what it can reject, that is, in reference to its freedom *from* other disciplines, not a freedom *for* language. In the end Barth's attempt to write a free theology is captured by an ontology which limits the sciences to objective and descriptive disciplines.

59. For Umberto Eco, this combination of hyperbole and irony is the mark of post-modernism. To make his point, he uses an example that is strikingly similar to my analysis of "God is love": "I think of the postmodern attitude as that of a man who loves a very cultivated woman and knows he cannot say to her, 'I love you madly,' because he knows that she knows (and that she knows that he knows) that these words have already been written by Barbara Cartland. Still, there is a solution. He can say, 'As Barbara Cartland would put it, I love you madly.' At this point, having avoided false innocence, having said clearly that it is no longer possible to speak innocently, he will nevertheless have said what he wanted to say to the woman: that he loves her in an age of lost innocence. If the woman goes along with this, she will have received a declaration of love all the same. Neither of the two speakers will feel innocent, both will have accepted the challenge of the past, of the already said, which cannot be eliminated, both will consciously and with pleasure play the game of irony . . . But both will have suc-ceeded, once again, in speaking of love" (*Reflections on the Name of the Rose*, 67–8). Postmodernism, note, should be distinguished from deconstructionism; the latter lacks the hyperbole which makes irony both necessary and productive.

INDEX OF NAMES

LaCapra, Dominick, 37, 43, 44
Leff, Michael, 2
Lindbeck, George, 205n.27, 206n.34
Locke, John, 21, 22
Lovin, Robin, 208n.40
Lowrie, Walter, 124, 125
Lukács, George, 203n.4
Luther, Martin, 80, 105, 106

Mackie, Louis, 124, 130
de Man, Paul, 3, 8, 19, 148, 180n.14,
   201n.12
Mann, Thomas, 119, 123, 151, 169
Marquardt, Friedrich-Wilhelm, 208n.41
Marvick, Louis Wirth, 85–87, 89, 90,
   123, 177
Megill, Allan, 53, 92, 95, 197n.7
Muecke, D.C., 118–122, 128, 133

Nehamas, Alexander, 92–94
Nelson, John, 19, 20
Nietzsche, Friedrich, 22, 33, 53, 63, 76,
   77, 91–98, 104, 109, 110–112, 124,
   126, 132, 138, 170, 194n.43
Norris, Margot, 198n.21

Otto, Rudolf, 87, 193n.32
Overbeck, Franz, 63, 64, 91, 194n.43

Pascal, Blaise, 195n.51
Pauck, Wilhelm, 9
Pepper, Stephen, 52
Perelman, Chaim, 84, 87, 88
Phillips, Donald, 156
Placher, William C., 206n.34, 208n.40
Poland, Lynn, 206n.34

Ramsey, Ian, 50
Richards, I.A., 24
Ricoeur, Paul, 18, 26–38, 44, 45
Rorty, Richard, 26, 27, 118
Ryle, Gilbert, 32

Schlegel, 118, 129
Schleiermacher, Friedrich, 2, 54–56,
   152, 180n.9
Scott, Nathan A., Jr., 206n.36
Searle, John, 119, 120
Socrates, 20, 93
Smart, James, 60
Snow, C.P., 154
Soskice, Janet, 23, 26, 32, 33, 49, 50,
   51, 80

Thurnesen, Eduard, 65, 152
Tillich, Paul, 9, 12, 13, 145, 152, 176
Todorov, Tzvetan, 19, 204n.12
Torrance, T. F., 4, 7, 156
Tracy, David, 1, 52, 176, 179n.4,
   191n.14, 210n.55

Updike, John, 5, 182n.21

Vico, Giambattista, 22, 26, 40, 43
Voltaire, 21, 89, 118

White, Hayden, 38–45, 53, 123, 149
Wiene, Robert, 16–18
Wilde, Alan, 166, 207n.37
Willett, John, 150
Wittgenstein, Ludwig, 33
Wiles, Maurice, 4

Yoder, John Howard, 209n.42